NERVES AND NARRATIVES

NERVES AND NARRATIVES

A CULTURAL HISTORY OF HYSTERIA IN NINETEENTH-CENTURY BRITISH PROSE

PETER MELVILLE LOGAN

Foreword by Roy Porter

University of California Press
Berkeley • Los Angeles • London

University of California Press
Berkeley and Los Angeles, California

University of California Press, Ltd.
London, England

© 1997 by
The Regents of the University of California

Library of Congress Cataloging-in-Publication Data

Logan, Peter Melville, 1951–
    Nerves and narratives : a cultural history of hysteria in
nineteenth-century British prose / Peter Melville Logan;
foreword by Roy Porter.
        p. cm.
    Includes bibliographical references and index.
    ISBN 0-520-20473-5 (cloth : alk. paper)
    1. Hysteria in literature.   2. Literature and mental
illness—Great Britain—History—19th century.
3. Literature and society—Great Britain—History—19th
century.   4. Mental illness in literature.   5. Mentally ill
in literature.   6. Body, Human, in literature.   7. Psychology and literature.   8. Narration (Rhetoric)
I. Title
PR778.H95L64   1997
828'.80809353—dc20   96-43866
                                                                        CIP

Printed in the United States of America
9 8 7 6 5 4 3 2 1

To Cathleen A. McCoy

It is an usual observation, that if the body of one murthered be brought before the murtherer, the wounds will bleed afresh. Some do affirm, that the dead body, upon the presence of the murtherer, hath opened the eyes.

Francis Bacon, *Sylva Sylvarum* (1627)

Contents

Foreword by Roy Porter   xi

Acknowledgments   xv

Abbreviations   xvii

Introduction   1

ONE   THE BODY WITH THE STORY TO TELL

1. The Narrative of Nervous Bodies in 1800:
   Thomas Trotter's *A View of the Nervous Temperament*   15

TWO   THE BODY TALKS

2. The Nervous Narrator's Paradox:
   William Godwin and *Caleb Williams*   45

3. Narrative and Self-Violence: Framing
   Mary Hays's *Memoirs of Emma Courtney*   59

4. *Suspiria de Machina:* De Quincey's Body
   and the *Confessions of an English Opium-Eater*   73

5. Harrington's Last Shudder: Maria Edgeworth
   and the Popular Fear of the Nervous Body   109

THREE   VICTORIAN BODIES

6. The Body in Need of Nerves: Working-Class
   Insensibility and Victorian Sanitation   143

7. The Story of the Story of the Body:
   Conceiving the Body in *Middlemarch*   166

Notes   197

Bibliography   229

Index   243

Foreword

One of the most exciting recent developments in the humanities has been the interaction between literary criticism and the history of medicine, mediated through studies of the body. Thanks to new approaches to texts stimulated by various forms of postmodernism, we can no longer regard poems and novels as disembodied works of the spirit; we see them now as works that are subject to modes of production that have a challenging (and long-neglected) physical life of their own. For its part, the history of medicine has finally ceased to limit itself to the biographies of great doctors and has addressed itself to the wider social and cultural history of health and sickness, ideas whose ramifications spread far beyond medicine proper. The rediscovery of the body as a subject of scholarly discourse has many sources—to my mind, feminism has been the chief impetus—and draws inspiration from the work of Bakhtin, Elias, Foucault, and many others. Combining these new trends, *Nerves and Narratives* is a particularly clear and fruitful instance of our new perception of the sympathetic connections between the human body and the body of a text.

As the merest mention of Cheyne, Smollett, Sterne, or Diderot will show, the era in which Professor Logan's story starts was especially alert to the relations between writing and health, both physical and mental. The fascinating correspondence between Samuel Richardson and his physician, George Cheyne, focused upon the possible psychopathology of obsessive writing; and the very topos of *Tristram Shandy* was the discrepancy between the chronology of writing and the tempo of life itself. The many moralists preoccupied with the supposed epidemic of masturbation likened writing and reading to illicit sexual activity; and excessive stimulation of the solitary imagination formed the grounds for the widespread condemnation of the (supposedly largely female) cult of novel reading.

Books and bodies were connected in Enlightenment thinking by influential discourses about the civilizing process. On the positive side, the spread of literacy and the freedom of the press were believed by many to be crucial to the wider emancipation of mankind, not least the realization of forms of progress that would directly affect the body itself. William Godwin (whom Professor Logan discusses) and, in France, Condorcet were both confident that intellectual advancement would lead to greater longevity and even to a kind of earthly immortality; the dangers of such scientistic dreams were, of course, pointed out in Mary Shelley's *Frankenstein*. More broadly, moralists and medical thinkers alike expressed the fears—illuminatingly analysed by Professor Logan—that the civilizing process, with its sedentary occupations, its incessant traffic in opinions, and its quest for heightened sensibility might overstimulate the mind and the passions while sapping bodily strength. Professor Logan documents such views through the writings of Dr. Thomas Trotter, correctly observing that they were the common coin of a popular medical critique of the dangers of modernity, which thought in terms of "diseases of civilization."

The concepts that linked doctors with the literary world were "nerves" and (in Trotter's phrase) the "nervous temperament." Enlightenment medicine set the nerves center stage, and its nineteenth-century heirs further developed the exploration of "nervousness." Elevated nervousness was both the fulfillment of human potential and an expression of hysterical or hypochondriacal sickness. It was a malady visible in and on the body, and one of its symptoms was a compulsive tendency to talk about itself. Physicians of the late Enlightenment and the Romantic era diagnosed such nervousness as one of the characteristic maladies of the age, and the more reflective of them—including the Bristolian friend of Coleridge, Thomas Beddoes—perceived that their own habits of writing incriminated them, too, in the disorder. It is this problem that forms the conceptual core of Professor Logan's study: When talking and writing behavior becomes a disease symptom, what happens to the authority of the author?

That is what is explained in this book. One of its pleasures is its long time perspective, moving from Thomas Trotter, born at the very beginning of the reign of George III, to George Eliot's *Middlemarch*, that classic expression of the humanism/science anxieties in the age of Darwin. By taking the extended historical view—Mary

Hays, Thomas de Quincy, and others are examined en route—Professor Logan can tackle the problem of "recovery" (the recuperation of authorial truth) and examine how Victorian narratives sought to overcome the difficulty of the hysterized body as well as the unreliable tale.

It goes without saying that gender plays a key part in Professor Logan's account; the hysterical body and the nervous narrative were automatically considered feminine, even when they were associated with males. In an analysis reinforcing those of J.G.A. Pocock's *Virtue, Commerce and History: Essays on Political Thought and History* (Cambridge / New York: Cambridge University Press, 1985) and F. J. Barker-Benfield's *The Culture of Sensibility: Sex and Society in Eighteenth-Century Britain* (Chicago: University of Chicago Press, 1992), wider questions are raised of the prevalent fears of a loss of manliness attendant upon the nervous sensibility of the novel. But as well as discussing gender, Professor Logan demonstrates the importance of class. The body under threat toward the close of the eighteenth century was that of the middle-class man (or woman) of feeling. There was a widespread tendency to idealize in a Rousseauian manner the sturdy peasant or laborer as totally immune to hysterical conditions. By the early Victorian era, it is suggested, all had changed. The "condition of England" novels of the 1840s and 1850s problematized the proletarian body as being simultaneously subject to medical and moral contagions of its own.

One of the great gains of the last decade or two has been the breaking down of old disciplinary boundaries in the humanities and the consequent recognition that the very business of writing in earlier centuries produced transformations in sensibility and hence in the very bodies and being of authors and readers. Traditional literary critics were interested in the narratives of novels; traditional historians of medicine noted how in earlier days the art of diagnosis was that of "taking a history." It is only recently that the immense common ground between both sorts of narration has been grasped. Professor Logan's book affords a signal example of reading the stories the body tells.

Roy Porter

Acknowledgments

The personal encouragement and professional support given to me throughout the years by scholars more learned than I have made it possible to conceive and complete this project. In particular, Catherine Gallagher from start to finish helped make this into the book I wanted it to be. Nancy Armstrong's responsiveness to my ideas was a significant factor in seeing this book finished. Equally important, Thomas Laqueur, Jack Pressman, and Elaine Scarry all provided me with the central concepts and critical responses needed to develop the larger trajectory of the manuscript at crucial points in its development. Gillian Beer, John Bender, Carolyn Dinshaw, Steven Goldsmith, David Lloyd, Mitzi Myers, Guenter Risse, Stephanie Smith, Eleanor Ty, and Athena Vrettos offered helpful critiques and suggestions that made this a better book than it could ever have been otherwise. I am also indebted to a number of colleagues at the University of Alabama whose ideas contributed to developing threads of this narrative that would otherwise never have been woven: Salli Davis, Claudia Johnson, Elizabeth Meese, David L. Miller, Richard Rand, Diane Roberts, George Starbuck, and William Ulmer.

I am grateful to Roy Porter for supplying a foreword to this work and to Doris Kretschmer at the University of California Press for arranging it. Larry Borowsky also deserves thanks for his superb job of copyediting. Without my research assistants at Alabama, this manuscript would neither have been so thorough nor so timely. Jessica Hollis proofread the manuscript, tracked down endless quotations, and researched the history of the novel. Jake Honeycutt discovered a wealth of information on the history of crowd theory. For Robert Boliek's legal research and fact checking, I am further grateful. The graduate students in my Hysteria and the Novel seminar at the University of Alabama in 1994 also kept these ideas developing through their fascination with the different definitions of hysteria and their engagement with the writers discussed in Part Two: Dana Barnett,

Lucinda Burchel, Lisa Eno, Cynthia Hartley, Jessica Hollis, Tamara Horn, Rhonda Knight, Mary Lanford, Waits Raulerson, Nina Ronstadt, Blair Simmons, Nan Smith, and Merrie Winfrey.

Work on this manuscript was funded in part by the University of Alabama Research Grants Committee, whose summer research grant in 1992 made possible an extended research trip and supported final drafting in the summer of 1994. I am grateful to James D. Yarbrough, dean of the College of Arts and Sciences at the University of Alabama, for supplying me with leave time to pursue this project. Hank Lazer and Stanley Jones, assistant deans of the college, provided additional small-grant support at a critical late juncture.

Chapter 7 was originally published in a slightly different form as "Conceiving the Body: Realism and Medicine in *Middlemarch*," in *History of the Human Sciences* 4 (1991): 197–222. Chapters 1 and 2 appeared in a very different form as "Narrating Hysteria: *Caleb Williams* and the Cultural History of Nerves," in *Novel: A Forum on Fiction* 29.2 (1996). Copyright NOVEL Corp. © 1996. Reprinted with permission.

Abbreviations

Frequently referenced works are identified by the following abbreviations in the text and notes:

CW   Godwin, William. *Caleb Williams; Or Things as They Are.* Edited by David McCracken. New York: Norton, 1977.

EC   Hays, Mary. *Memoirs of Emma Courtney.* 2 vols. London, 1796; New York: Garland, 1974.

M   Eliot, George. *Middlemarch: A Study of Provincial Life.* Edited by David Carroll. Oxford: Clarendon Press, 1986.

NT   Trotter, Thomas. *A View of the Nervous Temperament: Being a Practical Enquiry into the Increasing Prevalence, Prevention, and Treatment of Those Diseases Commonly Called Nervous, Bilious, Stomach and Liver Complaints; Indigestion; Low Spirits; Gout, &c.* London: Longman, 1807. Reprint, New York: Arno, 1976.

OE   De Quincey, Thomas. *Confessions of an English Opium-Eater.* Edited by Alethea Hayter. New York: Penguin, 1971.

PJ   Godwin, William. *Enquiry Concerning Political Justice: And Its Influence on Modern Morals and Happiness.* New York: Penguin, 1985.

SR   Chadwick, Edwin. *Report on the Sanitary Condition of the Labouring Population of Great Britain.* Edited by M. W. Flinn. Edinburgh: Edinburgh University Press, 1965.

TN   Edgeworth, Maria. *Tales and Novels.* Vol. 9, *Harrington; Thoughts on Bores; and Ormond.* London: Routledge, 1893; Hildesheim, Germany: Georg Olms Verlagsbuchhandlund, 1969.

Introduction

A new body appeared in Britain in the late eighteenth century, one marked by its susceptibility to hysteria and a host of related nervous conditions, variously called hypochondria, spleen, vapours, lowness of spirits, melancholia, bile, excess sensibility, or, simply, nerves. These complaints were not themselves new; they had previously been the exclusive province of the English aristocracy. But their appearance as an epidemic in the middle class of the late Georgian years reflected a new set of assumptions about the bodies of speculators, traders, and businessmen and their wives, daughters, and servants. As a consequence, nervous disorders such as hysteria became the leading category of illness, accounting for two-thirds of all disease, and the new middle-class nervous body was viewed with considerable alarm.[1]

The emergence of this new body was explained by the rationale George Cheyne developed in *The English Malady* in 1733. Responding to the European view that the English aristocracy had a constitutional melancholy, Cheyne—who was Samuel Richardson's physician—argued that this malady was a "disease of civilization" resulting from the consumption of too many luxuries. Physicians at the century's end such as Thomas Beddoes, Thomas Arnold, and the provincial Thomas Trotter argued that the new middle class was finally falling prey to the same dangers, having itself amassed considerable wealth.[2] The new nervous body, however, was not simply a repetition of the one defined by Cheyne's aristocrats. Its disorders were the consequence of a class-specific form of social life, and they were brought on by such middle-class conditions as year-round urban residency. The nervous body of the speculator was a corporeal response to the dynamics of the stock market. The hysteria of his wife was an embodiment of her being confined in a townhouse, unable to walk out by herself. The hypochondria of the retired tradesman followed from his sudden loss of acquisitive activity. The lower class, by virtue of its poverty and constant labor, was still considered immune to the diseases of wealth, and so the fear of a nervous epidemic was singularly focused on the middle class and its social environment.

Because of this linkage between nervous bodies and social conditions, nervous complaints became a useful tool for writers engaged in social criticism. The leading characteristic of this new body was its excessive impressionability; it was permeated by the artificial world in which it lived, having lost the ability to resist the harmful effects of England's new social environment. Like a canary in a mine shaft, this body, with its mysterious symptoms, was singing its warning song. An author could credibly use the health or sickness of the body to ground a commentary on the British way of life, or, more precisely, on the structure of British social power, which had brought the nervous body and its protean complaints into being. Because its disorders were broad and causation vague, it made possible an unlimited range of naturalized critiques of unnatural life.

Its use for this purpose in literary narratives of the period was widespread. The disorders of Mary Wollstonecraft's heroines in both *Mary: A Fiction* and *The Wrongs of Woman* are well-known indictments of the punishing social experiences that cause them. Nervous manifestations range in severity from the intensity of the crisis (as with Marianne Dashwood's nearly fatal ailment in Jane Austen's *Sense and Sensibility*) to the diffuseness of the chronic: Miss Milner's impulsiveness in Elizabeth Inchbald's *A Simple Story* has a pathology familiar to medical texts of the time. Each of these variations functions in its own way as a commentary on the order or disorder of the social conditions that produced it.

Nerves and Narratives is an archaeology of that nervous body and its implicit social critique. In particular, this study focuses on one of the central characteristics of the nervous body: its tendency to talk, especially to talk about itself. The nervous patient spoke incessantly about her or his body, its pains and sufferings, and its history. As Part 1 discusses, this body's tendency to narrate the story of its nervous condition was itself a sign of the condition. Thus, this association of nerves and narrative makes problematic the narratives of social criticism in the period that depend on a nervous narrator to testify from personal experience to the injustice of society.

What happens when that nervous body tells its story? A significant cluster of first-person literary narratives in this period featured precisely such a nervous narrator, and four examples are analyzed in Part 2: William Godwin's *Caleb Williams* (1794), Mary Hays's *Memoirs of Emma Courtney* (1796), Thomas De Quincey's *Confessions of an English Opium-Eater* (1821), and Maria Edgeworth's *Harrington* (1817). Each of these examples is a full-scale nervous narrative—that is, one in which the nervous narrator is the central narrating voice—and they demonstrate a need to simultaneously negotiate two wholly opposite narrative problems. First, these narratives strain to avoid the negative implications of the narrator's hysterical speech, as the hysteria threatens the authority to speak. However, the texts also pose an opposite and more intractable problem caused by the relationship between the speaker's illness and the speaker's voice. In each case, the narrator's illness serves a positive purpose, for it gives rise to the narrative voice. Without the disease there would be no narrative, not even one with the social utility of warning against the social conditions that created it in the first place. And so, paradoxically, the nervous narrative promotes, in its formal structure, the same disorder it cautions against by transforming the narrator's debility into a narrative premise. This problem only intensifies as the narrative gets increasingly convincing. The more compelling it is aesthetically or intellectually, the more valuable the nervous condition ultimately appears as a precondition to the act of speech. Thus, these narratives have to negotiate two contradictory problems, one in which hysteria implicitly undermines the authority to speak, the other in which it becomes the basic condition of speech.

Each of the four narratives discussed in Part 2 represents a different response to the problem of the nervous narrative form as a means of social commentary. The two opposite endings William Godwin wrote for *Caleb Williams* create opposite relationships between narrator and narrative, and so they serve as an introduction to the paradoxical difficulties the form presented. Godwin's narrator finally disowns his narrative, losing all interest in it as self-representation. However, this kind of detachment, in which the past is thrown off or tossed aside, is rejected by the early feminist philosopher Mary Hays in her *Memoirs of Emma Courtney*, a novelistic response to *Caleb*

Williams. Hays instead constructs an ongoing relationship between the narrator and her earlier narrative, one she links to the social condition of woman.

The writers of this first pair of narratives were political radicals who utilized the instability of the nervous narrative form to expose unresolvable conflicts within the existing social order. Both narratives insist on the instability of the narrator's voice, and that instability ultimately serves as a metonym for the social instability the narratives seek to represent. Politically conservative writers who used this form adopted a very different approach to its problematic structure. They insisted on resolution rather than instability. Two examples are examined in the second pair of narratives, Thomas De Quincey's *Confessions of an English Opium-Eater* and Maria Edgeworth's *Harrington*. Both writers tried to contain the instability of the form by constructing narrators who describe their escape from a past nervous condition. That escape is the precondition of speech for both narrators, and thus they attempt to tell the story of recuperation and reconciliation, rather than disorder and alienation.

Nervous narratives continued beyond the brief life span explored here, and nervous conditions in the Victorian age were a major subject of discussion, but the nervous body did not continue in the same fashion.[3] Part 3, "Victorian Bodies," looks at two qualitatively different kinds of historical developments that affected the earlier idea of the nervous body and impinged on its cultural status. The first development was a relative change. The nervous body was a paradigm that the middle class used to explain itself to itself and to differentiate itself from other classes. With the rise of the new urban working class, that self-definition underwent a change, and we can see that shift by looking at the new discourse of public health, which arose as the medical science of the working-class body. In this new genre of middle-class discourse, the working class became the inheritor of the problem of an excessive environmental determinism. In comparison, the middle-class body appeared to be relatively healthy.

The second development was an internal shift in the Victorian medical conceptualization of the nervous system, which is outlined at the beginning of Chapter 7. George Eliot was aware of this paradigm shift, and in *Middlemarch* the novelist looks at medicine as, itself, a narrative in transition about the body. Rather than embracing or deploying the fixed medical concept of the body, George Eliot portrays medicine as engaged in a business of conceiving bodies, and thus she questions the basic structure of medical knowledge itself. Because it is set in 1832, at the close of the medical generation with which this study begins, *Middlemarch* also makes it possible to return symbolically to the early century, and to revisit the questions—medical authority, epistemologies of the body, their bearing on the forms of literature—of that era. The question takes on a radically different meaning in this paradigmatic novel of Victorian high realism.

The combination of an extended analysis of the theory of narrative in an outdated, noncanonical medical text with analyses of narrative problems in literary narratives of the time is a deliberate means of establishing the methodological field within which my object of study can come into view. That object is not the individual works, whether medical, fictional, or autobiographical, that constitute this study, nor their different genres, but rather the cultural episteme in which they participate. I term that episteme "the nervous body." It is the basic literary claim of this study that the nervous body is a defining characteristic of late Georgian literature. The basic historical claim is that the nervous body enjoyed its clearest moment of cultural ascendancy in the late Georgian period, when specifically middle-class disorders became part of the official discourse of medicine, and that its cultural status changed with the emergence of the working-class body in the early Victorian years.

The "body" with which this study is concerned is not a given that exists outside of history. It is a flexible group of narratives used by members of late Georgian culture to explain their physicality to themselves. The assumption that the body could serve as a natural locus for social criticism rested on a second series of assumptions about how this body was structured, how it functioned, and why it reacted in one way and not in another. And so the physiology of experience became a cultural language through which this social critique operated. The cultural episteme of the nervous body made it possible to appeal to physicality as a meaningful source of social commentary. It was the precondition for meaning, the theoretical structure that followed from the physical structure. The narratives about nervous function that this culture told itself permitted some kinds of bodily meanings and not others. And so this cultural episteme was not a specific message but rather the grammar in which a variety of messages could be constituted.

This body resists being reduced to a cultural construction that can be understood in relation to a given or "real" body, a body understood to be outside of cultural interpretations. "I can offer material for how powerful prior notions of difference or sameness determine what one sees and reports about the body," Thomas Laqueur writes, describing how cultural assumptions about gender came to define the physical structures that were then appealed to as the body's given sex.[4] The distinguishing feature of the nervous body, the one that made it particularly useful for social criticism, was that it was highly responsive to cultural conditions. Each occupation produced a distinctive body type, for example, which was then further differentiated through the inheritability of acquired characteristics.[5] The physical material of the body had more pliability than it now appears to have. And so, from the perspective of the late twentieth century, it is tempting to say that this antiquated nervous body is clearly different from the real body because this mutability is a (mis)representation.

But this cultural variability was premised on an essential physical structure that could respond to cultural conditions yet retain its integrity. This body allowed for variation within limits, and the center of this conceptual structure, the presence that both enabled and constrained its play, was the physiology of the nervous system. These physiological principles (sensibility, irritation, nervous power, excitability) were present in all bodies and were necessary to account for the observed physical variations between bodies.[6] That these principles were rudimentary, that they were vaguely understood, that they were purely hypothetical—all of this uncertainty was fueled by the underlying belief that the "real" body did function in a particular fashion, or at least within observable parameters. In recognizing that they did not quite have it right, writers on nerves were doing two things simultaneously: They were asserting that the culturally limited views of the available science were necessarily misrepresenting the real body, and they were outlining the space, outside of culture, where that real body resided. They knew without question what the real body was *not*. It was not structured humourally, as their Renaissance predecessors had thought. And that realization in itself began to shape what the body might be, so the space of the real body, that which is not understood but is always present, shifted. The real body existed in a space very different from the one that I, in my cultural perspective, would ever imagine, because I, too, know what the real body is not. I know that it is not nervous.[7]

Thus, although the nervous body has an intimate relationship to late Georgian culture, and although nervous characteristics are thought to be highly responsive to cultural events, the cultural episteme of the nervous body also affects the sense of the body as a given, because it shapes the area against which that natural body can be thought. Though it is tempting to view the nervous body as purely a product of discourse and as a cultural (mis)representation of the given body, we cannot do so without eliding the way this episteme also shapes the "real" body, the one that exists apart from all cultural understanding. I find it impossible to distinguish, ultimately, between what a culture takes for granted about "the body" and the body as something that is given. For that reason, this study is ultimately concerned not with *the* body but rather with the means through which a culture produces its version of *the* body as that which exists outside of culture.

The same problem appears when trying to differentiate between "actual" psychological states and a culture's beliefs about its own psychological processes. The nervous system had an "intimate association with the phenomena of mind" because, despite disagreement on a somatic site for the mind, "it was generally recognized that the nervous system did represent an interface between the material and psychic realms."[8] As a result, the late Georgian era is called "the age of physiological psychology." The defining feature of the nervous body was its susceptibility to nervous disorder. But although all bodies had nerves, not all nerves were susceptible to nervous disorder, and the way in which that line was drawn, in terms of gender and class, is a central preoccupation of this study.

"Hysteria" was the term most often used for nervous conditions. It derives from the Greek word for uterus, *hystera*, and was used in classical antiquity to describe complaints caused by the "wandering womb," which traveled around within the female body.[9] The Middle Ages attributed supernatural causes to hysteria, and it became associated with witchcraft and possession, but naturalistic explanations advanced during the Renaissance viewed it as a physical, rather than spiritual, condition. Hysteria became known as a disorder of the nervous system rather than the uterus during the Enlightenment and remained so throughout the nineteenth century. Though theories of causation and consequence changed, hysteria remained a functional organic disease—that is, a disease assumed to originate in physical causes even though empirical evidence of the physical cause was unavailable. However, at the end of the nineteenth century Breuer and Freud redefined hysteria as originating in mental, rather than physical, causes, so mental states that were physical in origin again ceased to qualify as hysterical, as in the Middle Ages.[10] More recently, "hysteria" has all but disappeared as a diagnostic category in clinical usage. In 1987 it still existed parenthetically, as an antiquated alternate term, in the *Diagnostic and Statistical Manual of Mental Disorders: DSM-III-R*, the official taxonomy of disorders published by the American Psychiatric Association. Those references disappeared in *DSM-IV*, published in 1994.[11]

Even after reviewing this brief history, however, it is difficult to avoid the implication that hysteria, variously labeled, has an ontological status apart from its labels. The idea that one could write a history of hysteria presupposes that, at some level, there is something to write a history of, something that is consistent enough to be traced through various representations over 2,000 years.[12] And yet the purpose of this study is not to gesture toward the transhistorical reality of hysteria but to outline the shape that category took in the late Georgian period.

Today, at the same moment that hysteria is disappearing from clinical practice, it is enjoying a renaissance in academic writing.[13] In a survey of this phenomenon, Mark S. Micale locates four hundred separate publications on hysteria, most of them published between 1980 and 1995. He calls this phenomenon "the new hysteria studies" and lists the separate disciplines involved as follows: "within the health sciences, neurology, psychiatry, clinical psychology, and psychoanalysis, and within the humanities, intellectual history, medical and science history, legal history, women's studies, psychoanalytic studies, art history, and literary history and criticism" (*Approaching Hysteria*, 5). Each discipline defines hysteria differently, and different definitions exist within the disciplines.

The predominant definition of hysteria used in literary criticism derives from psychoanalytic theory. Hysteria is associated with woman's exclusion from the sphere of representation, the symbolic that is necessarily gendered male. In elegantly theorizing hysterical narrative, Mary Jacobus writes: "Women's access to discourse involves submission to phallocentricity, to the masculine and the symbolic: refusal, on the other hand, risks re-inscribing the feminine as a yet more marginal madness or nonsense. When we speak (as feminist writers and theorists often do) of the need for a special language for women, what then do we mean?"[14] Within this interpretive paradigm, hysterical narrative can become valorized as a radical social critique because it is the means of evacuating the phallocentric space of the symbolic and opening up a space in which the theoretical paradox, a language for women, becomes possible.[15]

As the point of departure, psychoanalysis uses the opening act in the twentieth-century conceptualization of hysteria, the publication in 1895 of Breuer and Freud's *Studies in Hysteria*, and its foundation text, the case history of Fräulein Anna O., in which the "talking cure" originates. Anna O., the paradigmatic hysteric, is unable to tell the story of her own past. As Breuer sees it, "she would complain of having 'lost' some time and would remark upon the gap in her train of conscious thoughts" (*Studies on Hysteria*, 24), and that inadequacy is the central symptom of the disorder. Through the talking cure, she slowly works her way backward in memory, moving through layers of unconscious resistance until she finally remembers the originary event she had repressed. Her hysteria disappears once she becomes able to tell the story of her past. Through this case history, hysteria has become regularly associated with aphasia and the inability to tells one's story. Hélène Cixous's formulation is memorable: "Silence: silence is the mark of hysteria. The great hysterics have lost speech, they are aphonic" ("Castration or Decapitation?" 49).

Aphasia was one of the grab bag of hysterical and hypochondriacal symptoms before Freud, but so too was a contradictory impulse to speak, and we must account for those other parts of the constellation of hysterical stars. One can see definite prefigurations of Freud's ideas within the tradition of writing on nerves.[16] Freud began his career as a neurologist, and so his early training was in the school of medical ideas about nerves in the late nineteenth century that, in turn, originated in the Enlightenment redefinition of the body as primarily nervous.[17] The most well-known intellectual history of hysteria, Ilza Veith's *Hysteria: The History of a Disease,* shows how tempting it is to read the record of hysteria as a slow parade toward the concepts Freud would later articulate.[18] But this synchronic narrative obscures the diachronic coherence of those pre-Freudian hysterias. Emphasizing those elements of nervous thought that are continuous with Freud's ideas and ignoring those that are discontinuous is a useful strategy for understanding Freud and psychoanalysis, but it comes at the expense of the materials necessary to conceptualize the structural center of earlier hysterias.[19] For the purposes of cultural history, the value of hysteria as an object of study lies precisely in its protean, wide-ranging, and frequently unrestricted semiology. This conceptual flexibility allowed the disease construct to be adapted to the different circumstances of time and place.[20] Hysteria is always thought to be enigmatic, and so it is necessary to account for the local context in which it is deployed, the individual decision that *this* is hysterical and *that* is not.

Roger Chartier points out that the object of cultural history has shifted over time.[21] What began as an attempt to define a prior social reality has focused instead on an analysis of the process of its representation. "Reality thus takes on a new meaning. What is real, in fact, is not (or is not only) the reality that the text aims at, but the very manner in which it aims at it in the historic setting of its production and the strategy used in its writing" (*Cultural History,* 44). This is the basic premise of this study and is why, in writing about Thomas Trotter and Edwin Chadwick's ideas, for example, I place them in a prominent relationship to their profession-building projects. My approach toward the topic of the working-class body is to interrogate it as a middle-class representation and to focus on the discourse in which that body was constructed. As with hysteria and the body, I am not locating the social reality of working-class experience in these middle-class studies. I am solely concerned with the middle-class idea of a working-class body and with understanding why it was imagined in the way that it was.

I do not know whether these literary writers read the medical texts under discussion. It is worth noting that medical texts at the time were not the province of specialists that they are now, that their language was still accessible to any well-educated reader, and that all the literary authors discussed in Part 2 were exceptionally well read in that broad category of discourse then known as "letters." My argument is not one of influence but rather that this nervous body was an integral part of the culture in which these writers lived.[22] And if they did not think about the body and its psychological life in the precise detail of medical writers, they could not think at all about these things without using the basic grammar of its nervous structure as the means through which the amorphousness of personal experience was organized and explained.

My assumption is that the structural premises on which the nervous body rests are most accessible in the grammar of physicality contained in the language of medical writing, where the physiology of the body receives its fullest discussion. I also assume that this grammar exists outside of any individual medical text and that it is not restricted to medical discourse. To avoid an overly specialized treatment, I have chosen to concentrate on a medical text that is more representative than innovative, to do a formal analysis of its structural assumptions, and to use those assumptions as representative beyond this specific text. This is a manageable procedure because I am ultimately writing not about late Georgian culture in its entirety but rather about a slender, horizontal section of it. Although I utilize primary texts from a variety of discursive practices—philosophy, medicine, fiction, colonial history—all are written by middle-class writers for an assumed middle-class readership. Indeed, all can be traced to the thinnest band, a narrow intellectual segment of that contentious class, because almost all are written by people, men and women, who made their living through writing or the educated professions.

I have thus tried to focus my analysis as specifically as possible on a localized context of nerves, as they were conceived by members of one class in one place and at one time. And if this nervous body and its narratives appear more strange than familiar, that at least indicates progress. To take this problem further by going backward to the epigraph from Francis Bacon, if that body were to "bleed afresh"—Bacon thought it might even open its unseeing eyes—then we, its post-Freudian "murtherers," will finally know we have got the right corpse.

PART ONE

THE BODY WITH THE STORY TO TELL

1

The Narrative of
Nervous Bodies in 1800

Thomas Trotter's A View of the
Nervous Temperament

The British physician Thomas Trotter began his literary career in 1777 publishing conventional poetry in *Edinburgh Magazine*, and he ended it with a collection of verse in 1829.[1] But by far most of his writing was on medical subjects. He received his M.D. at the University of Edinburgh in 1788, and from 1794–1802 he served as one of four doctors to the British Navy. Admiral Howe named him physician to the Channel Fleet, a particularly important appointment because it gave Trotter full responsibility for health conditions aboard forty warships and supporting boats during the height of the naval war with Revolutionary France. Howe was impressed by the obscure physician's first book, *Observations on the Scurvy* (1786), written before he entered medical school. Trotter went on to write a second book on the topic and another on naval medicine in addition to writing on health conditions in coal mines. While a student at Edinburgh, he had written his M.D. thesis on alcoholism and, in 1804, published the first medical text to categorize drinking as a medical condition rather than a moral failing, *An Essay on Drunkenness*.[2]

As a naval physician, Trotter observed a direct relationship between the diseases of sailors and the environmental conditions aboard ship. Shortly after his retirement to private practice in Newcastle, he extended the concept of environmental causality to write about the broader English social environment and its relationship to nervous conditions in *A View of the Nervous Temperament* (1807).[3] This text stands out in its time as one of the few full-length treatments of that characteristically late Georgian condition, excess sensibility, which Trotter calls the nervous temperament.[4] The medical ideas he proposes on the subject are not, themselves, so much original or unique as they are exemplary and influential; his study pulls together many different strands of Georgian thinking about the nervous patient and rearticulates them in images that would persist throughout the nineteenth century. *The Nervous Temperament* also sold well, going through three editions in Britain and becoming the first book on mental medicine ever printed in the United States. Today, medical historians view *The Nervous Temperament* as the culmination of a series of popular books on nervous disorders by medical writers.[5]

Trotter, echoing many of his contemporaries, warns that nervous conditions are so widespread in England that they pose a threat to the nation's commercial greatness and independence. The epidemic, "if not restrained soon, must inevitably sap our physical strength of constitution; make us an easy conquest to our invaders; and ultimately convert us into a nation of slaves and ideots" (*NT*, xi). Despite their ubiquity, these disorders are notoriously difficult for doctors to read. Hysteria is defined as a protean condition, one that has no reliable signs of its own. As Trotter notes, the symptoms "vary in every constitution" (*NT*, xv), and so the best he can offer is an impressionistic description of his own, gleaned from practical experience. He calls it a "cursory" list and limits it to only five symptoms, the most consistent indicators of an inconsistent disease. The symptoms of the nervous body are:

> An inaptitude to muscular action, or some pain in exerting it; an irksomeness, or dislike to attend to business and the common affairs of life; a selfish desire of engrossing the sympathy and attention of others to the narration of their own sufferings; with fickleness and insteadiness of temper, even to irrascibility; and accompanied more or less with dyspeptic symptoms.
>
> (*NT*, xvi)

Each of these five symptoms deserves comment, but the one at the center of the list stands apart. For although Trotter otherwise refers to physical sensations, his claim that nervous people are forever demanding "the sympathy and attention of others to the narration of their own sufferings" describes an act of speech. As an act, it differs qualitatively from the other symptoms. An "inaptitude" to action, or a "dislike" for it, indicate constrained or inhibited acts, whereas narration is not only uninhibited but actually in need of constraint. A nervous condition impedes most actions, but it enables the act of speech. The type of speech it generates is remarkable, too, in its specificity. Trotter describes not just any narration but one with an identifiable form, a specific content, and a distinct rhetorical function.

This symptom is far from being an eccentric element in Trotter's list. Indeed, the idea that nervous disorders can cause one to talk excessively about her or his bodily condition persists today. Such people are still called "hypochondriacs," the term used for male hysteria in the eighteenth century.[6] But whereas hypochondria, like all nervous disorders, originally had an endless parade of symptoms, only this particular narrative act has survived to become the primary meaning of the term in current usage.[7] This observation, first, suggests that this narrative act has had a lengthy and intimate connection with nervous conditions. Second, it allows one to glimpse the centrality of this narrative act in the construction of nervous disorders and thus to see that its appearance within Trotter's list, far from being idiosyncratic, is a foregone conclusion. It is, to him, so much a matter of common sense that it occurs within his most "cursory" thoughts on what most likely indicates a nervous condition.

Hysteria in Lacanian psychoanalytic theory today is more generally associated with aphasia than with speech and often privileged as an index of the imaginary, which exists outside the symbolic system of language.[8] But in confronting the physiological premises for pre-Freudian ideas about hysteria, the cultural logic they embody, and the boundaries for the fluid implications that follow from them, strange bodies come into view. The association of hysteria with a compulsion to speak is one of the most foreign, as it is the point on which hysteria in 1800 differs most dramatically from what is meant by hysteria in psychoanalytic discourse.[9] Yet within the assumptions about nerves as a mechanical entity, this association is unavoidable. As I will argue here, narrative became a central sign of nervous disorder because the nervous body had a narrative structure, and so there was an intrinsic link between nerves and narrative. But to understand why the nervous body was associated with narrative, we need first to understand what that body was like in 1800 and what kind of narrative it contained within it.[10]

Trotter derives his ideas about the structure of nerves from two founding figures in British neurology, the Scottish physicians William

Cullen (1710–1790) and Robert Whytt (1714–1768). In his *Observations on the Nature, Causes, and Cure of Those Disorders which Are Commonly Called Nervous, Hypochondriac, or Hysteric* (1764), Whytt argues that hysterical maladies are due to the "delicacy and sensibility of the whole nervous system" rather than an imbalance of bodily humours.[11] Cullen, one of Trotter's teachers at Edinburgh University, invented the term "neuroses," defining them as "all those preternatural affections of sense or motion."[12] Thus, a neurosis was originally any disturbance in either of the nervous fibers' two basic functions, the communication of physical sensations to the brain or of the brain's motor impulses to the body. Physicians of the eighteenth century were uncertain how the fibers actually conveyed these messages, whether through an ethereal fluid that flowed through the nervous tubes or through an exquisite vibration of the fibers. But they took a functional approach to the problem, inferring the presence of a *vis nervosa* from observations. Whytt thus notes, "But altho' the minute structure of the nerves, the nature of their fluid, and those conditions on which depend their powers of feeling . . . lie much beyond our reach; yet we know certainly, that the nerves are endued with feeling . . . and [I] have thought it better to stop short here, than to amuse myself or others with subtile speculations concerning matters that are involved in the greatest obscurity" (Whytt, *Works*, n.p. [Preface to *Observations*, p. 2]). Trotter also draws on an established tradition of medical writing that associated the rise of nervous conditions with the rise of civilization. His greatest indebtedness is to George Cheyne (1671–1743), Samuel Richardson's physician.[13] In his popular *The English Malady* (1733), Cheyne argues that two-thirds of the English aristocracy have fallen prey to a host of nervous conditions, variously called spleen, vapours, lowness of spirits, hysteria, or hypochondria.[14] In his meliorist view, however, the English malady is a sign not of failure in the character of the English aristocracy but of England's singular economic success. Too many luxuries, spicy foods, sensual pleasures, and indulgent excesses have degraded the delicate nervous constitution of the upper class. "Nervous Disorders," he insists, "are the Diseases of the Wealthy" (*English Malady*, 158). Laborers, in his view, lack the physical fineness in their nervous fibers required to develop nervous disorders: "*I seldom ever observed a* heavy, dull, earthy, clod-pated Clown, *much troubled with* nervous *Disorders, or at least, not to any eminent Degree; and I scarce believe the thing possible, from the* animal oeconomy *and the present Laws of Nature"* (*English Malady,* 180, original emphasis). Rather than melancholy, the poor suffer from simple laziness.[15] Nervous conditions thus became an index of wealth and of the breeding that produced delicate sensibility. It was because of the class-specificity of the disease, as articulated by Cheyne, that nerves became fashionable during the eighteenth century as a sign of social stature or of the acute sensibility associated with the disorder.[16]

The Romantic-era epidemic that Trotter describes is thus an aristocratic disease whose class boundaries have been redrawn.[17] In Cheyne's era nerves were "little known among the inferior orders," Trotter notes, but in 1800 they "are by no means limited to the rich" (*NT,* xvii). Indeed, Britain's consumption of luxuries has grown to such an extent that now *"nervous disorders . . .* may be justly reckoned two thirds of the whole, with which civilized society is afflicted" (*NT,* xvii, original emphasis).[18] Because of the sedentary nature of their occupations, bankers, vendors, and investors from the rising commercial and bureaucratic branches of the middle class now "make up the bulk of hypochondriacs in this country" (*NT,* 43). Their daughters and wives are victimized by misguided social conventions that keep them confined indoors reading passion-inflaming novels. Because of the widespread availability of tea, tobacco, opium, and especially alcohol, even the working class has become susceptible.[19] But Trotter's concern with laborers is limited; he holds that their physical activity keeps their bodies strong enough to resist the worst effects of debauch. Conditions endemic to poverty, such as starvation and exhaustion, pose a danger, he acknowledges, but one that does not compare in significance to the infinitely more dangerous diseases of wealth: "[A]ll the diseases which are caused by hard labour, poverty, and want, are much easier of cure, than those which arise from indolence, luxury, and debauch. A constitution that has been weakened by subtraction of nourishment, may soon have its energies restored by suitable regimen, diet, and medicine: but the frame that has been wasted of its vital powers by excessive stimuli and debilitating pleasures, has seldom or never been brought to its former strength" (*NT,* 47–48). At the opposite extreme from poverty, we are told, "to be born a prince, is to be the most unfortunate of mankind," for of all individuals, he most lacks the hardiness to endure the dangers of excess and simultaneously is "exposed to greater temptations" than others (*NT,* 221). Like Cheyne, Trotter remains concerned with the diseases of wealth. His interest in the working class is always contingent on the danger it poses to the health of his middle- and upper-class audience. Thus, he warns readers to beware the condition of a wet nurse, who might communicate her debility to their delicate children.[20]

This expansion of the epidemic across class lines necessitated a revision in the traditional method of diagnosing nervous diseases. Interpreting psychological disorders had always presented a major difficulty for the physician because of the indefiniteness of their signs. Robert Burton, in 1621, writes, "The tower of Babel never yielded such confusion of tongues, as the chaos of melancholy doth variety of symptoms."[21] A century later, Whytt is still able to observe that the label of nervous disorders, "having been commonly given to many symptoms seemingly different, and very obscure in their nature, has often made it to be said, that physicians have bestowed the character of *nervous,* on all those disorders whose nature and causes they were ignorant of" (Whytt, *Works,* n.p. [Preface to *Observations,* 1]). Whytt explains this confusion by contending that nervous diseases are by definition imitative of other diseases. As he conceives it, the nervous system touches all the organs of the body, so any disruption of the nerves affects the performance of one or more of the bodily organs. A nervous disorder might impair the function of the intestines and present itself to the outside observer as dyspepsia or constipation. Or it might appear in the lungs as congestion, in the heart as an elevated pulse, as typhus, or as delirium. Nervous disorders "imitate the symptoms of almost all other diseases," writes Whytt; "the shapes of Proteus, or the colours of the chamaeleon, are not more numerous and inconstant" (*Works,* 530). Trotter agrees: "In the body we observe symptoms, that counterfeit every other disease" (*NT,* 289). Thus the "migratory power which these affections possess, of traversing every part of the body, is the inscrutable *idiosyncracy* of the NERVOUS TEMPERAMENT" (*NT,* 216, original emphasis). The primary problem represented by nervous disorders, then, is this seemingly insurmountable epistemological dilemma caused by their imitative nature. Nervous disorders are everywhere, but they are everywhere disguised as something else. Whytt summarizes the problem as "the difficulty, perhaps the impossibility, of fixing a certain criterion by which nervous disorders may be distinguished from all others" (*Works,* 528).

Like his predecessors, Trotter uses the concept of predisposition to tame the protean shape of nervous disorders. As he notes, the irregularity of their symptoms must lead the investigator to look elsewhere: "A methodical history of these diseases, at least a narrative of the symptoms as they appear in succession, is almost impossible. They assume such variety in form and manner in different persons, that we look in vain for regular order. The only thing certain and peculiar in their character, is *predisposition*" (*NT*, 166). This prior susceptibility that constitutes the nervous temperament, not the manifest disease itself, is the subject of Trotter's book. This temperament is an invisible first stage in a two-stage disease model. In the first stage, a hidden temperament is first formed and creates a predisposition to nervous disorders. In the second stage, an actual disorder, such as hysteria or hypochondria, is manifested. The temperament is itself created by exposure to the same kinds of events that, when continued, will later aggravate it into a manifest disorder; the danger lies in repeated exposure to a broad class of causes rather than to a single catastrophic event. As Trotter notes, "Many of these causes, of both the mental and corporeal class, act for a length of time before they bring forth actual disease; but this mode of operation would seem to happen only where there was no predisposition. They may therefore be said first to create predisposition, and when this is sufficiently done, a train of symptoms appears which constitutes real disease" (*NT*, 196–97).

This hidden temperament also can be inherited. When a mother or father is in the second stage and actively suffering from a nervous disorder, the acquired temperament of the parent will be inscribed on the body of the child, who is born with an inherited nervous temperament and so is predisposed to the protean host of nervous disorders. It is in this manner that the nervous temperament has become, by 1800, an integral part of the British "constitution," according to Trotter. This inherited condition resembles Cheyne's theory of blue-blood aristocratic sensibility, but it is more closely related to the acquired condition. It extends into the next generation what was acquired in the first. And so the middle-class nervous temperament always originates in social factors rather than in some "naturally" predisposing condition in the body, such as the innate delicacy of the aristocracy. But by allowing for the function of inheritance within the structure of the temperament, Trotter is able to extend the class range of the condition yet retain its traditionally aristocratic characteristics. The specific predisposing factors, however, can no longer be restricted to the narrow range of experiences and inherited sensibilities unique to an idle aristocracy. Trotter's explanation of the specific conditions within the middle class—primarily their sedentary occupations and confinement indoors—that eventually create the predisposition is the central object, and the central accomplishment, of *A View of the Nervous Temperament.*

Although the predisposition is hidden, those conditions that create it are readily accessible to the physician. Thus, Trotter insists on a type of social realism in the practice of medicine: "Early habits, pursuits in life, modes of living, moral character, preceding diseases, amusements, professions, seasons, climate, &c. must all be taken into the account" (*NT,* 208). Through such a broad knowledge of the individual's circumstances and personal and family history, the doctor can gauge the likelihood that the patient's complaint represents a given disease or its nervous counterfeit. The division of labor in modern society, he argues, generates unique body types; each occupation produces "a different species of being" (*NT,* 31). Because bodies literally embody their social role, the first step in the proper interpretation of the body is to place it in its social context to establish the body type:

> The physician of a cultivated understanding, who knows how to appreciate the resources of his art . . . would not confound the complaint of the slim soft-fibred man-milliner, with that of the firm and brawny ploughman; nor would he mistake the nervous cramp of the delicate lady, for the inflammatory pleurisy of a nut-brown country girl. If both expressed pain on the same spot or organ, he would, in consideration of original temperament, along with the concourse of symptoms, resolve into first principles what belonged to each constitution; and thus analyze the morbid phenomena, so as to give a degree of certainty to his indications of cure, and a decision to his practice, that would insure success, if the disease was at all remediable.
> (*NT,* 25–26)

Because nervous disorders imitate all others, bodies must be resolved into their different constitutions as a means of establishing whether symptoms represent established disorders or their nervous doubles. Thus, identical signs in two different bodies do *not* have the same meaning; the sign of nervous disorder in the urban "lady" means a simple cold in the rustic "girl," whose active life in the open air rules out the presence of a nervous disease. The same rationale marks his distinction between the plowman and the milliner. The ambiguity of nervous symptoms is thus resolved by interpreting the individual physical body as a product of its role in society, using information on occupation and parentage as the primary criterion in determining the presence of a nervous predisposition.

Trotter represents the effects of the nervous temperament in his different images of the sensible and insensible body. Both occur under various guises and in changed circumstances, but throughout his discussion they take two paradigmatic forms, each of which needs to be considered separately. The first is the urban female, "where the sensibility trembles at every breath" (*NT*, 36).

The female body in modern society has become, as Trotter terms it, "a subject for medical disquisition" (*NT*, 49). Hysteria began as a disease-construct specific to women, and its name was taken from the Greek word for uterus, "hystera." But in the eighteenth century, when the body became redefined in terms of its nervous system rather than Galenic humors, hysteria became one among many recognized nervous disorders and less frequently was viewed as intrinsically connected to the uterus.[22] Nonetheless, the new nervous medicine continued to associate the female body with a greater susceptibility to nervous disorders by ascribing to it a nervous system more impressionable than that of the male body. Whytt explains, in his *Observations*, that in women "the nervous system is generally more movable than in men," and it is because of this hyperacuity that women "are more subject to nervous complaints, and have them in a higher degree" (*Works*, 540). Trotter inherits this assumption and makes it conform to his theory of predisposition. In terms of the two-stage model of the temperament, the female body, because of its "greater delicacy and sensibility than [that of] the male" (*NT*, 49), is naturally in the first stage and is never free of the nervous temperament. Male bodies, by contrast, are naturally born without the temperament. "Hence the diseases of which we now treat, are in a manner the inheritance of the fair sex" (*NT*, 51–52), the bodies of which are always predisposed to the protean horde of nervous disorders. When to its intrinsic sensibility is superadded the "preposterous customs of fashionable life" (*NT*, 52), the female body rapidly succumbs to the multiform disabilities of the nerves: "[T]he modern system of education, for the fair sex, has been to refine on this tenderness of frame, and to induce a debility of body, from the cradle upwards" (*NT*, 49). In consequence, he laments, "these diseases, from innate delicacy of frame, fall mostly on the fair sex" (*NT*, 249). The nervous temperament is thus indivisible from the female body; it forms a constituent part of Trotter's gender construct.

His attitude toward this female body is two-sided. In his argument against the "modern system of education" for females, he takes the position that women are victimized at an early age by the very practices intended to protect female delicacy from harm. Against enforced inactivity, he argues that the young girl should be allowed to run "with her brother, to partake of his sports, and to exercise herself with equal freedom" (*NT*, 50). Because of her inherent predisposition, she is even more in need of this exercise than her brother. It is sadly misguided, thus, that "we indulge our boys to yoke their go-carts, and to ride on long rods, while little miss must have her more delicate limbs crampt by sitting the whole day dressing a doll" (*NT*, 50–51). Yet the female body, though victimized by confinement, is also the contagious source of the nervous epidemic; the nervous mother, in her debility, infects her offspring with a constitutional nervous temperament. Trotter quotes Deuteronomy (38:56) for emphasis:

> "The tender and delicate woman among you, which would not venture to set the sole of her foot upon the ground, for delicateness and tenderness, her eye shall be evil towards the husband of her bosom, and towards her son, and towards her daughter."
>
> No text in scripture, or any other book, ever conveyed a more just censure on the indiscreet conduct of a parent to the offspring. From having injured her own frame by refinements in living, the mother thus sows the seeds of disease in the constitutions of her children: hence a weak body, delicate nerves, and their consequence, a sickly existence, become hereditary.
>
> (*NT*, 52)

Instead of being a passive victim of its condition, the female body thus represents the active principle of contagion. More significant than the mere fact of its activity is the way in which it acts. The disease it "sows" in the frame of its children, that "weak body" with its "delicate nerves," is the essential sensibility that Trotter defines as a constituent part of the female body. So he argues, ultimately, that the female body not only spreads disease but spreads the particular disease of femininity by reproducing its female nerves. In his analysis, it is this specifically female contagion that threatens England.[23]

The suggestion that the nervous temperament is a female contagion is made explicit in Trotter's images of contaminated males who are literally being transformed into females. Clerks, merchants, and vendors, for example, are debilitated by the sedentary nature of their employment, and they are infected by the female clients with whom they associate each day. Trotter claims these males thus suffer peculiar "degeneracies in corporeal structure," which he describes as follows: "These persons are commonly pale and sallow, soft-fibred, and of a slender make. Not a few of them behind the counter, approach in external form towards the female constitution; and they seem to borrow from their fair customers an effeminacy of manners, and a smallness of voice, that sometimes make their sex doubtful" (NT, 41). As nervous disorders imitate other diseases, they also mask themselves in changed social mannerisms. Society itself becomes a form of nervous masquerade as males discard their supposedly natural gender roles, adopting those of the female. Male nervous personalities undergo a similar transformation. In business, such men are "indecisive, unsteady, and impracticable. Their friendships are often puerlish, and their resentments unmanly" (NT, 163). In government, the emotionalism of a nervous legislator can endanger the state: "Every plan he devised, would partake of the mood he happened to be in at the moment" (NT, 161). The common characteristic in these nervous men is a mercurial inconstancy—variously called fickleness, changeability, or a "wavering and capricious principle of action"—which is a hallmark of female gender stereotypes in eighteenth-century thought (NT, 163).[24]

The uncontaminated male body is absent from Trotter's representation of the present, and the author describes this opposite of the nervous female paradigm as belonging to the distant past of ancestral Britain's tribal life. Drawing on Gibbon's account of Tacitus, Trotter devotes a full chapter to describing the historical transformation of the human body.[25] The savage tribe's constant exposure to the elements hardened their bodies and dulled their susceptibility to dangerous sense impressions. This leads Trotter to the conclusion that "insensibility or passive content of mind, are the inheritance of the untutored savage" (NT, 29). This inheritance, because it forms the exact reverse of the sensibility that is "the inheritance of the fair

sex," suggests that Trotter's primitive world was primarily a masculine one, even as his contemporary world is feminine. Thus, the ancestors had "large limbs and muscular form" (*NT,* 21). As gender
roles in Trotter's day blur sexual differences toward varieties of feminization, the earlier savage state blurred them toward the male: "It
was part of the matrimonial contract," he writes, "for the wife to
share with the husband his labours and dangers; and to be his companion in peace and war" (*NT,* 22). Trotter's image of the savage female body is a significantly masculinized one in the gendered terms
of Trotter's day; it is characterized by physical strength, vigor, and
stamina as well as stature. In this way he constructs an overall historical narrative that tells the basic story of the decline of the healthy
and therefore male body and the rise of the sick and female body.[26]

These two paradigms of the insensible and sensible body establish a fundamental antagonism between bodily health and the basic
capacity for feeling. Trotter claims that the savage's insensibility was
accompanied by a remarkable "health and vigor of body" and total
freedom from "bodily disorder" (*NT,* 20). Thus, he reflects, "if his
enjoyments are limited, his cares, his pains, and his diseases are also
few" (*NT,* 29). This absence of enjoyment was not due to any lack of
beauty in nature, which Trotter frequently praises. Instead, Trotter's
point is that insensibility dampens the feelings of pleasure as well as
pain. This absence of *all* feeling, both "enjoyments" and "cares," was
the guarantor of the savage's perennial good health. Thus, health is
predicated on an inability to feel. At the opposite extreme, civilized
bodies of both sexes quickly develop a feminine sensibility, which,
we are told, "disposes alike to more acute pain, as to more exquisite
pleasure" (*NT,* 25). From the earliest age, the child's body in civilized
society is sensitized by a stimulation that makes it alive to all sensual
delights: "He is no sooner brought into the world, than he is taught to
admire every thing that dazzles, glitters, or makes a noise" (*NT,* 221).
But this same urban body is simultaneously weakened by luxury
and its physical confinement, becoming thus both physically weak
and sensitive to sensation. Sensibility and illness combine in the civilized body as intimately as insensibility and health combine in the
savage. In Trotter's model of nervous function, then, feeling itself en-
dangers health. To be capable of feeling pleasure is to be unavoidably exposed to the dangers of pain.

By medicalizing sensibility, Trotter sacrifices the positive qualities associated with the ability to perceive sensations at the beginning of the nineteenth century. For although it poses a peril to the body, sensibility is equally a necessity for the individual. The nervous system, as the site at which sensations enter the mind and motor impulses move outward, is also the medium between the individual and the world. Being insensible implies a type of individual isolation, a lack of sympathy for others, and it is this absent capacity by which Trotter defines the savage.[27] The savage's nervous system "was fully excited for all the movements of vital energy" (*NT*, 27). It was not inert; his mechanical sensations were functioning well, as they would have to be for adept hunters and warriors. What remained absent was a theoretically higher level of functioning, the excess of sensation that generates the capability to experience "higher" sentiments or those "elevated" feelings associated with refinement, as well as the despair that forms their unavoidable shadow.[28] There was no artistry or inventiveness in the savage's most un-Athenian world, and Trotter consistently regulates any implication in his description that there might have been an aesthetic component to it. There were martial tournaments, for example, but even these dramas "were only kinds of palaestrae for exercising the body so as to enure it to martial fatigues" (*NT*, 23); they served a purely functional end, rather than including displays of color or artistry. As Foucault has noted, "On one hand, nervous sufferers are the most irritable, that is, have the most sensibility: tenuousness of fiber, delicacy of organism; but they also have an easily impressionable soul, an unquiet heart, too strong a sympathy for what happens around them. . . . From now on one fell ill from too much feeling; one suffered from an excessive solidarity with all the beings around one."[29]

It is precisely because the nervous temperament implies qualities in excess of mechanical sensation that the condition of sensibility embraces at once the body's greatest triumph and its most abject failure. For, as Trotter acknowledges, although the nervous temperament is the cause of Britain's degeneration, it is also the seat of sympathetic understanding: "On the other hand, the nervous temperament is often found to be the soil of numerous virtues: the noblest feelings are cherished here. Sensibility to excess marks the constitution; and affliction cannot address it without meeting its sympathy. It is this degree of feeling, that too often makes it the sport and victim of passion. It loves and hates beyond bound. Hence those corroding sorrows, which sometimes overtake the most tender of all attachments, and which ultimately bring the possessor to the grave" (*NT,* 164). The conflict between what are simultaneously the "noblest feelings" and feelings "beyond bound" is unresolved (and unresolvable) in Trotter's pristine encapsulation of the paradox of sensibility. Virtue and despair thus join hands in a bodily condition where to feel "tender attachments" is also to suffer under the most "corroding sorrows." It is this problematic body represented by the nervous female, rather than the absent body of the healthy male, that Trotter faces in the present.

The difference between these two bodies rests on their opposite relationships to narrative. Trotter defines sensibility and its nervous consequences by explaining that "the living body possesses the faculty, if I may so call it, of receiving impressions, and retaining them, even to the hazard of its destruction" (*NT,* 199). The hazard of nervous disorders is caused by the problem of retained impressions. In Trotter's nervous physiology, healthy nerves receive and transmit impressions without ill effect, operating as transparent media between the subject and the world. But the nervous body "retains, or records as it may be termed, all the effects of vicious indulgence" (*NT,* 211). These retained impressions produce a physical record of the past that is "hoarded as it were in the structure of [the body's] nerves" (*NT,* 210). Thus, as a physical condition, the nervous temperament consists in a new receptivity to impressions that are incorporated into the fibers of the nerves, taking on a new materiality as they become permanently etched in the body rather than passing through as transient sensations. This process of retention, however, cannot continue indefinitely, for it is limited by the finite capacity of the nerves; eventually they "accumulate the quantum of predisposition, and a nervous fit, or a *bilious attack,* is the immediate consequence of every new trouble of mind, and of every recent debauch of the body. Thus the habit may become so completely nervous . . . that the faculties of the soul will be worn out, and fatuity takes place; and the body will be so enervated as to be in a state of constant pain, tremor or convulsion" (*NT,* 211). The essential quality of the nervous temperament, thus, is that it destroys the body's assumed ability to resist the ill-effects of impressions. It creates an overly inscribable body, one that is too easily written upon by the stimulus of its day-to-day experience.

These gradually accumulated impressions create a narrative within the nervous body that details its interaction with the larger social order. Within each nervous body lies the story of the social conditions that created it and, having created it, compel it to act out its nervous fit. This narrative is also a history of its own production, a somatic *bildungsroman* that tells the story of how it came into being, of how this particular body came to have a story to tell. Trotter's medical text on the genesis of nervous disorders is thus a critical treatise on how and why these nervous narratives originate.

Trotter's two paradigmatic bodies thus have essentially opposite relationships to this nervous narrative. The nervous female body contains a narrative within the fibers of its nerves. That narrative details the body's interaction with the social world around it, and so within each nervous body lies the story of the social conditions that created it. The non-nervous male body, certainly, has a history, but it is not pressed into its material structure, waiting to come forth at a moment of crisis. The nervous female body, however, possesses a constitutive relationship to narrative. It has a story to tell, whereas the healthy male body has none. In the medical view, nervous disorders as well as narrative itself are inextricably bound up with the female body and with the feminization of the non-narrative male body. To assert, then, as this medical writer does in his brief list of nervous symptoms, that a particular narrative act is symptomatic of nervous disease is to presuppose the narrative structure of the disease. He is saying that, having acquired the body with a story to tell, the nervous sufferer characteristically tells it.

When this body tells its story, it is going to tell it in a recognizable form, that of "engrossing the sympathy and attention of others to the narration of [its] own suffering." And, because of its association with the female body, this form is unavoidably gendered female. In this nervous narrative, the speaker pleads for the listener's sympathy and so will appear blameless or essentially victimized. She narrates her own sufferings, describing in the first person the events in the past that produced her nervous condition. It is a retelling of the narrative in the body; the narrator tells the story of how she acquired the body with a story to tell, of how she came into being as a narrator. This is also a self-canceling narrative, because the narrator's authority to speak is compromised by the nervous disease that the story reveals. To a trained ear, the form of this narrative immediately identifies the speaker as a medical object, not an authentic speaking subject. It demands treatment, not attention: a house in the country, fresh air, and energetic horse rides are the proper response. If it is heard in the prescribed manner, as a type of hypochondriacal speech, we know that this narrative asks only to be made to disappear, regardless of what it might say. And it will disappear, of its own accord, as the nervous narrator is recuperated to the realm of health and silence. Because she has acquired the body with a story to tell, the nervous narrator is disqualified from telling it.

That authority shifts to the practitioner. His minute attention to the individuality of the nervous body allows him to represent, in the third person, the narrative that has been written on its nerves and produces its disease. From the vantage point of the practitioner, the new nervous body is a body in need of his narration. And his job as a nervous doctor is to tell the story his feminized patient has been disqualified from telling.

Trotter's brief list of symptoms reflects the new social reality of 1800. Defining as a medical condition a "dislike to attend to business and the common affairs of life," for example, is a way of naturalizing the new importance the middle class attached to efficiency and routine. Trotter's nervous temperament is a middle-class disease, as he points out, and his configuration of its symptoms tends to reflect the concerns of his own newly important class by medicalizing behaviors that contradict its values. He also defines the specific conditions that are responsible for the new epidemic within the day-to-day experience of this class. These social conditions have changed since the day of Cheyne and have brought into being this new nervous body. So Trotter's construction of the epidemic has two separate aspects to it: the naturalizing of middle-class values and a critique of middle-class social reality.

We can see his ideological assumptions at work in his most frequent complaint about modern life, the lack of physical activity caused by sedentary occupations. Nervous diseases "are chiefly the offspring of a life of sloth and inactivity" (*NT*, 156). Thus he lists as the first of his five nervous symptoms an "inaptitude to muscular action, or some pain in exerting it." This physical passivity forms an important trope in his litany of conditions contributing to the

present, debilitated state of the physical body. Prior to Trotter, inactivity was commonly used to explain the mental maladies of the
aristocracy. But because Trotter is concerned with the middle class,
his focus on the ill effects of inactivity involves a criticism of middle-
class forms of property that do not require productive activity. When
Trotter argues that inactivity leads to "the most confirmed habits of
nervous affection," he explains that "[s]uch cases are chiefly to be
seen among people enjoying easy fortunes, who had formerly been
active, but are now without any of those urgent motives which preserve energy of mind, so conducive to health" (*NT,* 246). Their former activity indicates that these sufferers are not perennially idle
aristocrats but successful entrepreneurs who have found a way to
invest safely their ample fortunes. Trotter in fact makes this suggestion explicit, and his comment emphasizes the relationship between
the condition of possessing an "easy fortune" and the social effect of
commercial investments: "The public funds of this country are one
great cause of those torpid habits of living; where the security of
property is so compleat, that any care about its safety is needless. A
vast capital is by this means unproductive of any thing to the public,
but is a source of bad health to its owner. All interprize is thus
checked among a large part of the community, who become victims
to diseased feelings, and to those kindred glooms which prey on still
life" (*NT,* 246–47).

Trotter formulates a direct causal association between the investment in "public funds," or government stock, and the sedentary
habits that generate the nervous temperament. Once alerted to the
implicit criticism of "unproductive" uses of capital within his references to "sedentary" habits, one rapidly perceives that his argument
against the dangers of "civilization" is specifically aimed at a credit
society's commercial investments, which make this idleness possible. As we have seen, Trotter reserves his greatest opprobrium—
and the greatest degree of effeminization—for "men of business." In
that class he includes "[a]ll those employed in the public offices of
government, and in the houses of trading companies and banks"
(*NT,* 43)—that is, those most closely associated with the stock market and capital investment, or more generally the commercial and
bureaucratic branches of the middle class. This segment of the middle
class, in particular, has inherited the mantle of the English malady
from the young lords of George Cheyne's day. Instead of aristocrats,

Trotter tells us, in "this age, when riches are so generally diffused," men of business now "make up the bulk of hypochondriacs in this country" (*NT,* 43). In the middle class, the figure of the sedentary, successful man enjoying his "easy fortune" is repeatedly discussed: "When he comes to retire he is of all men the least satisfied; for his easy circumstances become the root of all his evils; and from having no longer any motive for action, he falls a certain prey to low spirits" (*NT,* 42–43). What matters in the ideological underpinnings of this observation, ultimately, is the social arrangement that makes that "easy retirement" possible for a man whose new independence comes not from land but from successfully invested capital.[30]

The consequences of such a secure means of wealth on the national character are disastrous. Surveying Britain of 1805 and its response to the imminent danger of French invasion, Trotter describes a nation lost in the delusions of its own hypochondriacal fears. Whereas early Britons repelled invaders with a calm spirit of self-reliance, modern, effeminized Britons instead have "projected the inundation of Essex, and hoarded up the current gold coin, as tokens of being afraid of the French. These alarms are to be considered as so many symptoms of a nervous temperament appearing in our national character" (*NT,* 147). Given his years of naval experience, Trotter is as certain of the groundlessness of such fears as he is about their source: "[A]t this moment she has a navy capable of fighting the whole fleets of Europe united; yet she trembles at a flotilla of cock-boats. It is that puddle of corruption, the Stock Exchange; that Delphi of Plutus, where stock-brokers pay their vows, and expound prophecies, that has filled the nation with degenerate fears, apprehension, and hypochondriacism" (*NT,* 147). Thus, Trotter blames the system of public credit, the stock market, and commercial investment generally for the rising disorders that are effeminizing the "national character" through the nervous diathesis.

In a broader sense, the "effeminizing" threat to society posed by commercial exchange lies in its redefinition of relations within that society. Commerce transforms relations between otherwise independent individuals into mutually dependent relationships, and Trotter loathes this transformation. His indictment of "commercial society" draws heavily on a coherent tradition of eighteenth-century political rhetoric, recently elaborated by J.G.A. Pocock.[31] This oppositional tradition raised an ideal of agrarian independence against the corrupting relations of commercial exchange. It relied on a resurrection of the patriot-citizen ideal of the Greek *polis,* in which land enables the individual to become an independent, and therefore virtuous, civic actor. This oppositional discourse originated in response to the Financial Revolution of the 1690s, when the government instituted the national debt and financed the country's political operation through an offering of public stock. Pocock points out that this new system of public credit "transformed the relations between government and citizens, and by implication those between all citizens and all subjects, into relations between debtors and creditors" (*Virtue,* 110). An elaborate system of patronage, or favoritism in appointments, arose between the government and its creditors, who wielded a new influence in the control of preferments, so that the entire government was seen as operating through a web of mutual dependencies that destroyed self-sufficiency and created instead a nation ruled by corruption.

This commercial creation of dependent relations was not limited to the operation of public stock but included, by association, trade in general. As Pocock notes, "The merchant became involved in the indictment of capitalism, and the credit society became known as the 'commercial' society, because it was observed that there was a fairly obvious relation between trade and credit" (*Virtue,* 110). Commerce transformed isolated and self-reliant societies, such as those of Trotter's ancestral ideal, into societies that now depended on others for their economic well-being. In Trotter's idealized past, "when commerce has made no progress," each localized group was self-reliant because each was isolated from "intercourse with its neighbours" (*NT,* 25, 143). But commerce between groups erodes their capacity for independent action: "A commercial people merely, can never be an independent nation. They owe to foreigners the consumption of their manufactures; and when these chuse to do without them, or to buy them elsewhere, such a people must become bankrupts in finance" (*NT,* 150). Buying and selling thus produce mutually dependent relations, and it is this dependency that Trotter views with the greatest alarm, associating it with the effeminization of British society.

Trotter does not offer a coherent scheme of social relations to replace those of the effeminized commercial society. But his remedy implies a retreat from exchange-value to a social order founded on use-value. He advocates a direction away from the stock exchange and back toward rural life. Cheyne had been obligated to defend himself for adopting a similar course, which led to the accusation that he "advis'd People to turn *Monks,* to run into Desarts, and to live on Roots, Herbs, and wild Fruits; in fine, that I was at Bottom a mere Leveller" (*English Malady,* ii). Rather than prescribing an actual return to a life of nuts and berries, Trotter generalizes that the "lesson is only so far in point, as it tends to confirm general truths . . . or to illustrate a precept by showing an example" (*NT,* 233). Yet the "simplified mode of living" that Trotter recommends as an anodyne for the disease of civilization promises to renew health in the face of contemporary hysteria, and it aims to do so by implicitly reforming society's property relations, eliminating "unproductive" forms of labor involved solely in commercial exchange and favoring the "productive" labor represented by the farm. Trotter's solution to the nervous temperament consists of a modified return to the agrarian life of the past, with an emphasis on "simplicity of living and manners" (*NT,* xi). Thus, his specific remedies always entail altered economic relations. Ideally, the businessman or artisan and his family must move "from the city to the village," where they will begin anew as gentleman farmers (*NT,* 245). He endorses a new society to promote a scheme "to regenerate the physical strength of the country, by recalling mankind to agricultural life. . . . No man who possesses the smallest spark of love for his country, but must with full success to the undertaking" (*NT,* 149–50). Where such a removal is not possible, he recommends intermediate steps, such as daily rides into the country "beyond the effluvium of smoke and mud" and extended vacations there (*NT,* 248). But where an agrarian way of life is impossible, Trotter is pessimistic; for "the town-bred female"—more in need of an energetic country life than the male, yet more restricted in her options—he advises, "[i]f she cannot look to a country residence, her situation must be pitiable" (*NT,* 249). Against the commercial dependencies symbolized by the rise of the city, he thus prescribes a return to the limited intercourse of agrarian independence.

This dichotomy between the healthy virtue of agrarian independence and the avaricious patronage of urban politics permeates Trotter's text. The healthy masculine savage is also a paradigm for the modern agrarian individual, rendered self-sufficient (and thus masculine) by virtue of his land. The modern female, we have already seen, is closely allied to the urban man of business. His contamination by her femininity is a dramatization of the dependent relations in which he is placed by the process of commercial exchange and by his dependency on the good will of the buyers and sellers with whom he deals.

Trotter's political rhetoric was a conventional part of the ongoing debate between competing elements of the middle class. The standard commercial response to claims about the corrupting effects of commerce on social virtue, first articulated by writers such as Addison and Defoe, was to transform commerce into the primary source of social good.[32] According to this point of view, commercial intercourse destroys the isolation of societies by bringing them into closer communication with one another. Rather than creating servile dependency, commerce leads to an increased understanding between individuals and between societies, thus enlarging the scope of social sympathy. It progressively expands a society's knowledge of the world. "Refinement" and "manners," far from the transient "fashionability" Trotter complains about, represent an accumulation of social wisdom that distinguishes civilized people from their ancestors, who are conceived as unsocialized barbarians rather than as the noble savages of Trotter's mythology. Thus, when Trotter claims that nervous diseases "receive a stronger tincture from the manners of the age, than any others" or that they "increase in proportion to the deviation from simplicity of living," his rejection of "manners" and endorsement of "simplicity" is a criticism aimed at the heart of the ideology of eighteenth-century commerce.

Sensibility plays a central role in this commercial ideal as a product of the progressive refinement of the individual's capacity to feel. It represents the remaking of the individual personality by the accumulated improvements in social organization made possible by the rise of commerce. Thus, Trotter's medicalization of sensibility as the nervous temperament at its most fundamental level makes pathological what are otherwise seen as the beneficial effects of marketplace dynamics on social development. Sensibility is indivisible from coffee, opium, tobacco, tea, spice, and other "luxuries," which both cause nervous disorders and function as metonyms for commercial trade and commercial social values. It is for this reason,

Trotter claims, that the "produce" of Britain's trade "only tends to weaken her manly character, and overwhelm her with nervous infirmities" (*NT*, 144).

Because Trotter was himself a middle-class professional, his critique of middle-class values cannot be disinterested. The medical profession in 1800 was still emerging from the patronage system of eighteenth-century medicine, in which doctors were servile dependents of their aristocratic patients. Though major professional reform would not be instituted until the 1830s, Trotter was one of the earlier voices to argue for it; he wanted to end medicine's dependence on wealthy clients and to establish an independent social basis for medicine's professional authority.

Few biographical details are available, and most of those are supplied only by his own writing, but it appears that Trotter himself was victimized by the system of government patronage at the time he was writing *The Nervous Temperament*.[33] His appointment as physician to the Channel Fleet by Admiral Howe in 1794 brought the obscure young doctor into a demanding, high-profile position, and his efforts were noticed. In 1802, at the age of forty-two, he retired early after injuring himself climbing aboard ship. Despite his accomplishments, testimonials on his behalf, and the service-related nature of his disability, his pension was only half what his colleagues received, the minimum of £200 per year. Trotter was convinced that the parsimonious award, inadequate to live on, was the result of professional jealousy by the other naval physicians and their patrons, who resented his success and his evidently high reputation (*Sea Weeds*, xix). Nor was this an unwarranted assumption. His Edinburgh degree placed him outside the institutional structure of power in the British medical profession, as virtually all political authority within the Royal College of Physicians was held and jealously guarded by graduates of Oxford or Cambridge, despite the fact that medical education at Edinburgh was clearly superior to that of Oxbridge.[34] Because he was an outsider, Trotter appears to have made serious enemies by gaining Howe's appointment and improving his reputation, and Howe's death in 1802 left Trotter vulnerable.[35] It is certain that Trotter was excluded from the increase in pensions awarded to ship's doctors shortly after his retirement and that his appeals for a redress of his grievance were first ignored and then dismissed in 1805 and again in 1808. Thus, his remarks on patronage and nervous disorders in *The Nervous Temperament*, written in 1805, have a timely autobiographical resonance: "Some of the severest instances of these diseases, which have come under my care, were in officers: men endued with acute sensibility of mind, of fine parts, and with high notions of honour. They had been long tantalized by promises of promotion, and lived to see unworthy favourites put over their heads. Similar cases are too often met with among other conditions of life; where worth, virtue, and talents, must give place to wealth, servility, and intrigue" (*NT*, 88–89).

Having been on the losing end of the system of political patronage in medicine, Trotter is uncompromising in describing its adverse effects on the profession as a whole.[36] He establishes a melodramatic rivalry between the physician of a "manly spirit and dignified independence" and his avaricious counterpart, "the gossiping physician" or "wheedling apothecary" (*NT*, vii, 232). Trotter's battle with degeneration in the profession is a substantial element of his treatise.[37] It is the opening subject of the book's dedication and appears more than fifteen times during the course of his text. Degenerate doctors cater to their patients' hypochondriacal ailments rather than adopting an independent and medically principled position. Such doctors contribute to the spread of nervous disorders, rather than curing them, by subjecting patients too frequently to courses of physic that weaken their constitutions; opium and mercury, in particular, create a nervous temperament where it does not yet exist. In a world of "the poor, sick, and lame," Trotter complains, the "physician and apothecary are seen gliding in their chariots, with retinues sometimes not much like men who are conversant with human affliction, and enriched by the luxuries and vices of their fellow mortals" (*NT*, 145).

His description of degenerate, sycophantic doctors bears a close resemblance to that of the "men of business," particularly in their exaggerated effeminacy and in the author's palpable sense of disgust: "A man who carries for ever on his face the sleek simper of artful insignificance; who has a bow and a smile ready for every person that addresses him, will be very apt to accommodate his prescription to a fashionable folly" (*NT*, 313). As eloquent and dissembling as his business counterparts, the avaricious doctor is a vendor of physic and a dependent on the good opinion of his patron-clients. His engagement in commerce thus leads him away from principled self-reliance and moral virtue.

The primary market for medical care in Trotter's time was still among the wealthiest part of the population.[38] For a physician or surgeon to sustain a full-time private practice without resorting to farming on the side or writing books (as Tobias Smollett did), pleasing his querulous and often powerful patients was essential. In the relationship between practitioner and patient, the latter frequently held the balance of power over the former, who was the patient's social inferior and so was expected to accommodate the treatment to his or her desire for a particular remedy or favorite physic.[39] Nowhere was the subservient role of the practitioner more evident than in the treatment of nervous disorders, where the clientele was historically drawn from the wealthy and the protean disorder impossible to identify. As Trotter acknowledges, "This branch of medical practice has commonly been reckoned one of the most lucrative; for the subjects of it are generally found among the affluent" (*NT*, 231). When the only evidence for a nervous complaint is the patient's testimony of some discomfort, a difficulty sleeping, anxiousness, or lethargy, the medical attendant is wholly dependent on the patient's report to make the diagnosis.

Trotter's placement of that same patient narrative at the center of his list of nervous symptoms is thus part of a professional strategy to minimize the patient's authority within the new doctor/patient relationship, and his definition of the doctor as narrator is the necessary counterpart to that goal. His construction of middle-class hysteria is part of the ongoing campaign to professionalize medicine. He writes that the purpose of his book is "to familiarize the junior members of the profession with the genius of nervous disorders" (*NT*, x). In this process of educating members of the profession, he aims to alter the professional relationship between patient and doctor by contributing to an elite basis of specialized knowledge on which the practitioner can claim an independent basis of authority.[40] He would have physicians be as independent as any idealized landholder, beholden to none and none to him, and therefore able to act with perfect, uncompromised virtue. He thus seeks to rescue the physician from the cesspool of patronage and from the influence of his feminized patients and so establish him as an independent civic actor in the model of the agrarian ideal of virtue.

But this rhetoric of dependence and independence directly conflicts with the larger goal of professional reform. For professional independence depends on a base of specialized knowledge, not land. Establishing independence for the physician means accumulating knowledge and progressively refining techniques, processes that presume a network of social intercourse. Trotter draws on the ideas of his predecessors Cheyne, Whytt, and Cullen; he quotes from Tacitus, Horace, Virgil, the Bible, Shakespeare, and Goldsmith; and he cites contemporary medical and historical texts, borrowing their ideas in a perfect example of how commerce promotes the accumulation of knowledge and progressively refines social wisdom.

The social function of Trotter's book is to establish a knowledge base for professional independence. But by thus participating in the exchange of ideas and the process of refinement that make up the central defense of the commercial ideology, Trotter symbolically elevates commerce into a necessary virtue. Even as he attacks commercial values, his attack serves a professional function that endorses the commercial ideal. His protest against the effects of commercial exchange is ultimately a reassertion of commerce's progressive underpinnings. As the voice of the new medical professional, Trotter relies on the ideology of commerce to supply him with the authority to criticize the diseases of commerce.

Indeed, the nervous doctor does more than just rely, in an abstract or formal sense, on the virtues of commerce. He makes its offspring, sensibility, the central element of medical work. The physical body, he explains, is a site of mystery and infinite subtlety. Its material truth can never be fully known "without overstepping the bounds which divine Providence has prescribed for the ingenuity of mankind" (*NT,* 142). Thus, to be empirically effective, medicine must rely on more ephemeral qualities in the physician, qualities that few possess and that exceed the quantitative sum of rational knowledge: "Nature has endowed so few minds with that superior intelligence of being equal to this task, that we cannot be surprized when told, that medicine is still in many respects *'a conjectural art'* " (*NT,* 142).[41] He insists on the need for practitioners to develop a most refined sensitivity to exquisitely subtle sense perceptions in order, for example, to judge the internal condition by signs in the patient's face: "Persons accustomed to study the variations of feature in the human countenance, such as physicians, sometimes acquire a wonderful expertness in developing the passions. This physiognomonic experience is of great utility to the practice of medicine: it is the gift of genius; and in this respect, the physician like the poet, may be said to be, *'nascitur non fit'"* (*NT,* 81–82). This "wonderful expertness," this "gift of genius," is the essential quality of the physician, distinguishing between the true *artiste* and mere mechanical imitators. "The want of this eminent quality of intellect, makes the laborious plodder a dangerous visitor at the sick bed, particularly to the nervous patient: nature refuses to draw her veil aside to a clumsy observer; who, being denied access to her mysteries, is very apt to pervert the purpose of what she discovers" (*NT,* 82). Wanting to avoid self-incrimination, Trotter refuses to brand this ineffable attribute "sensibility," yet the two are indistinguishable. Sensibility, thus, is not simply advisable in the physician; it is, in fact, the central ingredient in his interpretive work.

Trotter's construction of the nervous temperament transforms the work of the physician from what it had been in Cheyne's day. Cheyne insisted that the presence of a nervous temperament was discernible in immediate bodily signs; abnormally fragile hair suggested weak nervous fibers, for example. He carefully listed the essential physical qualities—skin color, texture, complexion, muscle tone—that could guide the physician in distinguishing a disease from its nervous double, all empirically observable qualities (*English Malady,* 99–105). Trotter, however, insists that such stable signs are misleading. The physician must see through the deceptive appearances of present signs into their past, and he must see through the surface of signs to a deeper level of hidden significance within the present moment. The epistemological problem posed by the nervous temperament demands the development of uniquely acute observational powers in the doctor. Hence, the epidemic of nervous disorders, which transforms the male body into that of the female, requires that the physician become feminized in order to combat the disease of feminization. It is precisely because of the ubiquity and ambiguity of the nervous temperament that the doctor must rely on the same nervous temperament he seeks to cure in his patient. Thus, Trotter's construction of the disease makes his own implication within it inevitable. In his inconstant—one might say "fickle" or "capricious"—wavering between the fear and praise of sensibility, Trotter becomes himself an example of the nervous temperament at work, and his text ultimately mimics the very disorder it claims to describe.

Although the simultaneous insistence on the physician's sensibility and the medicalizing of it as the nervous temperament are in conflict, they nonetheless work hand in hand in advancing the medical profession's social authority. Trotter's text claims to be responding to an epidemic of nervous disorders in British social life. It seeks to convince the reader of the existence outside the text of the nervous disorders it describes by organizing particular events and sequences of events, incorporating them into its own model of nervous function and social decay. But by relabeling as "nervous" events that otherwise would not be seen as such, the text creates a new social perception of these events as diseased. That is, *A View of the Nervous Temperament* argues for a "re-viewing" of the world. Where effeminate mannerisms in men, for example, were previously seen as a matter of manners and social bearing, among Trotter's readership they become medicalized as a nervous disorder. *The Nervous Temperament* is not simply responding to events outside of its text. It is in fact creating, in the minds of its readers and thus in social life, the disease it pretends to react against.

Trotter creates the phenomenon of a nervous epidemic and then uses it to justify medicine's existence as an independent profession. The epidemic creates a new social role for the physician; society now needs his "expertise" to rid it of the disorder he has "discovered" in its midst. And so Trotter's professional project cannot be restricted to establishing a new mode of treatment for disease, which then becomes the source of professional authority. It extends to creating the epidemic his new treatment will remedy.

In the history of mental medicine, disease constructs are frequently designed to expand the boundaries of professional authority, and in this respect the nervous temperament differs little from Esquirol's monomania in the first half of the nineteenth century or Charcot's reworking of hysteria at the century's end.[42] However, in Trotter's case this pattern is further complicated because the physician's "expertise" is intimately related to the disease he creates. The central ingredient in the physician's work is the same sensibility, or nervous condition, he seeks to cure in the world. In effect, then, Trotter creates a belief in the nervous temperament as an empirical reality but simultaneously elicits an acknowledgment, through the back door, of the related phenomenon that becomes the essential skill of the physician. The reality of that "wonderful expertness," which exists somehow in the nebulous sphere of excess knowledge and sensation, cannot well be denied in a world where its shadow looms in every nook and cranny of human behavior as the protean nervous disorder. Thus, there are two distinct but related elements to medicine in Trotter's text. The first, discussed earlier in its relationship to commerce, is based on the accumulation and exchange of knowledge and its role in the professionalization of medicine. Here the text tries to advance the development of medicine as a science. The second element, which enters on the coattails of science, is its justification of medicine as an art. In the best Romantic tradition, Trotter is *"creating* the taste by which he is to be enjoyed."[43] He does so by creating a need for his expertise as well as a belief in the empirical reality of his own refined sensibility.

PART TWO

THE BODY TALKS

2

The Nervous Narrator's Paradox

William Godwin and Caleb Williams

William Godwin's *Caleb Williams* (1794) contains an intricate representation of the nervous body in the novel. Because that body belongs to the narrator, the novel also illustrates the particular narrative act that was associated with nervous conditions. "All is not right within me," Caleb reports, and he tries to explain what has gone wrong within his body by looking back over the sequence of impressions it received.[1] Because he is isolated by the point late in the story where he begins to construct his narrative, he addresses an unknown future reader, one who will "render me a justice which my contemporaries refuse" (*CW*, 3). He rehearses for this imaginary but sympathetic audience the litany of social injustice that caused his condition, and this retelling helps him to endure the intolerable present: "I derive a melancholy pleasure from dwelling upon the circumstances which imperceptibly paved the way to my ruin" (*CW*, 123). Trotter describes precisely this form of narration in his sparse, reluctant list of nervous symptoms, discussed in chapter 1: "a selfish desire of engrossing the sympathy and attention of others to the narration of their own sufferings" (*NT*, xvi). The nervous condition, then, does not only stem from a narrative within the body; it is also associated, in early nineteenth-century culture, with a characteristic narrative act.[2]

Because the nervous narrative was viewed as the product of the speaker's disease, what is remarkable is not that it was routinely discounted because of its formal qualities but that—quite the reverse—it was routinely deployed by writers in the late Georgian period. William Godwin, after using it for *Caleb Williams,* used it again in his next novel, *Fleetwood* (1805). Mary Hays also used it for *Memoirs of Emma Courtney* (1796), Mary Wollstonecraft for Maria's memoir in *The Wrongs of Woman* (1798), Maria Edgeworth for *Harrington* (1817), Mary Shelley for Victor's narrative in *Frankenstein* (1818), Thomas

De Quincey for his *Confessions of an English Opium-Eater* (1821), and James Hogg for Colwan's half of *The Private Memoirs and Confessions of a Justified Sinner* (1824). In each case, the first-person narrative begins with the narrator's nervous body and sets out to explain the specific social conditions that produced it. The opening words of *Caleb Williams* typify the narrative stance that characterizes these nervous narrators: "My life has for several years been a theatre of calamity. I have been a mark for the vigilance of tyranny, and I could not escape. My fairest prospects have been blasted. . . . I have not deserved this treatment" (*CW*, 3). The balance of the narrative will expand on this statement, restaging the exact conditions of the calamity, and it will denounce those conditions on the basis of the narrator's illness.

This form proved inviting to writers of the period, despite its suspect nature, because people widely believed, as our nervous doctor did, that the social and physical environment had a determinant effect on individual development and, more generally, that it shaped the character of the English as a "race"—that is, as defined by a distinctly English physical body. The late Georgian period saw the beginning in England of the utopian faith in reform-oriented institutions based on the effects of control over external impressions.[3] York Retreat, the Quaker asylum for the insane founded by William Tuke in 1792, was a significant practical manifestation of this new faith. One of the earliest of the new breed of institutions, it eliminated physical restraint and punishment in favor of a new therapeutics based on the beneficial effects on the mind of a domestic physical environment combined with a carefully structured model of social interaction.[4] Prison reformer John Howard, whose 1777 book on the conditions within England's prisons is cited within *Caleb Williams*, also contributed to the new focus on the power of environmental conditions to shape individuals (*CW*, 181).[5] Institutional structures were given a utopian power to remake inmates in a predictable fashion, and this trend led to the appearance of the new reform-oriented institutions—penitentiaries, insane asylums, orphanages—that characterized the early to mid-nineteenth century. Novels such as *Caleb Williams* utilized this larger cultural paradigm.

However, this social critique produces an inherent paradox within this narrative form. For although the narrator's illness condemns the social conditions that produced it, that same illness also constructs the narrating voice. Without it, there would be no narrative, for the illness enables—in fact, compels—the narrative act. So the literary genre of nervous narration promotes, in its formal structure, the same disorder it cautions against. In this, it reenacts the paradox that Trotter's writing exemplifies in its attack on excess sensibility, for like him the novelist relies on the same condition he or she condemns. Trotter makes sensibility the center of the doctor's interpretive skill. In the novel, the narrator who criticizes sensibility does so from the position of experience, testifying to its terrors. The result is a conflict of narrative authority within the sizable group of first-person novels attacking sensibility that appeared at the same time sensibility was being medicalized by writers such as Thomas Trotter. How does the speaker of the nervous narrative criticize the sensibility that forms the basis of his or her authority to speak without negating that authority? By founding their critique on their own suffering bodies, these narrators invite the diagnosis of Trotter that the narrative itself is an expression of their disorder and hence not to be trusted. Similarly, the more compelling and admirable this narrative's aesthetic qualities, the more it valorizes the disorder that produced it. The more it succeeds, the more it fails in its critique.

Because there is no firm ground on which to base narrative authority within such a dynamic, novelists attacking sensibility must devise extraordinary strategies to develop some alternate foundation for their criticism, distancing the nervous speaker's narrative from the disease it criticizes. Godwin wrote two separate endings for *Caleb Williams,* and the changes he made directly respond to this nervous paradox, as he tried to avoid implicating his hero in the disease he constructed.

Although they were at opposite ends of the political spectrum in counterrevolutionary England, the radical Godwin shared with the conservative Trotter basic assumptions about the body's responsiveness to its social environment.[6] In his major philosophical work, the *Enquiry Concerning Political Justice* (1793), Godwin goes even further than the nervous doctor to argue that *all* disease is caused by social factors. He predicts that in the future, when social power is rationally distributed, all disease will disappear. He even holds forth the ultimate possibility that, freed of the prejudices and errors that produce social conflict and disease, people will no longer age, and so we might realize "the possibility of maintaining the human body in perpetual youth and vigour."[7] Thus, both writers interpret illness as a product of external impressions on the body, impressions that are defined as originating in the social structure. Godwin expands the role of social events further than Trotter, because he more fully enfranchises the working-class body in the new nervous democracy. The doctor allows for the presence of nervous disorders among *some* servants and laborers, but he preserves a partial role for inheritance in the production of the nervous body. Godwin, however, dismisses *all* theories of inherited sensibility as "the refuge of indolence" (*PJ*, 107). In the mold of Locke, he regards sensibility as entirely a social product: "In fine, it is impression that makes the man, and, compared with the empire of impression, the mere differences of animal structure are inexpressibly unimportant and powerless" (*PJ*, 107). Thus, the nervous body expands more noticeably across class lines in Godwin's writing than in Trotter's. It shows up in a rustic servant such as Caleb as well as in his aristocratic master, Squire Falkland.

Godwin's novels pointedly expose the specific machinery at work in the relationship between the social body and the individual. The author afterward said of *Caleb Williams* that he was primarily interested in "recording the gradually accumulating impulses, which led the personages I had to describe primarily to adopt the particular way of proceeding in which they afterwards embarked."[8] Like Trotter, he focuses on the relationship between an observable sequence of events in the external world and its consequence in the individual, trying to demonstrate a cause-and-effect explanation for present, inexplicable behaviors—the murder of a rival, the fickle behavior of a stock trader—in the body's intercourse with its social environment. This accumulation of impulses, because it represents that external social order, forms a social narrative of incidents, a narrative first produced by the order of society, then impressed on the inscribable body of the individual, and finally enacted in that individual's conduct.

The entire structure of *Caleb Williams* revolves around the problematic of the inscribable body and the social narrative that impresses itself upon it.[9] The novel ends with the nervous body of the narrator. It begins with the nervous body of Falkland. And it follows the story of the unnecessary conflict the social narrative creates between these two fundamentally honorable individuals. Falkland's story forms only the principal case history nested within the narrator's own case history. Within Falkland's tale lie further histories, each stressing the accumulation of sensations, the cascade of unwelcome shocks that lead to a given physical manifestation, either in action or illness. The squire Tyrell, a petty tyrant, is subjected to a series of "innumerable instances that every day seemed to multiply, of petty mortifications" (*CW*, 23). He is "accumulating materials for a bitter account" and "[s]marting under a succession of untoward events" (*CW*, 23). The farm boy on trial for murder commits the act only after being harassed with "a course of hostility" by his brutish victim (*CW*, 129). The sentimental heroine, Emily Melvile, uninured to hardship, develops a fatal fever due to unremitting persecution. These bodies, including Falkland's and Caleb's, are reservoirs for the social narrative, which is gradually written upon them and hoarded in the structure of their nerves. Each is the product of a slowly accumulated sequence of sensations rather than of a single catastrophic event. As the steward Collins asks of his master, Falkland, "Did any man, and least of all a man of the purest honour, ever pass in a moment from a life unstained by a single act of injury to the consummation of human depravity?" (*CW*, 103). Within the assumptions of the novel, the answer is in the negative. Despite Falkland's guilt, he is not traduced "in a moment" into the act of murder but is led into it, ineluctably, through a lifetime of socially acquired conventions, particular incidents, and recent aggravations that finally accumulate to produce the disordered fit that constitutes murder itself.

Godwin believed that his novel was going to do more than just critique society. Indeed, he wrote it immediately after completing the *Enquiry Concerning Political Justice*, with the stated intention of broadcasting his ideas to a broader readership through a more accessible representation of British social life. But Godwin felt that, in addition to conveying his philosophy, his novel was going to change the society it represented by changing the readership. "I will write a tale," he explained, "that shall constitute an epoch in the mind of the reader, that no one, after he has read it, shall ever be exactly the same man that he was before" (*Fleetwood*, ix). The statement contains three assumptions that need to be addressed: first, the reader is male; second, this male is somehow in need of change; and third, the novel can remedy this reader's problem.

That reader's problem is that he is not quite male enough. God-win's nervous body is always, like Trotter's, an effeminate one. In his utopian philosophy, he describes the ideal future as one in which "[t]he men . . . will probably cease to propagate. The whole will be a people of men, and not of children. Generation will not succeed gen-eration" (*PJ*, 776). With the elimination of disease, longevity will be infinitely extended, and reproduction, no longer necessary to the survival of the species, will cease.[10] In this disease-free utopia, then, the female body, as the site of reproduction, disappears, along with its inherent nervous inscribability.[11] In Godwin's progressive his-tory, that utopia is egalitarian but also entirely masculinized, much as the savage past is masculinized in the conservative history of Trotter. In both cases, the present body represents an effeminate de-viation from a healthy and masculine ideal.

Godwin's presentation of Caleb reflects this gendered ideology. The critical problem posed by *Caleb Williams* is that the narrator has become effeminized. Godwin describes Caleb's body as riddled with the delicate "flutterings and palpitations" of his feminine sensibility (*CW*, 153). His ruling passion is an "ungoverned curiosity" that is itself gendered female (*CW*, 133). "Caleb Williams was the wife," wrote Godwin, drawing an analogy to the story of Bluebeard, "who in spite of warning, persisted in his attempts to discover the forbid-den secret" (*Fleetwood*, xii). His curiosity represents the ascendancy of female nerves within his body; similarly, Falkland's sensibility and hypochondriacal fits suggest his own effeminacy, within the older aristocratic model. What Caleb narrates is the process of his own gradual effeminization, as his abject position makes him in-creasingly nervous. He attributes that gendering process to the im-pressions produced in him by the irrational social environment. Caleb thus tells the story of how he acquired the body with a story to tell; and through Caleb, Godwin tells the story of how the narrative of social events produces female bodies. Within Godwin's philoso-phy, the population as a whole possesses an overly inscribable body, one that carries within it the narrative inscribed by the social envi-ronment, and this narrative is the reader's problem. So all readers, to some degree, are sick like Caleb Williams.

Caleb's sensibility also has a positive side to it: It gives him a heightened "involuntary sympathy" (*CW*, 133) that, like the sensibil-ity of Thomas Trotter, makes him "a competent adept in the differ-

ent modes in which the human intellect displays its secret workings" (*CW*, 123). His role within the first half of the novel closely resembles that described by the nervous doctor. The enigma of Falkland's secret hypochondriacal fits—in which the reserved but gentle
squire has to hide himself as he begins to turn brutish, palsied, and
violent—motivates Caleb to investigate, like a fictionalized Thomas
Trotter, the elaborate history of the nervous body and to reconstruct
the story behind it. At the climax, when he breaks into his master's
chest and glimpses Falkland's autobiography, it is as if he is prying
into Falkland's own breast to discover the narrative hidden within.[12]
His narrative curiosity, his desire to know the story, combines the
same two elements that structure Trotter's work: a need for the interpreter to construct narrative explanations and the feminization required by the work of interpretation. The ability to uncover the "secret workings" and move beyond what is made available on the
surface is associated by both writers with the exquisite sensibility of
the female body.

Godwin adds a new element in the relationship between narrative and the body, however. Although the problem of *Caleb Williams*
is the social narrative that produces conflict between individuals like
Caleb and Falkland, the solution to that problem lies in a new type
of narrative, the narrative of reason. In Godwin's philosophy, the individual is a reasonable creature who always behaves rationally
within the faulty dictates of his or her situation (*PJ*, bk. 4, chapter 7).
It is impossible for any person to persist in an action he or she knows
to be based on erroneous beliefs.[13] As he points out, "there is no conduct . . . the reasons of which are thus conclusive and thus communicated, which will not infallibly and uniformly be adopted by the
man to whom they are communicated" (*PJ*, 136). Thus he establishes
the principle, evident in each of his novels, that "[s]ound reasoning
and truth, when adequately communicated, must always be victorious over error" (*PJ*, 140). Because erroneous assumptions create the
prejudice and blind traditionalism that cause the world's distress
and illness, the cure for these bodily disorders is rational explanation and discussion.[14]

Caleb Williams repeatedly illustrates the compelling power of narratives based on "sound reasoning and truth," representing in fictional form the real power it claims to possess over its audience. Emily
and Falkland both move, briefly, the emotions of the "unfeeling"

tyrant, Squire Tyrell, through their direct appeals to his reason. Like Godwin, they reject eloquent conventions of speech, using a "plain-spoken" narrative to say what would otherwise remain politely unsaid. There is a teasing motion throughout the novel wherein the power of plain-spoken truth confronts the artful prejudice that characterizes the social narrative and, like a genie constantly threatening to break out of its bottle, almost overcomes it—but not quite. Caleb almost succeeds in persuading the guard to free him. He almost succeeds in the pastoral interlude with Laura. Not until the concluding scene, when Caleb tells his story to the court, does the narrative of truth finally emerge triumphant over the prejudice produced by the social narrative. Then Caleb's "naked" analysis of the joint errors that destroyed his friendship with Falkland, the "best of men," proves irresistible, even to an audience predisposed against him because of his reputation for having the charming eloquence of a charlatan. The "artless and manly story you have told," reflects his former persecutor, "has carried conviction to every hearer" (*CW*, 324). Caleb's story is gendered male by Falkland because it is a clear expression of reason, and so it functions as a harbinger of Godwin's male utopia of reason, when all discourse will take this form. Godwin's concept of the "manly story," or the narrative of reason, envisions a narrative form in which the first-person description of personal suffering is no longer bound by its constitutive association with the female body.[15]

To Godwin, reason is less a theoretical abstraction than a physical force. As he describes it, reason operates through the same mechanism as sensations. Caleb's climactic story has the power to move his audience to tears because Godwinian reason is experienced as a felt condition. It has a pronounced sensual element that distinguishes it from error: "Our perceptions can never be so luminous and accurate in the belief of falsehood as of truth" (*PJ*, 133). Truth for Godwin is always embodied truth, rather than disembodied abstraction. It "possesses an undisputed empire over the conduct" (*PJ*, 144) because it duplicates the physical mechanism of sensation and so has the same determinant effect as do physical impressions in Trotter. As a consequence, Godwin's concept of rationality contradicts the principle of independent free will; he describes bodies as responding with the same mechanical predictability to rationality as to sensations.[16] Caleb's own language best represents the conflation of the mechanisms of reason and sensation: "I conceived that my story faithfully digested would carry in it an impression of truth that few men would be able to resist" (*CW*, 303–4). Truth operates through "impressions" precisely as sensations do, as a form of writing on the body, and thus Godwinian truth opposes the determinist power of external sensations with a similar model for reason. It competes with the social environment for control of the body of the individual, offering an antidote to the effeminizing effect of the social narrative, one that will lead a world of effeminized bodies forward to a masculine utopia. The difference between these two forces, then, is simple: whereas the social narrative produces female bodies, Godwin's narrative of reason produces male bodies.

Caleb Williams was written as a narrative of reason, and it was on this basis that Godwin imagined it could transform the reader. But he encountered a problem late in the process of writing the novel. Four days after finishing the manuscript, and with the first volume already being set in type, he went back to the novel, canceled the original ending, and wrote an entirely different conclusion.[17] The differences between the two are critical, because the two endings frame the preceding narrative in opposite lights. In the conceit of the first-person narrative, Caleb does not sit down to write his story until almost the conclusion of the novel's action, during the two-year period when he is most discouraged. Ostracized, incessantly hounded by Falkland's agent, he suffers a progressive mental collapse even as he writes the history of that collapse. When the narrative arrives at the present moment, Caleb makes a final, journalistic entry in which he decides to bring the charges of murder against Falkland. Because this decision holds the danger of imprisonment for him, he entrusts his written narrative to Collins, hoping it will vindicate his actions should the trial end unfavorably and his voice be permanently silenced. This self-vindicating manuscript, then, is the body of *Caleb Williams,* and it includes all of the novel except the brief trial scene itself, which is framed as the postscript to the narrative proper.

As first written, the postscript has the trial going against Caleb, and he ends up under physical restraint in a madhouse controlled by Falkland.[18] In notes smuggled out to Collins, he explains that his overly impassioned testimony at the trial was "alarming to my hearers" and that the magistrate dismissed his story with the peremptory command, "Be silent!" (*CW*, 330). Caleb thus is situated as a nervous narrator, with the magistrate in the position of a Thomas Trotter, dismissing the speaker's narrative as a proof of disorder and thus one that begs to be silenced. In his last note from the madhouse, drugged and virtually inarticulate, Caleb can remember nothing: "I had something to say—but I cannot think of it" (*CW*, 333). He is finally deprived of his ability to construct a narrative out of the sequence of events: "[T]here is one thing first, and then another thing, and there is so much of them, and it is all nothing" (*CW*, 334). Although the magistrate does not believe Caleb, the reader knows his testimony to be truthful. Thus Caleb's voice is suppressed, and his fugitive narrative, wisely entrusted to Collins, becomes the recovered voice of resistance to tyranny. The narrative stands as Caleb intends it, as a narrative of reason vindicating him and exposing the tyranny of the social narrative which, in an extreme form, the asylum restraint symbolizes.

The cancellation of this ending is particularly significant because Godwin conceived it first and then designed the rest of the novel to explain the sequence of events leading up to it.[19] By eliminating it, Godwin did more than excise a supplement; he apparently had located a problem in the novel's central rationale. The revised ending supports this view. In it, Caleb succeeds in the trial through his triumphant speech but suddenly disavows the entire narrative. "I began these memoirs," Caleb says in his final words, "with the idea of vindicating my character. I have now no character that I wish to vindicate" (*CW*, 326). Instead of letting his story stand as a first-person narrative seeking sympathy, in the nervous form, Godwin reframes it as a documentary of Caleb's own errors. And so, like the medical patient described by Trotter, the nervous narrator of the novel is recontained as an object of study rather than a subject, as one whose diseased and effeminized body speaks and who, in the act of speaking, delegitimizes the content of his speech.

Godwin's retrenchment might suggest a fear that Caleb's original narrative would be routinely dismissed as the product of hysteria. But the need to contain it more convincingly suggests the reverse: that there is something transgressive in the original form, something that needs to be neutralized. This is the larger problem raised by the nervous narrative in the novel and autobiography. In a medical setting, the effeminate nervous narrator is a noisy object whose body must be disciplined into healthy silence. But in a novel, the speaker's effeminization becomes formally desirable as a necessary condition for the production of narrative. Without that nervous body, there would be no narrative launched into the world, not even to warn readers against the social conditions that brought it into being. In these narratives, the nervous condition transforms the narrator into a speaking subject, one who does the disciplining through his or her body's nervous critique. In *Caleb Williams*, the problem is not just that the speaker has become effeminized and needs to be restored to a non-nervous condition but that the narrative depends on this effeminization as the basic condition of its production. In its formal quality, the nervous narrative inevitably promotes the nervous condition it claims to warn against.[20]

It has been argued that Godwin canceled the first ending because it was overly doctrinaire and he had tired of his own dogmatism.[21] In terms of what Godwin called the "moral" of a text, or its "ethical sentence," this explanation makes sense.[22] However, Godwin differentiated the intended moral from the rhetorical effect of a text; he distinguished between the contained authorial statement and the uncontained constructions that could be made of it by the reader, which he called the "tendency" of the text. At the level of this larger and less containable statement, the basic problem with the original ending is not that it is overly doctrinaire but rather that it is not doctrinaire enough. Godwin's social critique has the tendency of investing those faulty social conditions with the positive quality of generating narratives like Caleb's. Indeed, his novel presents a picture of a comprehensive system of social power whose most extreme manifestation is located in the very production of the nervous narrative itself. Thus, to criticize that system for the nervous body it generates is simply to reaffirm, at a higher level, that system's value, for it is a system that makes Caleb into a speaking subject. Although the "moral" of *Caleb Williams* is a condemnation of the injustices in British social life, its "tendency" contradicts that moral by ascribing a creative function to the same social oppression. And so Godwin must recontain Caleb's narrative. Otherwise, his social criticism inevitably valorizes the system he wants to change.

In making his revision, Godwin does not entirely surrender the ideal of a new first-person narrative form, one that is to be gendered male instead of female. When his narrator disavows his narrative, something new happens. He becomes a different type of speaker, one defined by his resistance to the essentially feminine act of narration rather than by his original indulgence in its pleasure. His narrative is reframed as a protest against the compulsion of the body to speak.

This resistance to narrative appears at two critical junctures of the narrative. In the final trial scene, it constitutes the main change in Caleb's attitude toward the trial and his own part in it. The success of Caleb's testimony hinges on his paradoxical repudiation of the act of speaking. He narrates the story of all the forces that brought him to the fatal moment of his testimony, describing the "dreadful mistake in the train of argument that persuaded me to be the author of this hateful scene" (*CW,* 320). His "manly tale" indicts the sequence of events that brings it into being, and it works through the paradox of criticizing its own narration: "Would to God it were possible for me to retire from this scene without uttering another word!" (*CW,* 320).[23] He concludes, "Never will I forgive myself the iniquity of this day" (*CW,* 323). In the trial scene, the narrative of reason is carefully bracketed within this act of negation, in which the speaker denounces himself for speaking. The "manly" quality of the tale comes not from within the tale itself but rather from the narrator's negation of his own misguided act of speech. Narrative, that is, remains a feminized act. The existence of a "manly" narrative of reason is only revealed through the narrator's resistance to his essentially feminized impulse to tell his own story.

The postscript reframes the fugitive narrative in exactly the same way. Given the change of heart Caleb undergoes in the new trial scene, the function and status of his narrative need to be redefined, for its publication—we are, after all, reading it—contradicts the new narrative conceit, in which Caleb no longer seeks to clear his own name. In the final words of the postscript, Caleb redefines his intentions, adopting a biblical tone and addressing himself to Falkland as though to a saint: "I will finish them that thy story may be fully understood; and that, if those errors of thy life be known which thou so ardently desiredst to conceal, the world may at least not hear and repeat a half-told and mangled tale" (*CW,* 326). The original nervous narrative, then, written to clear the name of Caleb, becomes redefined as the narrative of Falkland's vindication. What was initially written as a self-vindication becomes recast as a self-denunciation, and through this transformation the narrative itself is redeemed, not as a rational narrative but as a protest against its own existence.

Because it is redefined as a vindication of Falkland, Caleb's narrative finally comes to occupy the position of the narrative that he imagines is hidden within Falkland's trunk:

> The contents of the fatal trunk from which all my misfortunes originated, I have never been able to ascertain. . . . I am now persuaded that the secret it incloses is a faithful narrative . . . written by Mr. Falkland, and reserved in case of the worst, that, if by any unforeseen event his guilt should come to be fully disclosed, it might contribute to redeem the wreck of his reputation. . . . If Falkland shall never be detected to the satisfaction of the world, such a narrative will probably never see the light. In that case this story of mine may amply, severely perhaps, supply its place.
>
> (*CW,* 315–16)

By rededicating his own narrative to redeem Falkland's reputation, Caleb's narrative does finally "supply its place," establishing a formal association between itself and the imaginary narrative in the trunk. That unseen manuscript of the new Saint Falkland perfectly symbolizes the masculine narrative of reason, a dreamlike narrative that can only exist hypothetically and comes into language itself only through negation.[24] The formal effect of the postscript is to reposition the reader, who now duplicates Caleb's action within the novel and peers into that trunk at Falkland's narrative.

Thus, the narrative of reason proves elusive in the novel. *Caleb Williams* is not, in the end, such a narrative; it only points to the presence of such a narrative elsewhere, outside the novel, through the final protest against its own feminized act of narration. Although Godwin can theorize a new male narrative, because of the nervous narrative paradox he cannot tell it. He can only point to it through the speaker's protest against the compulsion to speak, through the narrator's healthy resistance to the disease that produces narration.

In reading the nervous narrative, then, emphasis needs to be given to the moment of the speaker's resistance to the act of speaking, a resistance that is evident not just in *Caleb Williams* but more famously in *Frankenstein,* with Victor's reluctance to narrate his past, or less familiarly in Hays's *Memoirs of Emma Courtney,* where the narrator protests against having to revisit her painful past. The resistance points to a subject that is conceivably distinct from the socially determined subject whose narrative is itself an act of capitulation, an acquiescence in the system it condemns. In a culture that believes widely in the determinant forces of external events, there is no safe "outside" from which to criticize its effects. Self-negation at least enables a subject to recontain her or his own uncontrollable tendency to give value to an oppressive social order, and if this resistance is not exactly self-expression, nor even descriptive of an alternate mode of being, it is nonetheless the only available sign of social condemnation available to the nervous narrator. Made into a critic by an unjust society, the social critic must necessarily practice a self-criticism—more precisely, a criticism of the hystericized impulse to criticize.

3

Narrative and Self-Violence
Framing Mary Hays's Memoirs of Emma Courtney

Caleb Williams posits a particular relationship between the narrator and the narrating body, one in which the impulse to speak is itself identified as a product of the speaker's nervous disease rather than a response to it. His speech, initially seen as outside the structure of his disorder, is ultimately defined as its very essence. Two years after Godwin published his novel, Mary Hays revisited this narrative problem in *Memoirs of Emma Courtney* (1796). In this novel, the young and philosophical Emma writes a memoir of her relationship with Augustus Harley, a man she falls in love with but who is secretly married. This memoir is in turn framed within the remarks of an older Emma. She sees her earlier justifications as the outpourings of a diseased mind. She presents the narrative as a cautionary tale to her adopted son, who is in love with a married woman, a relationship he has justified through the same kind of reasoning Emma had practiced earlier. Hays's use of this narrative structure, however, differs significantly from Godwin's. The most evident difference is in her narrator's intense relationship to the earlier narrative. Whereas Caleb Williams has lost all interest in narration, Emma Courtney experiences it as a violation: "Rash young man!—why do you tear from my heart the affecting narrative?" are her opening words.[1] She is wounded by the necessity of retelling her story, and that retelling requires an involuntary self-violence that stands in stark contrast to Caleb's lack of narrative affect. This narrative position can be directly tied to the novel's representation of a social experience for women that differs from that of men. This experience produces a distinct relationship between the narrator and her nervous body, and it is this distinction that leads to the premium Hays places on this narratorial self-violence.

Hays was an outspoken feminist and English Jacobin in London's polarized political environment of the 1790s.[2] She is most known today as the woman who introduced Mary Wollstonecraft to William Godwin and who shared with Eliza Fenwick the sad duty of nursing Wollstonecraft through her final illness. Her publications include a second novel, *The Victim of Prejudice* (1799), and a collection of non-fiction writing, *Letters and Essays, Moral and Miscellaneous* (1793). Her philosophical book on the condition of women, *Appeal to the Men of Great Britain in Behalf of Women* (1798), resembles Wollstonecraft's *Vindication* in its major outlines. Katharine M. Rogers identifies Wollstonecraft as the more theoretical and decisive of the two in her break with sentimental ideology, whereas Hays's strength lies in her practical illustrations of the everyday hypocrisy that is inevitable within the patriarchal home under the ideology of sentimentality.[3] Despite the terror of the counterrevolution, Hays continued productive writing, publishing two works on distinguished women in history, *Female Biography* (1803) and the *Memoirs of Queens Illustrious and Celebrated* (1821).[4]

Although the philosophy in Mary Hays's first novel has been seen as derivative, a product of her "blind discipleship" to Godwin, her borrowings from Godwin are a means of pointing out the limitations of his ideas rather than an imitation of them.[5] The borrowings themselves are overt and frequent. In her preface to *Emma Courtney*, Hays cites Godwin's novel as one of her models and figuratively aligns Emma with Caleb by arguing that her work similarly explores the consequences of "one strong, indulged, passion," in this case the heroine's romantic passion for her enigmatic lover, Augustus Harley (*EC*,1: Preface 5). Emma also quotes directly from both *Caleb Williams* and *Political Justice*, citing them in footnotes for the reader.[6] The most substantive reference to Godwin is his inclusion in the novel as a character, the philosophical Mr. Francis, who befriends Emma and corresponds with her. His letters are recitations of specific elements of *Political Justice*, and their inclusion in the narrative is a means of importing Godwin's voice and philosophy directly into the novel. This fictionalized correspondence also reproduces an actual correspondence between Hays and Godwin.[7]

Emma's relationship with Mr. Francis suggests an ongoing debate over the position of women in Godwinian philosophy. The crux of this debate can be identified at a particular moment three-quarters of the way through the narrative, when the Godwin double disappears. Because of a combination of untoward circumstances, Emma finds herself in London in what she labels "my present unprotected situation" (*EC*, 2:146). A variety of factors lead to this predicament. She has too little fortune to live independently because of a consistent pattern of patriarchal improvidence, and she has no living family to rely on. An older female friend, Mrs. Harley, the mother of Augustus, serves as a substitute mother for Emma and provides her with a home, but when she dies Emma has only one option: she travels to London, where she takes a room she cannot afford, in the hope that Mr. Francis, her sole remaining friend, will offer her his help. She sends him a note on her arrival and waits, but for once he does not reply. His house, she soon learns, is tightly shuttered, and he is far away, on the continent, his date of return uncertain. Out of options, she contemplates for a brief moment two unpalatable alternatives: the "degradation of servitude" or a life of prostitution (*EC*, 2:149).

The sudden and unexpected departure of the Godwin double from the narrative—he does not reappear, nor is his name even mentioned after this disappearance—is similar in effect to the death of Mrs. Harley, for Mr. Francis, too, plays a sustained parental role. His ongoing correspondence with Emma on philosophical issues is a substantial part of the novel, as the letters are transcribed at length. Within the confinement of her monotonous existence, the younger Emma welcomes his philosophical letters as a rare and vital source of intellectual stimulation. He is also significant as a sympathetic listener; her letters to him are the only means she has to voice her complaints about the enforced idleness in her life, which stifles her ideals of virtuous and socially useful activity. Mr. Francis's replies, paraphrases of *Political Justice,* urge her to sharpen her powers of reason and resist the idleness that breeds excess sensibility and its hysterical manifestations. So his sudden absence opens a large hole in the web of Emma's life. But Mr. Francis, unlike Mrs. Harley, is not dead. Instead, at the moment Emma most needs him, he is nowhere to be found.

Emma occupies a position in which Godwin's ideas no longer apply, and so his character's permanent departure for regions unknown is symbolic. Godwin's philosophy, we have seen, elides the question of sexual difference by looking forward to a uniformly masculine utopia where reproduction is eliminated. Although he maintains a commitment to equality, any concept of woman as distinct from man disappears. However, in her unprotected situation,

Emma occupies a distinctly gendered social position. Rather than an experience common to both men and women, her unprotected situation is typical of the social position specifically imposed on women, one that makes women's social experience distinct from that of men. *Emma Courtney*, then, describes a social narrative that is unique to women rather than one predicated as universal and hence male, as in *Caleb Williams*. The very moment at which Emma enters on this gendered terrain of a compulsory female dependency, when she faces the choice between service and prostitution—at that moment she discovers that the male voice of Godwinian reason resides in a foreign land. She is "alarmed by this silence" (*EC*, 2:147), and well she should be. What had once seemed so near and helpful, an unconventional and hence reliable friend for an unconventional woman, appears now remote, alien, and inaccessible.

In the last exchange of letters between Emma and her Godwinian mentor, immediately preceding his disappearance, his failure to account for woman's social experience is specifically addressed, so the relationship between the letters and the incident is that of theory and practice. The exchange takes place at the dramatic climax of the story, immediately after Emma learns that Augustus is secretly married. She has actively pursued him, even against his stated wishes, and finally proposes to live with him without the ceremony of marriage because she believes that he returns her love, and reason tells her to proceed.[8] She is right about him. When she discovers that he has a wife and children, however unloved, she concludes that her pursuit of him has in fact been an act of passion, not reason. In lengthy epistles to both Harley and Mr. Francis, she had carefully justified that pursuit in Godwinian terms, reasoning through the thicket of social proscriptions that prohibit women from actively pursuing men. But in retrospect she sees her actions differently. She was in fact the most deluded at the moment she felt most convinced of her rationality. As a result, her letters to Mr. Francis after the discovery are written in a state of wholly ungrounded perception, for she has come to doubt her basic ability to distinguish desire from reason, fantasy from reality. In this state, she initiates the final correspondence with Mr. Francis, and what she writes is substantial: the narrative of her life that we later read as the *Memoir*.

His critique of her narrative is blunt. Her pursuit of Augustus, Mr. Francis opines, was a "moon-struck madness," which "the smallest glimpse of sober reflection" would have brought to an end (*EC*, 2:99). With this, Emma is in full agreement. But he goes on to claim, in a perfect paraphrase of Godwin, that her "disappointed love" is not one of the "real evils," such as "bodily pain, compulsory solitude, severe corporal labour" (*EC*, 2:99). By indulging her excess sensibility, she has created an imaginary pain, a form of self-inflicted violence caused by "hunting after torture" (*EC*, 2:99). He explains: "Evils of this sort are the brood of folly begotten upon fastidious indolence. They shrink into non-entity, when touched by the wand of truth" (*EC*, 2:100).

At the center of this self-indulgent condition is the social dependency that leads to such indolence. It is not excess sensibility itself that is at issue in this hunt for torture so much as the underlying social dependency that generates the tendency to inflict wounds on oneself. "May every power that is favourable to integrity, to honour, defend me from leaning upon another for support," he writes; ". . . I will not be weak and criminal enough, to make my peace depend upon the precarious thread of another's life or another's pleasure. I will judge for myself" (*EC*, 2:100–101). He faults Emma for allowing her happiness to depend on the emotional whims of Augustus, thereby surrendering her independence.[9] This kind of emotional dependency impedes the independent function of reason, and that is why Mr. Francis calls it "criminal," for all rational judgments are disinterested, in his view, and not prejudiced by the needs or desires of others. "The first lesson of enlightened reason," he emphasizes, " . . . is *independence*" (*EC*, 2:100), without which reason itself is not possible. Because she has surrendered her independence, her wounds are self-inflicted.

But it is precisely this independence that is systematically denied women in Emma's narrative. Her "unprotected situation," at the moment of Mr. Francis's disappearance makes manifest the compulsory social dependency that all women face. As she states the problem, when alone in London, "[a]ctive, industrious, willing to employ my faculties in any way, by which I might procure an honest independence, I beheld no path open to me, but . . . the degradation of servitude" (*EC*, 2:148–49). Servitude is inherently degrading because it entails the surrender of independence. It is not that she does not share Mr. Francis's view on dependence but that there is no "path" to independence for women. This is the point on which she directly challenges Godwin's philosophy in her last letter to his double: "Why call woman, miserable, oppressed, and impotent, woman—*crushed,* and then *insulted*—why call her to *independence*—which not nature, but the barbarous and accursed laws of society, have denied her? *This is mockery!*" (*EC,* 2:107). Because women are denied independence by their social condition—that is, because dependence is part of the social narrative written into women's bodies—Emma's pain is not self-willed, as Mr. Francis would have it, but a genuine social evil. As she twice asks, quoting Godwin against himself, "Are we, or are we not (as you have taught me) the creatures of sensation and circumstance?" (*EC,* 2:104). Mr. Francis's refusal to accept as "real" the pain she experiences is a refusal to acknowledge the gendered condition of women, for his philosophy treats women as if they had equal access to independence and, with it, the rationality that would cure her romantic love and her pain at its disappointment.

Self-violence, as Janet Todd points out, is the definitive characteristic of this (as well as Wollstonecraft's) fiction.[10] It is also a characteristic that is constantly under interrogation in the *Memoir* and one that the frame story shares with the inner narrative. As we have seen, through its opening words the novel connects self-violence with the basic coming-into-being of the narrative. Within the narrative, self-violence is explicitly under discussion in the exchange between the female and male philosophers, but it is implicitly *always* under discussion, for the competing interpretations of Emma's painful actions—that they were avoidable, that they were unavoidable—are the issues at stake in the story of her life. Self-violence is both the specific issue in the break between Emma and Mr. Francis and the general issue against which the question of a distinctly gendered woman's social experience is formulated.

The disappearance of Godwin, as Mr. Francis, reflects a general pattern in the novel in which Emma's relationship to reason—and not just to its metonym—is marked by a tenuous unpredictability. Emma goes through three separate cycles in which she appears to recover from a distemper, acts in what she believes is a rational manner, and then rediscovers that "my own boasted reason has been, but too often, the dupe of my imagination" or that her philosophy "was swept before the impetuous emotions of my passions like chaff before the whirlwind" (*EC,* 1:84, 1:85). For Emma, the certainty of her own rationality becomes the primary symptom of its absence. Whereas reason in *Caleb Williams* is a present, palpable force, in *Emma Courtney* it is itself bracketed as an object of desire, a shadow that one wants to embrace but that always eludes one's grasp. There is no triumphant moment for the narrative of reason to rival that in *Caleb Williams*. There are moments in which rational truth should have this compelling force, as when Emma proposes a completely rational discourse with Augustus: "Let us walk together into the palace of Truth, where . . . every one was compelled by an irresistible, controuling, power, to reveal his inmost sentiments!" (*EC*, 1:180).[11] But such moments, including this, are consistently redefined as products of passion, suggesting that she does not know her own "truth."

Hays's version of self-delusion is more insistent than Godwin's, a characteristic that can be traced to differences between her framing device and that of *Caleb Williams*. Godwin's novel uses only a closing frame, in the postscript, to reveal the narration as a self-delusion, and so it is only in retrospect that the reader comes to perceive the extent of the narrator's distemper. In contrast, Hays fully frames her novel, opening it with the letter (and its defining self-violence) from Emma to her adopted son, making it clear from the start that the narrative is a cautionary tale. The author's preface reinforces the framing perspective, explaining that "the errors of my heroine were the offspring of sensibility" (*EC*, 1: Preface 8). The story itself is littered with apostrophes in which the older Emma labels her younger writing as "reasonings, so specious, so flattering, to which passion lent its force" (*EC*, 2:54). In extended quotations from the letters, the older Emma inserts footnotes warning against the rhetorical force of the diseased writer's reasoning. At a particularly dark philosophical passage in one letter, for example, a footnote cautions, "This is the reasoning of a mind distorted by passion" (*EC*, 2:94 n). It is not that the novel fails to celebrate Godwinian reason; it clearly does. But these multiple framing devices make reason significantly less accessible to the subject in Hays's novel than in *Caleb Williams*. In consequence, the novel has a more pronounced emphasis on the female's incarceration within her nervous body than does its male predecessor, *Caleb Williams*.

That incarceration is represented as an inescapable product of woman's social condition. Emma's story details the evolution of her disorder as a form of excess sensibility in the protagonist, one that is explicitly compared to Caleb Williams's uncontrollable curiosity. But the conditions that create the protagonist's "distempered imagination" (*EC*, 1:89), as Emma calls it, are explored in much greater detail in Emma's narrative than in Caleb's. Whereas Caleb's early years are sketched in a few paragraphs, Emma gives a sustained history of her childhood and adolescence, methodically demonstrating the wholly ordinary events that, one after the other, with compelling force, produce the excessive sensibility that finally compels her distempered condition. An educated narrator, Emma approaches the topic of her past scientifically, delineating the sequence of impressions—being weaned, being overly indulged as a child, reading romantic novels, being deprived of stimulating companionship— that molded her mind and made her susceptible to her romantic despair.[12]

The central moment in this development occurs when she falls in love with a portrait of Augustus, before ever meeting him, and his idealized image becomes all-in-all to her.[13] As she explains, "Cut off from all the society of mankind, and unable to expound my sensations, all the strong affections of my soul seemed concentrated to a single point" (*EC*, 1:113). She floods the representation of Augustus with desired qualities and invests him with a fairy-tale aura of perfection. She also recognizes that she is in love with "an ideal object" of her own making, but, she concludes, it "was in vain I attempted to combat this illusion; my reason was but an auxiliary to my passion, it persuaded me, that I was only doing justice to high and uncommon worth; imagination lent her aid, and an importunate sensibility . . . completed the seduction" (*EC*, 1:116). Where Godwin would identify this delusion as self-inflicted, she represents her romantic love as if it were as inevitable as an infection, to which she later compares it: "[A]rgue with the wretch infected with the plague—will it stop the tide of blood, that is rapidly carrying its contagion to the heart?" (*EC*, 2:103). To her, the condition is an occupation of the subject by a compulsory and unwanted sexuality. Her romantic feelings signal her containment within the female social narrative.

The causes of her disease are represented as conditions typically experienced by middle-class daughters, implying that her distemper is a general condition for women, not one unique to the heroine. In a pattern similar to that outlined by Wollstonecraft in *Vindication of the*

Rights of Woman and later by Florence Nightingale in *Cassandra*, she identifies the underlying condition as the restricted social role of women and an economy of energy in which enforced female passivity leads the mind to turn inward:

> While men pursue interest, honour, pleasure, as accords with their several dispositions, women . . . remain insulated beings, and must be content tamely to look on, without taking any part in the great, though often absurd and tragical, drama of life. Hence the eccentricities of conduct, with which women of superior minds have been accused—the struggles . . . of an ardent spirit, denied a scope for its exertions! The strong feelings, and strong energies . . . forced back, and pent up, ravage and destroy the mind which gave them birth.
> (*EC*, 1:169)

Emma Courtney is thus less one woman's story of disappointed love than an examination of how late Georgian social conditions create a psychology that is unique to women and that results in a debilitating form of romantic love. Once created, it remains permanently etched in Emma's body, "written upon my own mind in characters of blood" (*EC*, 1:2), constituting an irresistible part of her nervous physiology.

In Emma's distemper, her entire being becomes focused on the object of desire to the exclusion of all else. It causes her body to tremble and blush; she feels faint in his presence; her passions run out of control. Hays's representation of excess sensibility constructs female sexuality as a diseased product of woman's social condition. Trapped within bodies that are sexualized by their early education and by restrictions on social activity, women become immersed within an isolated and overpowering sensibility. Sexuality in *Emma Courtney* perpetuates that isolation by subverting women's rational social ties, which are abandoned in the face of a selfish and individualized passion. Thus Emma refers to her passion for Augustus as "an excess, perhaps, involving all my future usefulness" (*EC*, 1:116), because it compels her into self-centered, and self-indulgent, forms of behavior rather than enabling outward-directed, socially useful activities. This prediction is realized during her marriage to Montague. Having spent her passion on Augustus, she has none left for Montague, whose offer of marriage ultimately resolves the problem of her "unprotected situation." She marries him in the same way that the spent Marianne in Austen's *Sense and Sensibility* marries the spent Colonel Brandon. And that's good. The early period in Emma's marriage becomes for her a time in which "every hour was devoted to active usefulness, or to social and rational recreation" (*EC*, 2:164). This outward-directed activity contrasts favorably with Emma's previous transformation from enforced idleness to romantic incapacitation. Like Austen's Marianne, she develops a rational friendship with her husband. Montague "became more dear to me" after the birth of a child, and her capacity for controlled emotion seems to recover. Emma feels "new and sweet emotions" and tastes "a pure, a chaste, an ineffable pleasure" in watching a maternal tableau of husband caressing child (*EC*, 2:165).[14] At the sudden reappearance of Augustus, however, her new social relations evaporate into nothingness, as the old passion reemerges. "For a moment," she tells us, "conjugal, maternal, duties, every consideration *but for one subject* faded from before me!" (*EC*, 2:174). As if she were back before the portrait, all else fades from view when this isolating sexuality—permanently inscribed in her nervous body—directly conflicts with her participation in any outward-directed activity.

Although Emma's memoir represents as unavoidable her confinement within this debilitating social condition, the fact of the memoir's existence threatens formally to undermine that claim. Because the memoir exists as a form of social intercourse, Emma appears to have the social agency she represents as being categorically unavailable to women. And so *Memoirs of Emma Courtney* raises a problem for narrative agency similar to that raised in *Caleb Williams:* how to construct a subject-position for a narrator who articulates her own lack of agency without contradicting that statement through the agency involved in being a narrator.

Hays constructs two distinct subject-positions, the younger and the older Emma, and each has a different claim to narrative agency predicated on a distinct relationship between narrative voice and narrating body. The narrative, as has been noted, is initially written when the young Emma learns about her lover's secret marriage and her distemper is at its height. She writes as a self-justification to Mr. Francis, her intended reader. Looking back, the older Emma explains, "I drew up a sketch of the events of my past life, and unfolded a history of the sentiments of my mind (from which I have extracted the preceding materials)" (*EC*, 2:96). Like Godwin's novel, then, the narrative is originally produced by a disordered mind as a supposedly rational explanation for the narrator's actions. Writing the narrative at the time is therapeutic, she explains, for "[w]hile pouring itself out on paper, my tortured mind has experienced a momentary relief" (*EC*, 2:95). The original act of narration soothes her nerves, as it relieves Caleb's, by releasing the story written within her body and giving it voice.

The younger Emma, in her letters and in the remnants of the earlier "confessions" (*EC*, 2:115), writes as if she has the status of an agent, as if she possesses a basic independence and, with it, access to reason, despite all the suffering to which she has been subjected. She writes, that is, as if her body is not real—a heavy, physical presence—but is instead a transparent and distant object whose inscriptions do not bear on her narrative authority. Combined with her remarkable role as a sexualized agent in pursuit of the passive Augustus, this seeming detachment gives her the bearing of an intelligent, independent-minded woman who rebels against her own incarceration within the constricted female role. Thus, it is possible to read *Emma Courtney* as a transgressive narrative of female agency founded on desire, one that is not effectively contained by the "modicum of damage control" represented by the framing devices.[15]

But in terms of the feminist philosophy that Hays and Wollstonecraft shared and promoted, the younger Emma's actions are problematic, because they tie her agency to her culturally constructed sexuality.[16] In *Vindication of the Rights of Woman*, Wollstonecraft articulates the ideological nature of female sexuality and shows it to be, first, socially constructed and, second, used against women as though it were a natural attribute of the female body.[17] Wollstonecraft, like Godwin, defines sexuality, particularly female sexuality, as a social disease, one that has no place within a rational marriage, in which partners have a more intellectual appreciation of one another and can better perform their social obligations as parents: "In order to fulfill the duties of life . . . a master and mistress of a family ought not to continue to love each other with passion. I mean to say that they ought not to indulge those emotions which disturb the order of society, and engross the thoughts that should be otherwise employed" (*Vindication*, 114). It is because, paradoxically, Emma does not have a romanticized love for Montague that the marriage becomes for her an interlude of social usefulness.

Unlike Godwin, Wollstonecraft separates this disruptive sexuality from the female body's reproductive capability. Whereas Godwin predicts the eventual disappearance of the distempered female body, with its interrelated feminine nerves and sexuality, Wollstonecraft constructs a future body in terms of maternity rather than diseased sexuality. Because of this theoretical distinction, she is able to articulate a separate social role for woman that is still founded on biological difference but is no longer limited by a disabling sexuality. By recurring to the image of the widowed mother, charged with the duty of caring for and educating children single-handedly, she argues the social necessity of educating women; they will need to assume an independent, socially useful maternal role as educators of the next generation of rational citizens, ready to contribute to social improvement.[18] Thus, Wollstonecraft divides the concepts of female sexuality and reproduction in order to justify an active social role for women that preserves difference, and she does it by grounding that social role in a nonsexualized concept of the maternal.

Hays's novel incorporates Wollstonecraft's argument as the symbolic form of the narrative's structure. The memoir is originally produced as a history of Emma's sexuality, recording its production in her body's excess sensibility and expressing it through her diseased reasoning. This original narrative is also a nervous narrative, one written to Mr. Francis as an appeal for sympathy, drawing attention to the narrator's pain, and so it is also the product of the sexuality it records. In the frame story, Hays redefines this narrative precisely as Wollstonecraft redefines the female body: by discarding an agency based on sexuality and substituting one based on reproduction. The older Emma produces the narrative as the fulfillment of her maternal duty to her child, and so she gives it a clearly defined, outward-directed social function, treating its sexuality as a disease produced by an oppressive society and locating its social value in the sphere of reproduction. Thus, Hays constructs a narrative that formally enacts the redefinition of the social place of woman it proposes in its content.

The maternal Emma's voice, with its characteristic self-violence, is complex because *Emma Courtney* is not a utopian novel; the heroine cannot, by an act of philosophical insight, transcend the narrative that has been written on her body. Thomas De Quincey makes that claim an integral part of his *Confessions,* but Emma Courtney's immanence in the material does not allow escape. She cannot *not* be sexual, cannot recreate herself as a rational being, certain of the reason she does not have access to, because she can never differentiate between reason and the past sexuality that remains inscribed on her body. As it reemerges at the sight of Augustus, so too it is revisited in the act of telling the story, which recalls him to mind and brings his image again before her.[19] This sexualized past lives on in the shape of a present and tangible pain caused by the act of narration. This is why this maternal narrator describes her narration again and again as self-violence: "It has been a painful, and a humiliating recital—the retrospection has been marked with anguish . . . my lacerated heart . . . has been again torn" (*EC,* 2:218). So she chastises her son and figurative reader for the "inconceivable misery" it causes her (*EC,* 1:1). "[I]t will cost me some pain to be ingenuous in the recital . . . and I feel an inclination to retract. . . . But . . . you entreat me to proceed" (*EC,* 2:2).

The difference between the younger and older Emmas resides precisely in the opposite relationships they assert between narrative and body. The younger Emma feels pleasure as she writes: "While pouring itself out on paper, my tortured mind has experienced a momentary relief" (*EC,* 2:95). Writing is a means "to beguile my melancholy thoughts" (*EC,* 2:95), and so it eases her feeling of despair and brings her comfort when nothing else will. This early act of narration accedes to the demands of her sexualized body; she yields to her sensations in the act of writing, and so it is a pleasurable and a sexualized act. In contrast, the older Emma defines her narration as a maternal act of "sacrifice" (*EC,* 1:6) in which she must overcome the demands of her body in order to tell her story. This new act is predicated on resistance to the sexualized body and its demands, and this resistance produces her pain.

Given the way Hays has described the condition of women—as uncertain of reason, denied agency, and unable to trust their own feelings—the only available sign of narrative authority is this narrator's pain. It does not guarantee the presence of reason. It simply implies that her reason is no longer the "dupe" of her desires. That pain is the closest Emma can come to a position of intellectual disinterestedness and, so, to Godwinian rationality. Hays has created a structure that paradoxically valorizes female self-violence, not as a plea for sympathy but as a sign of a woman's right to speak. It appears to be an agency of self-effacement or subordination—that is, a self-contradicting subject-position in which the only time a woman can know she has something to say is when her body tells her not to say it. But this pain also needs to be recognized as a sign of resistance, for what is effaced is not the female subject but the corporeal effects of an oppressive society. That resistance does indicate, obliquely, the persistence of another subject somewhere within this frame narrator's voice, one who distinguishes herself from her body and whose presence, however tentative and unstable, is nonetheless more substantial than the fiction of agency in the younger Emma's illusions. This complex, incarcerated voice, which can only indicate itself by turning on itself, ignoring its feelings and undermining its earlier assertions, is the consistent and larger response to Godwin and his symbolic disappearance from Emma's story.

4

Suspiria de Machina

De Quincey's *Body and the* Confessions
of an English Opium-Eater

In writing his original *Confessions of an English Opium-Eater*, Thomas De Quincey had to negotiate a fundamental conflict between his subject matter and his narrative authority.[1] As we have seen in the previous chapters, any early-nineteenth-century narrative of a personal history filled with painful sensations raises questions about the narrator's present clarity of mind. Thomas Trotter demonstrates that the suffering of excess sensibility produces a characteristic form of first-person narrative, one that an educated segment of the middle class could and did interpret as the verbal equivalent of a nervous fit. In this historically conditioned paradigm of reading, the narration of one's own past suffering is a symptom of bodily disorder rather than a rational critique of social disorder. Thus it can be discounted as a product of the material body rather than a willed production of the intellect. De Quincey's narrative is filled with descriptions of his suffering—his starvation in London, the ongoing nervous complaint in his stomach, the despair surpassing words of his opium habit—and so the writer's central problem is how to avoid implicating the narrator within these events. He has to negotiate the paradox of the nervous narrative before he can produce a personal tale that is not dismissed as a product of his material condition. His strategy is to rigidly police the boundary between body and voice, past and present, experience and consciousness, in order to prevent the narrator's body from entering into the narrating voice.

The *Confessions*, as its essential claim, asserts the narrator's gradual achievement of this independence from the body. It describes opium addiction as a past condition wherein the narrator was entirely contained within and defined by his material being; his escape from that state is the precondition to his narration. Though his is an experienced voice, one that has suffered deeply, it differs from the characteristically sadder but wiser voices of Godwin's, Wollstonecraft's, and Hays's narrators. These earlier narrators describe an ongoing condition of indebtedness to their past, as the history of each admittedly lives on within his or her bodily condition, damaging the authority to speak. In comparison, the narrator of the *Confessions* has a more robust voice, one that asserts a more complete independence from its material condition. He tells us that he has broken the chains of addiction, and his escape indicates a severing of the ties that once bound him to his body and compromised his authority. Through his past suffering, he has acquired a body with a story to tell, and in the relation of his progress through addiction he tells its story. But he is not defined by that body. Through this escape he has become a "transcendent philosopher," one whose authority to speak is predicated on his intellectual independence from his material condition.

From the time the *Confessions* was first published to the present day, De Quincey's autobiographical claim to independence has been disputed.[2] The author contributed not a little to the problem by continuing to use opium habitually until his death in 1859, at the advanced age of seventy-four. In this century there has been a continued debate about how the material effects of opium worked their way into his writing.[3] M. H. Abrams holds that opium creates specific images and that there is a characteristic content in opium writing. Elizabeth Schneider takes a relativist position, arguing that opium intensifies elements that are already present in the writer as an individual but has no absolute effects. Alethea Hayter places less stress on the individual's psychology and more on the range of culturally specific images available to the writer. Opium influences a writer's selection from among these predefined images, she argues, and therefore similar images recur in opium writing, but not for the deterministic reasons that Abrams describes.[4]

This twentieth-century debate on the extent to which De Quincey's narrative is or is not a product of his material condition reproduces the earlier assumptions about narrative authority and the body that define the problem of the early-nineteenth-century nervous narrative. At stake within each of these three accounts is the authority of the narrator. Is this a trustworthy, autonomous individual? Or is there a controlling dependence at work, in which the material realm inserts itself into the narrator's speech? In each case, the amount of authority continues to depend upon the narrator's independence from the assumed contamination of the body. Implicit within this debate are several large assumptions that need to be questioned: first, that there is indeed a type of materiality that expresses itself in words; second, that this "body-talk" should be discounted; and, third, that there is a kind of self-expression that is not "body-talk." These assumptions are based on the same gendered distinction between competing forms of discourse that has been explored in the previous chapters. They valorize a "masculine" discourse predicated on the speaker's independence from the distorting influence of the body. And they discount a "female" discourse defined by the speaker's immanence in her or his material condition. Rather than providing yet another assessment of De Quincey's indebtedness to his body, this chapter looks at De Quincey's construction of the body and the strategies he devises to escape it.

The paradox of the nervous narrative gives us a starting point, for it demonstrates a generic problem with first-person narratives of personal suffering that compelled writers to adopt new and creative strategies in order to avoid implicating themselves within their own stories. This is a generative paradox in that it forces change within narrative form and thus keeps it unstable yet alive and growing. But De Quincey's narration presents new problems because it is also autobiography and because he was an inveterate tinkerer who could never leave off commenting on and revising this, his favorite production. In addressing the problem of narrative authority in the *Confessions*, we have to consider the original narrative and how it constructed a position of authority from which the narrator could tell his own story. But we also must look at his later writing for the same polite audience, because he modified the statements he made in the *Confessions* in a way that alters his earlier claim to authority. In 1856 he completely revised the *Confessions*, and the new narrative takes an entirely different approach to the problem of narrative authority. What emerges from this discussion as the quintessential De Quinceyan narrative strategy is his development of a fiction of independence that grows out of a self-conscious strategy to erase his body from his narrative, transforming a body-centered narrative into an intellectual product. Thus he makes over his *suspiria de machina* into a *suspiria de profundis*.

De Quincey's essential claim in the *Confessions* was that he had been a habitual user of opium and lived to tell about it. The significance of this claim changed during the course of the nineteenth century as the cultural construction of opium and its patterns of usage changed. Even by the time of his 1856 revision of the *Confessions*, opium had become a different cultural object than it was in 1821. Not until the early twentieth century did the modern view of opiates begin to take shape, and since then nineteenth-century assumptions have been wholly obliterated by the remarkably powerful and extended state discourse on drugs.

Opium was one of many new commodities that became increasingly popular in Britain during the eighteenth century as the colonial empire expanded and international trade made new "luxuries" readily available. British supplies of opium came mainly from Turkey and were imported under the Renaissance-era monopoly granted to the Levant Company, which it maintained until 1825. In De Quincey's day, opium was wholesaled at auction in London's Mincing Lane, where trade in most British pharmaceuticals was concentrated. The Society of Apothecaries was the largest single buyer, but the majority of the product went to suppliers for small retail shops, mostly grocers. Imports steadily grew during the eighteenth and nineteenth centuries as opium became both an increasingly popular home remedy and an important element of the official *materia medica*. The most popular of the over-the-counter opium preparations was laudanum, the mixture of alcohol and tincture of opium that was De Quincey's drug of choice. But it was also the main ingredient of the best-selling patent medicines, such as Godfrey's Cordial.

Opium in early nineteenth-century England was in common use. As one historian notes, usage of the drug was "quite normal," for it was "freely available and culturally sanctioned."[5] There were no legal restrictions on its sale or use, and its popularity increased steadily during the first half of the century, with the government's blessing. In 1826 the import duty on opium was relatively low at 9s per pound, and it steadily declined until 1860, when it was eliminated entirely. This policy encouraged its importation and kept the price low, so it was both cheap and in good supply. It was used by people of all classes and was routinely resorted to as a remedy for everyday aches and pains. Mild preparations were the only available anodyne for the discomfort of menstrual cramps, toothache, and influenza. It helped insomniac adults get some rest, and in lozenge form it soothed persistent coughs. A sedative for crying babies, known as Infant Quietness, was one of the leading preparations. And opium offered welcome relief for women in labor as well as for people with chronic pain and severe injuries. Because of its constipating effect, it had a therapeutic value in the treatment of cholera, which tends to kill through dehydration. The majority of usage was self-administered—that is, the individual used it without the involvement of a medical professional. Because of the expense of consultations, this practice was prominent among the working class, and it was a firmly established part of the traditional folk medicine that served as the primary treatment for the poor. In the Fens district, where opium was locally grown, poppyhead tea was a popular remedy for common maladies.[6]

It also formed a prominent part of the official *materia medica,* for it was the strongest drug available to the physician. The medical works of Thomas Sydenham, the seventeenth-century English physician who invented laudanum, were a standard part of British medical education well into the nineteenth century, and his adulation of opium as a providential gift was frequently repeated. "I cannot but break out in praise of the great God, the giver of all good things, who hath granted to the human race, as a comfort in their afflictions, no medicine of the value of opium. . . . Medicine would be a cripple without it; and whosoever understands it well, will do more with it alone than he could well hope to do from any single medicine."[7] The Edinburgh physician John Brown gave it a central role in his influential medical theory, contributing greatly to its rise in late-eighteenth-century medical usage. His praise was effusive: "[I]t banishes melancholy, begets confidence, converts fear into boldness, makes the silent eloquent, and dastards brave."[8] It was also used in the early century as part of the new nonrestraint therapy practiced in model insane asylums such as the York Retreat, where it was as effective as chains in controlling hysterics and melancholics, although it was said to have an adverse effect on maniacs. There is little to wonder at in the consistent praise and widespread use of opium, for it was the only significant painkiller available until the late nineteenth century.

It could calm and comfort a person at the extremities of physical pain, when all else was ineffectual. And it could relieve the despair of mental anguish, giving respite to the suicidal. In its various preparations, it served the many functions now reserved for aspirin, cold medicines, sedatives, and morphine.

Until the 1870s, the habit-forming qualities of opium were not a significant component of the English construction of the drug's effects. "[D]ependence on opium went largely unrecognized," claims one study. Another writes of addiction, "It was, for the most part, a non-issue. Medical men wrote about it rarely; popular writers almost never. And when people thought about it at all, they thought that addiction was a relatively infrequent, if unfortunate, by-product of the therapeutic use of an important drug." As John O. Hayden notes, De Quincey's London reviewers disputed his claim about the extent of addiction among the English, arguing that it was not a problem.[9]

The invisibility of addiction, at a time when opium was in wide use, had several causes. If a person regularly used opium to treat a chronic complaint, such as rheumatism, his or her habituated usage was not considered noteworthy. Nor was it necessarily evident in the user's condition. As Parssinen mentions, "when opium was taken at relatively modest levels, it did not *necessarily* lead to health problems other than mild constipation" (*Secret Passions*, 47). He cites examples such as a Victorian doctor who described how he carried on a strenuous practice while using laudanum daily for nearly half a century. De Quincey himself would later be cited as a similar example.

As the nineteenth century progressed, this benign view would slowly change. The preliminary challenge came during the Earl of Mar life insurance trial in 1829. After the earl's death, the insurance company refused to pay on his policy, contending that his habitual opium usage had shortened his life. Their refusal was debated before the court by medical professionals, and the case demonstrated the widespread lack of consensus on whether or not addiction damaged the user's health. Whereas the Earl of Mar trial addressed the issue of opium's effects on the body of aristocrats, its effects on the working class were debated during the public health movement in the 1860s. Campaigners for the reform of living conditions in the urban slums represented opium as an intoxicant that was primarily used as a cheap substitute for gin during periods of low wages. The alarmist claims of the sanitarians stand out because, apart from the *Confessions* itself, reports of the recreational usage of opium among laborers were exceedingly rare. As several writers have pointed out, during this same time period medical discourse is filled with reports on the recreational usage of ether, chloroform, and nitrous oxide but silent on any similar use of opium, suggesting that the specter of working-class indulgence was raised by the sanitarians as further justification for their plan of social intervention.[10]

This image of the working-class addict contributed to the relatively welcome political reception that greeted proposals by the Society of Apothecaries that their profession be given exclusive control over the distribution of opium. By having it classified as a dangerous poison, the apothecaries hoped to remove it from the corner grocery store and increase their own base of professional authority. The 1868 Poisons and Pharmacy Act was the first law regulating opium retail sales, but it was a weak statute with few practical consequences.[11] The ubiquitous patent medicines were exempted from regulation, and there was no effective provision for enforcement of its other restrictions. Nonetheless, the ongoing campaign of the apothecaries, along with that of the sanitarians, contributed to an increasingly guarded popular assessment of opium during the period from 1870 to 1910.

The development of the hypodermic syringe in the 1870s also affected the perception of addiction. When taken orally, morphine has little difference in effect from opium, and so although it had been isolated from opium in 1815, it was little used. Given intravenously, however, it delivers a much higher opiate dose than that derived through oral consumption, and so injected morphine is significantly more addictive. Because of its expense, this form of usage had an almost exclusively middle-class clientele. In the popular image, "morphinomaniacs" were predominantly women. These new addicts were still relatively rare, and because they were middle class, they were viewed sympathetically.[12] During this period there was an overall decline in the use of opium because of the development of aspirin and barbiturates. As medical use continued to decline in the early twentieth century, opium became increasingly viewed as an inexpensive recreational drug. Between 1910 and 1930 it became associated with the urban working class, especially the idle unemployed.

And through opium's association with this socially disaffected class, the modern construction, in which narcotics are seen as a social menace, finally came into being. Thus, one hundred years after De Quincey wrote his *Confessions,* the benevolent image of opium had been completely reversed.

De Quincey's readers were already familiar with opium as an everyday article of commerce. Indeed, they could hardly have avoided encountering it. It was in the grocers, the drapers, the circulating libraries, and the bookstores; it was probably for sale in the very store where they purchased the *Confessions.*[13] De Quincey's readers had been given it to quiet them as children, had given it to their own children, and had used it, much as De Quincey initially used it, on the advice of a friend, to allay a nagging complaint. Few of them, however, had experienced opium in quite the way that De Quincey described it. Instead of a slight euphoria and pleasant respite from pain, De Quincey experienced a sublime profundity, an overwhelming psychic upheaval, at his first encounter. For eight years his usage was completely recreational, with no medical utility. And when his use became habitual, it enslaved him mentally and physically instead of being a minor nuisance. As the *New Edinburgh Review* noted, De Quincey described "a new or unusual vice."[14] He presented an alternate view of the experience of opium, one that differed qualitatively from the prevailing view held by his audience, and the uniqueness of his literary representation of that experience needs to be explained.

De Quincey's experience draws on a second opium construct that was circulating at the time, one that was seen in travel literature but rarely applied to the English themselves. Derived from the British colonial context, this Eastern model differed markedly from the benign model of domestic use. As one historian notes, "Fears voiced about the immoral consequences . . . of opium were based largely on reports from missionaries returning from overseas."[15] The image of the degraded Asian opium-eater was present in popular eighteenth-century travel writings such as Baron de Tott's *Memoirs of the Turks and Tartars* (1786), in which opium is represented as a sensual luxury rather than as a medical drug, and so it had implications of heightened sexuality and a degraded, debauched existence.[16] Very rarely, this same view of opium addiction as a moral corruption also appeared within the official discourse of colonialism, and not just in the moral discourse of the missionaries. The most significant example appears in the writing of Sir Thomas Raffles, the former lieutenant-governor of Java, who published his *History of Java* in 1817.[17] This intimate study of Javan culture and agriculture, written with the objects of colonial exploitation in mind, condemns the British introduction of opium into the island, arguing that it is immoral to trade in such an "abominable poison" (*Java*, 1:115). Raffles's harsh description of opium's effects on the human body sharply contrasts with the mildness of the domestic British model:

> The effect which it produces on the constitution is different, and depends on the quantity that is taken, or on other circumstances. If used with moderation, it causes a pleasant, yet always somewhat intoxicating sensation, which absorbs all care and anxiety. If a large quantity is taken, it produces a kind of madness, of which the effects are dreadful, especially when the mind is troubled by jealousy, or inflamed with a desire of vengeance or other violent passions. At all times it leaves a slow poison, which undermines the faculty of the soul and the constitution of the body, and renders a person unfit for all kind of labour and an image of the brute creation. The use of opium is so much more dangerous, because a person who is once addicted to it can never leave it off. To satisfy that inclination, he will sacrifice every thing, his own welfare, the subsistence of his wife and children, and neglect his work. Poverty is the natural consequence, and then it becomes indifferent to him by what means he may content his insatiable desire after opium; so that, at last, he no longer respects either the property or life of his fellow-creature. . . .
> . . . Most of the crimes, particularly murders, that are now committed, may be imputed to opium as the original cause.
>
> (*Java*, 1:114–15)

In Raffles's Asian model of addiction, opium is primarily defined as a physical agent that produces a moral disease. As this "slow though certain poison" destroys the physical body, it similarly poisons the physiological site of morality in the body, the "faculty of the soul," which has a specific material locus in the brain.[18] Opium's definitive physiological effect is its action on this locus, destroying the individual's capacity for moral, self-willed action and replacing it with an "insatiable desire" for more of the drug.[19] Opium destroys the will, and without that primary human faculty the addict becomes dehumanized as "an image of the brute creation." Whereas the domestic model of addiction is characterized by its benignity and mildness, the colonial model describes an all-consuming condition of moral corruption.

In addition to serving as an example of this second model of addiction, Raffles's description is also significant, paradoxically, because of its uniqueness. Discussions of opium's effects are rare within governmental and mercantile discourse on the colonial trade in opium. This silence is all the more remarkable in light of the immense volume of the India-China trade, its crucial importance to the British economy, and the British public's thorough ignorance of it all.

During the eighteenth century, the British East India Company had a monopoly on the sale and production of all opium grown in India. Cultivation was centered in Bengal, where the company compelled Indian *ryots* to plant poppies as their primary, and often their only, crop. Its principal market was China, although the company had to smuggle it into Canton through private merchant ships because the Chinese banned the importation of opium in 1723. The British government renewed the company's monopoly in 1789 and again in 1814, despite the obnoxiousness of monopolies to its own laissez-faire economic policies, and this renewal emphasizes the importance to the British treasury of the revenue produced by the opium trade. Indeed, until it began selling opium to the Chinese, Britain had been suffering a severe outflow of British bullion to China because of the demand for Chinese tea. The British love affair with tea grew enormously during the eighteenth century, from 1 million pounds in 1730 to 20 million pounds by 1789. The Chinese, however, were uninterested in British textiles or manufactured goods, and so the tea trade was draining British reserves. The opium trade gave the British a commodity to sell to China in exchange for tea. The trade became essential to the national economy; the government's ability to fund the war against France after 1793, for example, depended on the sale of Indian opium to China, and thus Parliament continued to renew the company's monopoly. Inglis remarks, "As it held the controlling interest, parliament, in a sense, had become the chief shareholder in the opium business" (*Opium War,* 52). Between 1780 and 1819, the amount of opium smuggled into China was restricted to 4,000 chests per year in order to keep prices high, but competition and falling profits led to steady growth, first to

10,000 chests annually in 1830 and then a skyrocketing increase. When the first Opium War broke out in 1839, the trade had risen to 35,000 chests per year.[20]

The effectiveness of the official silence on the character of this vast trade can be gauged by the surprise that accompanied the reports in 1839 of the Chinese seizure of British opium that immediately preceded the first Opium War. The religious forces were quick to raise the morality argument against the trade, and in one of the first and most influential of these books, *The Iniquities of the Opium Trade with China* (1838), the Rev. Algernon Thelwall opens with a description of this public ignorance. " 'The Iniquities of the Opium Trade with China?' methinks I hear some one exclaim, on reading the title of my book: 'I never heard before that we carried on any such traffic; much less that any iniquities were connected therewith.' This ignorance ought not to surprise me: for I was, till very recently, equally ignorant myself."[21] As Inglis points out, until newspaper reports appeared on the events of 1839 in China, "people in Britain had scarcely been aware of the existence of the opium traffic, let alone its scale" (*Opium War*, 126). De Quincey himself became one of the leading conservative apologists for the trade; his two articles on the Opium War, written for *Blackwood's* in 1840, are saber-rattling homages to British pride, and they stress the extraordinary patience with which the nation had submitted to the Celestial Empire's insulting arrogance.[22] But, like Thelwall, he notes the general unfamiliarity with the trade and even provides readers with a history of it.[23]

The reason for this public ignorance is easy to locate. The British colonial reports and the parliamentary debate on the subject self-consciously elided the term "opium" from the discussion.[24] This concerted silence suggests an awareness by the mercantile elite and its governmental supporters of the basic difference in the meaning of opium as a commodity within the domestic and colonial contexts. In Britain, opium had a clearly defined use-value connected with its medical properties; thus, when addiction did occur, it was assumed to have followed on the treatment of a medical condition, as both De Quincey and Coleridge report. But there was no medical utility present in the context of the China trade. Instead, opium's only use-value in this exchange was defined by the British East India Company as its unique ability to create an escalating demand for itself in the consumer. The British directors of the company had invented a new economics of addiction, for the whole trade was predicated on the belief that opium could create its own market and that the Chinese, once habituated to it, would pay anything to get more. Thus, the practiced silence by those engaged in the trade can only be explained by the assumption that Raffles's views on the all-consuming nature of opium addiction were fundamental to the opium trade itself; those views were only exceptional in that they contained an objection to the practice and found their way into print.[25]

There were, then, two very opposite cultural constructions of opium's effects in circulation in early nineteenth-century Britain: a dominant model of domestic medical usage and a subordinate one of moral enslavement deriving from the Asian context. De Quincey's own representation of addiction derives from the discourse of the Asian colonial trade, not from the British context. The sources of his insights into this version of addiction and the reasons his representation of addiction varied so remarkably from the British version can be located in his family's connections to the opium trade. In the *Confessions,* he mentions the favorite of his five guardians, the one who "lived at a distance" and "was more reasonable, and had more knowledge of the world than the rest" (*OE,* 36). This was his namesake Thomas Penson, his mother's brother.[26] Penson was in Bengal, where he was a colonel in the military service of the East India Company. In 1802 this "bronzed Bengal uncle" was visiting De Quincey's mother, Mrs. Quincey, after ten years in India, when her seventeen-year-old son returned home after running away from the Manchester Grammar School.[27] Penson intervened with Mrs. Quincey to allow the truant to explore Wales rather than being summarily returned to the school. When De Quincey returned from London in 1803, Penson was still present and supplied him with the £100 per year that enabled him to enroll at Oxford in the winter of 1803.[28] As Lindop points out, "During the summer of 1803 De Quincey had spent much time at the Priory debating with his Uncle Thomas the rights and wrongs of British rule in India. . . . That such arguments could have been carried on without reference to the opium trade is not credible" (*Life,* 124). By the time of this visit, De Quincey had certainly encountered the colonial version of addiction that he would incorporate into his narrative. But he had other opportunities as well. His mother's family was intimate with Col. Henry Watson, one of the early proponents of smuggling Bengal opium into China. Watson made a fortune in the trade during the 1780s, and at his death it went to his daughter, De Quincey's beloved Lady Susan Carbery, the anonymous friend who supplied him with the initial money to run away from the Manchester Grammar School (Lindop, *Life* 124). Through Penson and Carbery, De Quincey was economically dependent on opium before his first physical encounter with the commodity. At an early age, then, De Quincey had the opportunity of encountering the assumptions of the colonial discourse of addiction, and these were the assumptions he used in his representation of addiction in the *Confessions,* giving it its unique and definitive characteristics.

At the beginning of the *Confessions,* De Quincey claims to have "at length, accomplished what I never yet heard attributed to any other man—have untwisted, almost to its final links, the accursed chain which fettered me" (*OE,* 30). For De Quincey's audience, this was a remarkable claim, for it was well established that one could never give up opium once addicted to it. There was disagreement over opium's effects, as we have seen, and addiction itself was thought to be a rarity among the British, though not among the Asians. But where it did occur, it was considered inescapable. The physician John Jones, who wrote the first significant British treatise on opium, *The Mysteries of Opium Reveal'd* (1701), hails it as a "noble *Panacea*" when used moderately, but in a chapter titled "Effects of sudden Leaving off of the Use of Opium, after a long, and lavish Use thereof," he warns of the "Great, and even Intolerable Distresses, Anxieties and Depressions of Spirits, which in few days commonly end in a most miserable Death, attended with strange Agonies, unless Men return to the Use of Opium" (Jones, *Mysteries of Opium,* 31).

The same belief is part of Raffles's comments on opium use in Java. It is still the basic assumption in the 1836 comments of a British merchant in China, who disdains De Quincey's writing on opium as fanciful but nonetheless asserts as an unadorned fact that addiction is inescapable:

> *There is no slavery on earth to name with the bondage into which opium casts its victim. There is scarcely one known instance of escape from its toils. . . .* We need not appeal to the highly-wrought narratives of personal experiences on the subject, which have of late years come

> before the public: they rather invite distrust than otherwise, by the
> exaggeration of their poetical style. But the fact is . . . that *there is
> in opium, once indulged in, a fatal fascination, which needs almost super-
> human powers of self-denial and also capacity for the endurance of pain,
> to overcome.*[29]

Indeed, the reviews of the *Confessions* in the medical periodicals—
where it generated considerable interest—took issue with many
other aspects of De Quincey's representation of opium but agreed
that "persons who accustom themselves to it can by no means live
without it."[30] In literary publications similar remarks appeared; the
reviewer for *The Imperial Magazine* described De Quincey's success in
breaking the chains as "a victory that has never been attributed to
any other person."[31] Thus, although De Quincey presented a novel
view of the felt experience of addiction, there was nothing novel in
his basic claim about the tenacity of the habit. Nineteenth-century
readers readily agreed with his assertion that he had never heard of
anyone having escaped addiction to opium. Except for De Quincey
himself, they had never heard of anyone having done it, either.

De Quincey's claim to have broken the chains of addiction, then,
was a remarkable one, and although twenty years later he would
claim that he was in fact on an opium binge as he wrote the *Confessions*[32]—a matter we will consider later—the narrator's assertion in
1821 is critical to appreciating the original reception of his narrative
and to understanding the work's formal structure. For it is only because he has broken these supposedly unbreakable chains that the
narrator can justify his basic narrative project of revealing the felt experience of opium addiction. The self-exposure of his *Confessions*, he
recognizes, entails a fundamental violation of the code of propriety
within "the decent and self-respecting part of society" (*OE*, 29). He
announces at the outset that his narrative will violate "that delicate
and honourable reserve, which, for the most part, restrains us from
the public exposure of our own errors and infirmities. Nothing, indeed, is more revolting to English feelings, than the spectacle of a
human being obtruding on our notice his moral ulcers or scars, and
tearing away that 'decent drapery,' which time, or indulgence to human frailty, may have drawn over them" (*OE*, 29). Although embracing this rule, he explains his violation of it by pleading for the
"useful and instructive" value of his narrative (*OE*, 29): "[T]he

benefit resulting to others, from the record of an experience purchased at so heavy a price, might compensate, by a vast overbalance,
for any violence done to the feelings I have noticed, and justify a
breach of the general rule" (*OE*, 30). His act of confession, he concludes, is justified by "the service which I may thereby render to the
whole class of opium-eaters" (*OE*, 31). It is by virtue of his unique
position, as the only one who had discovered a means to break the
chains, that the narrator is able to render this particular service. De
Quincey promises to reveal the fundamental secret of how he has
broken the chains and been restored to his place within the "decent
and self-respecting" society, to whose feelings and sensibility he is
so acutely alive. Teaching others how he escaped the addiction, then,
is the specific "benefit" to society offered by the narrative.

There has been a thorough confusion in criticism of De Quincey
on this point. Most writers assume, like Ian Jack, that "the professed
object . . . is to warn the public of the dangers of opium eating."[33]
But, as Jack recognizes, this interpretation cannot account for the
narrative's praise of opium unless the conflict is viewed as evidence
of an authorial "uncertainty of intention" ("De Quincey Revises,"
124). This conflict disappears, however, when we recognize that De
Quincey describes two entirely separate types of opium usage—
recreational and habitual—and that he praises one and warns
against the other. Twentieth-century readers have difficulty recognizing the gulf that separates these two forms because, in the "social
menace" model of addiction, the two forms are part of a continuum,
the first shading inevitably into the second; in practice they are
barely distinguished. So there is little credit given to De Quincey's
repeated denials of any causal relationship between his recreational
usage and his later addiction. Yet in his section on "The Pleasures of
Opium," he describes an eight-year period of recreational usage, an
extended period designed to show that occasional usage is safe and
can continue indefinitely. De Quincey is telling his readers, both explicitly and implicitly, that amateur usage does not inexorably lead
to habituation. The danger is caused not by recreational usage but
by extended medical usage for chronic conditions, such as his
stomach complaint, where occasional use gives way to daily doses.
This distinction lies at the heart of his otherwise enigmatic disagreement in the *Confessions* with the physician Awsiter, who wrote of
opium, "[T]*here are many properties in it, if universally known, that*

would habituate the use, and make it more in request with us than the Turks themselves" (*OE*, 32). De Quincey replies, "In the necessity of this conclusion I do not altogether concur" (*OE*, 32), because he does not agree that the pleasurable qualities of opium will, of themselves, lead to such habituation. Thus, he is not ultimately inconsistent, for he can praise opium itself yet warn against the daily use that produces addiction. He has, then, two separate "services" to perform: a caution for nonhabituated users to maintain their moderation and advice for addicts on how to escape the chains.

Because De Quincey uses the colonial version of addiction, his breaking of the chains is a fundamental precondition for the production of his narrative. As we have seen, Raffles describes Asian addiction as a destruction of the individual's capacity for self-willed action.[34] De Quincey describes addiction, similarly, as an absence of agency, and he expresses this idea through the terminology he uses. When he refers to opium as a "fascinating enthralment" (*OE*, 30), he describes an experience of enslavement combined with the power of magic. He uses the term "fascinate" in its primary sense—to bewitch or cast a spell—and in its more specific sense of depriving one of the power of escape, a sense illustrated by the image of the snake fascinating its prey and ensnaring it through an irresistible influence.[35] De Quincey, like other writers of the period, also uses the term "addiction" in reference to opium; this word's primary meaning was not then, as now, a negative sense of physical dependence but a juridical sense of being made over or bound to someone or something by legal restraint or moral compulsion. To be addicted, to be fascinated, to be enchained—each means to become subject to an alien power and thus to be deprived of the ability to act as an independent agent in the world.

The two forms of opium usage De Quincey describes have opposite relationships to the issue of agency. In "The Pleasures of Opium," he takes opium occasionally, and because he is not habituated to it he retains his ability to act as an agent in the world. He demonstrates this free will through his mobility: He walks around freely after taking opium, enjoying the Italians at the opera and visiting the districts of the working poor. These images emphasize his power for independent action. In contrast, the habituated form of usage described in "The Pains of Opium" produces total immobilization that deprives him of all power to act in the world but leaves intact his desire to participate in it:

The opium-eater loses none of his moral sensibilities, or aspirations: he wishes and longs, as earnestly as ever, to realize what he believes possible, and feels to be exacted by duty; but his intellectual apprehension of what is possible infinitely outruns his power, not of execution only, but even of power to attempt. He lies under the weight of incubus and night-mare: he lies in sight of all that he would fain perform, just as a man forcibly confined to his bed by the mortal languor of a relaxing disease, who is compelled to witness injury or outrage offered to some object of his tenderest love:—he curses the spells which chain him down from motion:—he would lay down his life if he might but get up and walk; but he is powerless as an infant, and cannot even attempt to rise.

(*OE*, 102)

De Quincey thus represents the lived experience of addiction as a disease of the will that prevents him from entering into the social scene around him. This moral disease is closely related to the colonial model of addiction. But his description differs significantly from that of Raffles in one particular. Whereas the Asian user is seen as "an image of the brute creation," De Quincey inserts a perfectly constructed, fully developed middle-class sensibility into the torpid material body of the addict. In doing so, he makes explicit what is always implied in the Eastern version of addiction. The primary difference between the Asian and British addict, at least until De Quincey, had been that the Asian was more susceptible to absolute moral enslavement than the British addict, who retained the ability to act autonomously. That resistance, we can assume, was evidence of the superior British racial inheritance.[36] Within this assumption of an inferior agency in the depiction of the colonial subject was the subtext of middle-class values, which insisted on the power of individual self-making as the essential condition of human status. By this valorization of the individual's ability to make his own way in the world, the middle class buttressed its own untitled place in the social order, elevating itself morally above an entrenched aristocratic power. The representation of colonial subjects as lacking in this quality reaffirmed the moral superiority of the mercantile colonists. And it had the secondary utility, within the British context, of representing those who did not participate in this new ideology of self-making as suffering from a pathological corruption of the body associated with racial inferiority. Thus, the subject of Asian opium habituation was transformed into a cultural metaphor for the failure of individual self-making.

Each of De Quincey's opium dreams is centrally concerned with this issue of lost agency. The resonant but enigmatic cry "Consul Romanus" that rumbles through De Quincey's dreams of immobility, for example, is a reference to the Roman penchant for action and for domination over the material realm. These were the primary racial qualities he attributed to the Romans, as he described them in his "Letters to a Young Man," written within months of the *Confessions.* The Romans possessed "the energy of the *will* victorious over all passions, " he explains, and his primary example is that of Marius, the original Consul Romanus.[37] In another dream—the climactic nightmare, from which he awakens screaming, "I will sleep no more!" (*OE*, 113)—the narrator faces a day of "final hope for human nature," which is on the verge of extinction (*OE*, 112). Again he wants desperately to intervene but explains, "[I] had the power, and yet had not the power, to decide it. I had the power, if I could raise myself, to will it; and yet again had not the power, for the weight of twenty Atlantics was upon me, or the oppression of inexpiable guilt. . . . I lay inactive" (*OE*, 113). A second dream describes a descent "into chasms and sunless abysses, depths below depths, from which it seemed hopeless that I could ever reascend. Nor did I, by waking, feel that I *had* reascended" (*OE*, 103). The sensation of being buried alive—which bleeds over into his waking life—shows up again in a third dream, when he is "buried, for a thousand years, in stone coffins, with mummies and sphinxes, in narrow chambers at the heart of eternal pyramids" (*OE*, 109). Each image repeats his fundamental description of the felt experience of addiction: lying immobilized, alive to the world around him, yet unable to participate in it.[38]

When De Quincey adapts this colonial image to describe the condition of a paragon of British middle-class sensibility, he constructs a powerful and horrifying picture in the eyes of the "decent and self-respecting part of society." De Quincey's narrator is one who embraces, as naturally virtuous, all the fundamental middle-class values. Above everything he values self-making, seeking to make his way in the world by virtue of his own merits. Robinson Crusoe–like, he leaves the Manchester Grammar School, with its authoritarian and incompetent headmaster and subservient fellow students, because of an irrepressible urge to embark on a course of independent action in the world. Throughout his "Preliminary Confessions," he fears nothing so much as new and varied forms of enslavement to his guardians' will. The money lenders, he imagines, plan "to entrap me, and sell me to my guardians" (*OE*, 55), as though he were an escaped slave about to be put on the auction block. To represent such an individual as subject to an invisible and incomprehensible set of restraints is to express one of the great cultural fears of the new middle class.

That sense of failed agency carries with it gender connotations of effeminization. The sensation De Quincey describes, as he lies helpless on the bed, is laden with the cultural experience of the female. His sense of being restrained from action, of being prevented from intervening in the unjust events around him, of being reduced to a silent, ineffective raving at them—these attributes bear less resemblance to the writing of William Wordsworth than to that of Mary Wollstonecraft and Mary Hays, who, like him, find themselves unable to enter into the social sphere, even to protect their loved ones. When De Quincey describes the "Circean spells" that "chain him down from motion," he suggests an effeminization of his body, as if he has been contaminated by the Circean touch and transformed into not a pig but a woman.[39]

When De Quincey presents himself, then, to his middle-class readers as one who has broken the chains, and when he promises to instruct those readers in the secret process, he is making a larger claim for the social function of his narrative than the simple medical utility of freedom from a particular addiction. His narrative proposes to hold out a hope of restored social agency for a readership that implicitly lacks it. It promises to remasculinize an audience that has become effeminized, precisely as Godwin's *Caleb Williams* does, by teaching them to shed their metaphorical chains and become independent actors on the social stage.

The importance of this claim to the form of the narrative is that the *Confessions* proves the narrator's success, for simply by virtue of its existence as a narrative in social circulation it enacts his claim to a renewed social agency. The ultimate proof that the narrator no longer lies immobile on his bed, unable to act or to speak, is the narrative the reader of the *London Magazine* holds in his or her hands.[40] Here is a vital new voice, released from the spells that chained it in its slavish silence, entering into the arena of middle-class discourse. The narrative as a formal object embodies the social agency the narrator claims to have regained, and how can the reader doubt his success?

De Quincey has a second, related obstacle to overcome in order to find his way into the public arena of polite discourse. He not only has to break the chains of opium enchantment in order to speak but also must commit "a breach of the general rule" (*OE*, 30). His essential subject matter—the physical body, its sensual qualities, and his own immersion in them—lies outside the realm of polite discourse, and thus he begins his narrative with the apology to his audience for raising the subject of his own "errors and infirmities." As he clarifies, having such flaws does not constitute the "breach" so much as the act of removing the "decent drapery" of British "reserve" by which all readers keep them to themselves. Thus, the impropriety lies in the confessional act of talking about his infirmities and bringing them into discourse. More specifically, the fundamental impropriety at the center of the *Confessions* lies in the act of making the flawed physicality of the narrator's own body into the subject of his narrative.

Underlying this exclusion is the problem of the nervous narrative, that self-reflexive speech produced by the nervous condition. Talking about the sensual aspects of one's own body implies a narrow, antisocial perspective, for it suggests the solipsistic outlook of one whose isolated physical sensations assume an undue importance in shaping his or her view of the world. A person who talks excessively about his or her body is a person whose interests do not extend beyond the perimeter of the skin, and because this narrow experience substitutes for the whole, an excessive interest in one's body implies an inadequate engagement with the external world.

De Quincey, careful to guard against this impression, frequently expresses a reluctance to describe the actual nature of his physical condition, focusing instead on the intellectual consequences of his material addiction. Where he does describe physical symptoms, he provides a careful and repeated explanation of his socially useful purposes, differentiating himself from the nervous narratives of the hysteric or hypochondriac. As he explains in the 1822 Appendix to the *Confessions:*

> These were my reasons for troubling my reader with any record, long or short, of experiments relating to so truly base a subject as my own body; and I am earnest with the reader, that he will not forget them, or so far misapprehend me as to believe it possible that I would condescend to so rascally a subject for its own sake, or, indeed, for any less object than that of general benefit to others. Such an animal as the self-observing valetudinarian I know there is: I have met him myself occasionally; and I know that he is the worst imaginable *heautontimoroumenos;* aggravating and sustaining, by calling into distinct consciousness, every symptom that would else perhaps, under a different direction given to the thoughts, become evanescent.
>
> (*Writings,* 3:471)

Such body-centered speech he then denounces as an "undignified and selfish habit" that he could never "condescend to." Although he appears to be overly concerned with his body, the appearance is deceiving, for his case is qualitatively different. He allows that he once had the "disease" of meditating too much on "the suffering" of his past life, and except for extraordinary "remedies" he "should certainly have become hypochondriacally melancholy" (*OE,* 82). But, as De Quincey observes, "No man, I suppose, employs much of his time on the phenomena of his own body without some regard for it; whereas the reader sees that, so far from looking upon mine with any complacency or regard, I hate it" (*Writings,* 3:472). The urgency of his denial suggests an awareness of how closely his narrative resembles the nervous narrative that was regarded suspiciously as a product of bodily disease. The *Confessions* run a continual risk of displaying "a selfish desire of engrossing the sympathy and attention of others to the narration of their own sufferings," to return to Thomas Trotter's list of symptoms of the nervous temperament (*NT,* xvi). De Quincey's narrative flirts with the danger of undermining its own narrative authority every time the narrator turns to the improper subject of his suffering body.

As discussed in chapter 1, this conflict is a gendered one between a "masculine" independence from the physiology of the body and a "feminine" or "effeminate" incarceration within it. Mary Wollstonecraft and Mary Hays both try to demonstrate an intellectual independence from their biology, but the conservative De Quincey perpetuates the ideological position that women write from their bodies rather than their minds. The highest praise he can bestow on a woman writer is to make her an exception to this general pattern, and this he does when describing his mother, as if to reassure his readers of his own physical inheritance. "For though unpretending to the name and honours of a *literary* woman, I shall presume to call her (what many literary women are not) an *intellectual* woman: and I believe that if ever her letters should be collected and published, they would be thought generally to exhibit as much strong and masculine sense . . . as any in our language" (*OE,* 61–62). He does not perceive female writers, presumably novelists, as "intellectual" because they are defined by their material condition, their constitutive nervous bodies. For his narrative to be associated with his physical condition implies a similarly effeminized form of discourse rather than an exercise of "masculine" understanding, such as that which he praises in his paean to political economist David Ricardo: "Thou art the man!" (*OE,* 100).

Nor is this restriction strictly limited to those conditions we now define as physical. The common conditions of hysteria and hypochondria are seen not as "mental" diseases but as physical ones because they result from a functional disorder of the nervous system. The effeminization attributed to body-centered narratives includes the wide-ranging symptomatology of nervous conditions, particularly the expression of abjection, overwhelming despair, or bleak unhappiness of the sort that appears in Wollstonecraft's *Mary* and *Maria,* in Hays's *Emma Courtney,* and in Godwin's *Caleb Williams.* It appears, of course, in the *Confessions* as well, in the image of De Quincey lying helpless on the bed, tortured by his inability to protect a loved one. De Quincey's masculine authority, however, remains intact because he frames the experiences within the physical fetters of opium addiction, and so he safely brackets it at a distance from the narrating voice. On the one hand, he acknowledges the physical basis of the experience, allowing it to rise out of his material condition, and thus it is gendered female. On the other hand, he has found a unique way out of that condition and so has become remasculinized and can write intimately about his prior personal tragedies in an authoritative voice of intellectual detachment. He has thus "broken the chains" that heretofore have precluded the appearance of this type of narrative voice from polite British literature, a voice we can now define by its two most salient gender characteristics: a "masculine" analytic mode combined with a "feminine" experiential content. His is an intellectual narrator relating a sensual experience, a masculine narrator telling a feminine story.

The idea that this narrating voice is independent of the body—that it is not constituted by the material impressions of the events it relates—is central to his definition of himself as a philosopher. He explains that a true philosopher needs to combine both a "superb intellect in its *analytic* functions" (*OE*, 33) and an exquisite sensibility to the experiences of others in the world. "For a philosopher should not see with the eyes of the poor limitary creature . . . filled with narrow and self-regarding prejudices of birth and education" (*OE*, 33); he or she must also be able to sympathize with, and so understand, the pains and pleasures of those from other classes, as De Quincey illustrates in his relationship with the prostitute Ann. As we have already seen in the work of Thomas Trotter, this sensitivity to others invites the dangers of nervous collapse because it leaves one defenseless against the repeated impressions—particularly from the lower class—of a world filled with the pain and suffering of widespread misery. This dangerous sympathetic ability is the birthright of the female, explaining why nervous disorders are predominantly female-identified. De Quincey argues the necessity of this sensibility for the male philosopher, precisely as Trotter made it central to the work of the physician. As a defense against its material ill-effects, he stresses the power of an independent intellect trained to resist these dangerous sensations:

> I do not often weep: for not only do my thoughts on subjects connected with the chief interests of man daily, nay hourly, descend a thousand fathoms 'too deep for tears'; not only does the sternness of my habits of thought present an antagonism to the feelings which prompt tears—wanting of necessity to those who, being protected usually by their levity from any tendency to meditative sorrow, would by that same levity be made incapable of resisting it on any casual access of such feelings:—but also, I believe that all minds which have contemplated such objects as deeply as I have done, must, for their own protection from utter despondency, have early

encouraged and cherished some tranquillizing belief as to the future balances and the hieroglyphic meanings of human sufferings. On these accounts, I am cheerful to this hour; and, as I have said, I do not often weep.

(*OE,* 52)

De Quincey's stern "habits of thought" allow him to resist the flood of impressions that would otherwise produce that "utter despondency" characteristic of nervous collapse. He possesses a masculine independence from his bodily sensations. When he mentions, in this passage, others whose "levity" leaves them ultimately incapable of resisting this despondency, he has in mind indulgent sensualists, such as the young men he describes in "The Daughter of Lebanon," who are given over to their drink and debauchery and thus are vulnerable to the immediacy of their sensations.[41] The contrast between himself, as a philosopher, and these indulgent bacchanalians is crucial to his self-representation as a philosophical opium-eater. For though he experiences opium's sensual qualities, his detachment from physical sensations ensures that his joy will derive from its "intellectual pleasure," as he calls it, rather than from the gross sensuality of the body, which would expose him to despair. De Quincey's solution to the problematic immersion within sensibility, then, is to maintain an intellectual detachment from his sensations and to study them from afar in order to escape their constitutive effect. As he explains, "[T]he calamities of my noviciate in London had struck root so deeply in my bodily constitution that afterwards they shot up and flourished afresh," but he is able to resist their deleterious effects "with a fortitude more confirmed, with the resources of a maturer intellect," because of that philosophical detachment from the body that defines his narrative authority (*OE,* 67). His attitude toward his own sensations is that of the naturalist conducting an "experiment," as he explains in the 1822 Appendix, and thus he avoids being trapped within the constitutive nature of his sensations by treating his body as a detached intellectual object. It is from this dynamic that the oppositely gendered characteristics of his narrative— the male voice and its feminizing experiences—arise.

The strong antimaterialist bias of his philosophy underscores his claims to have "broken the chains" and developed an agency that is finally independent of his physical body. His opium nightmares, however, could be called images of the revenge of materialism. He is tortured by the tables and sofas in a Chinese house that "soon became instinct with life" (*OE*, 110), as if the material realm were suddenly growing a monstrous crocodilian idea of sentience in its wooden brain.[42] His persistent dreams of "silvery expanses of water" seem in themselves placid and pastoral; yet they torture him, he explains, because "I feared . . . that some dropsical state or tendency of the brain might thus be making itself (to use a metaphysical word) *objective*; and the sentient organ *project* itself as its own object" (*OE*, 107).[43] If his brain produces images of water because of its own waterlogged condition, then what appears to be an independent product of the intellect is in fact a representation of the materiality of the body. Thus, his nightmares suggest a fear that his transcendence is a delusion masking his actual immanence. These dreams of consciousness incarcerated within the material realm express a fear of the dependency of the intellect on the body.

They are related to the primary addiction dreams discussed earlier through the connecting issue of agency, for most of De Quincey's dreams represent the internment of a once-autonomous agent within a determinate material condition. Whereas De Quincey's narrative authority hinges on his independence from the body, his narrative content describes the horror of entrapment within it, both through the specific entrapment of his middle-class sensibility within the body of the addict and through the more general representation of consciousness defined by its material structure. In each case, he describes the presence of a male voice trapped within a female body, and it is the gendered dynamic that he has implicitly overcome.

Given the formal and metaphorical importance of De Quincey's promise to teach his readers how to break their chains, it comes as a surprise when he changes his mind at the conclusion and decides *not* to fulfill his promise. "It now remains that I should say something of the way in which this conflict of horrors was finally brought to its crisis. The reader is already aware (from a passage near the beginning of the introduction to the first part) that the opium-eater has, in some way or other, 'unwound, almost to its final links, the accursed chain which bound him.' By what means? To have narrated this, according to the original intention, would have far exceeded the space which can now be allowed" (*OE*, 113). This is all to the good, he decides, for "on a maturer view," he believes that such "un-affecting details" would "injure . . . the impression of the history it-self" and "injure its effect as a composition" (*OE*, 113–14). And so he abandons his "original intention" and sets aside the whole business of explaining his escape from his material fetters: "Medical account, therefore, of my emancipation I have not much to give: and even that little, as managed by a man so ignorant of medicine as myself, would probably tend only to mislead" (*OE*, 115).[44] Instead of the promised advice, he substitutes a cautionary injunction warning the reader against the danger of entering that bondage in the first place: "If he is taught to fear and tremble, enough has been effected" (*OE*, 115). The distinction here is between an audience of occasional users, for whom caution will have some benefit, and habitual users, who cannot benefit from such instilled fear. Implicitly, the latter are abandoned by De Quincey's newly defined purpose.

Most of De Quincey's editors agree with him in the decision to move away from detailed instruction in opium withdrawal; they, like him, regard references to drops, grains, specific symptoms, and bodily effects as unwelcome intrusions of medical discourse into an imaginative work. There is an uneasy relationship in the *Confessions* between these two forms of discourse, which De Quincey calls the literature of knowledge and the literature of power, and his final turn away from the subject of the body and toward Romantic aes-theticism seems to resolve this conflict in favor of the poetic function of the narrative.[45] Reading the *Confessions* in this way, however, has led to an undervaluing of the importance of De Quincey's original claim about breaking the chains, and thus there has been slight con-sideration of its relationship to the structure of his narrative or to the imagery of his dreams. For the same reasons, this approach also has led to a consistent dismissal of the 1822 Appendix, in which De Quincey returns to that "original intention" and supplies the physi-cal details of how to renounce opium. At best, his editors reprint the text of the Appendix but label it a "disfigurement," primarily useful as an illustration of his capacity for "ingenious rigmarole when he was hard pressed for something better" (*Writings*, 3:10). At worst, they begrudgingly include a few excerpts, and this abridgement is buried among other miscellaneous comments on the work, as though it had no more formal claim to inclusion in the text of the original *Confessions* itself than any of De Quincey's later reflections on his most famous work.[46]

The Appendix was written for the first edition of the *Confessions* in book form in 1822.[47] After the initial reviews of the two periodical installments in 1821, De Quincey promised his *London Magazine* audience to write a "Third Part" elaborating on the pains of opium, as his reviewers had noticed an overbalance on the side of its pleasures.[48] He never completed the task, but he included the Appendix as a substitute, and it makes good on his promise to elaborate on the pains of opium by describing his physical sensations of withdrawal. Hence, there is no bibliographical ambiguity over the integral place of the Appendix in the text of the *Confessions*. Objections to its conclusion are solely based on value judgments about its content. It includes, for example, a most unpoetic table of figures giving the weekly schedule of his dosages, and it describes such banal symptoms of withdrawal as his incessant sneezing and profuse sweating. Yet, precisely because of these details, it clearly represents a reconsideration of that avoidance of physicality that marks the end of the main narrative. Because the first two parts fail to explain how the narrator recovered from his immersion in the Circean spell of opium, they leave open the issue of how he became able to write the narrative, of how he found his way into discourse. So there remains a distinct hollowness at the center of the narrative, one caused not by the incompleteness of his psychological profile, as is most frequently noted, but by the absence of his physical profile.[49] As De Quincey explains, "being the hero of the piece, or . . . the criminal at the bar, my body should be had into court" (*OE*, 96).[50] In the self-representation of the narrative, this is literally what has *not* been done. The narrator's body—his physical condition, his material being—disappears from the end of the narrative as thoroughly as that of the mercurial druggist near the Pantheon, who after selling him opium "evanesced, or evaporated" (*OE*, 71). The Appendix is the moment in which De Quincey finally, reluctantly drags that body into court, thus fulfilling his original narrative promise. Hence it needs to be considered an integral part of the overall work on both textual and substantive grounds.

The Appendix emphasizes and exaggerates the same claims to narrative authority made in the main narrative. Parts One and Two, as we have seen, assert a clear relationship between the writer's escape from the material fetters of opium and the act of writing. He acknowledges as much in the Appendix: "Those who have read the Confessions will have closed them with the impression that I had wholly renounced the use of Opium. This impression I meant to convey" (*Writings*, 3:467). As he goes on to explain, this escape is the fundamental condition of speech that enables his narrative: "[T]he very act of deliberately recording such a state of suffering necessarily presumes in the recorder a power of surveying his own case as a cool spectator, and a degree of spirits for adequately describing it, which it would be inconsistent to suppose in any person speaking from the station of an actual sufferer" (*Writings*, 3:467). An "actual sufferer" cannot speak authoritatively about his or her own body because he or she is implicated within it; authority flows from the rationality of the "cool spectator," one who is situated outside the body and thus can talk about it as an object.

This is the basis of De Quincey's transcendent philosophy, as we have seen. He is never more literally transcendent than in the medically oriented language of the Appendix itself. He denounces his "worthless body" as "a base, crazy, despicable human system," a "wretched structure" not even worthy of "any respectable dog" (*Writings*, 3:467). As a final proof of his contempt for it, and as his concluding rhetorical flourish, he offers his body to the Royal College of Surgeons for public study, explaining, "it will give me pleasure to anticipate this posthumous revenge and insult inflicted upon that which has caused me so much suffering in this life" (*Writings*, 3:472).[51] Indeed, by finally introducing that body into a discourse designed to make a contribution to "medical history," De Quincey gives his text and his body parallel functions; both are now made available for the purpose of "inspecting the appearances in the body of an Opium-eater" (*Writings*, 3:467, 472). De Quincey brings his body into court only to wash his hands of the troublesome thing, as if he were already detached from it. He needs that extraordinary detachment in order to speak, at last, about his own suffering in the intimate physical terms required of him by his original promise without being implicated within that suffering.

These extreme claims to independence are made necessary by the surprising revelation he makes: He was unable to write the promised Part Three because he had, in fact, never quite gotten free of his body. He was still addicted to opium, without quite realizing it, as he was writing the *Confessions*. He explains that he had originally thought, with good reason, "that the victory was in effect achieved. In suffering my readers, therefore, to think of me as of a reformed Opium-eater, I left no impression but what I shared myself" (*Writings,* 3:467). De Quincey is using a familiar technique here, pointing to a lack of correspondence between external appearances and internal motivation; thus, although it appears he lied, in fact he was honest. Fortunately, he tells us, in the months since then he has—really and truly—reached this goal. The "foremost purpose" of the Appendix is to "communicate this result of my experiment," as he calls his late escape, so that "Opium-eaters in general" may "benefit" from his account (*Writings,* 3:470). This time he makes that beneficial conclusion explicit: "[I]t establishes, for their consolation and encouragement, the fact that opium may be renounced, and without greater sufferings than an ordinary resolution may support" (*Writings,* 3:470). Thus, he belatedly fulfills his "original intention" in writing the *Confessions* and is able to invoke closure.

In typical De Quinceyan fashion, however, this fulfillment raises more questions than it answers. For it redefines the central relationship, which was established in the first two parts, between the narrator's voice and body. No longer is the speaker of the main narrative an independent agent; although he believed himself to be free, he had in fact spoken while still in thrall to the Circean spell. The Appendix reframes the preceding narrative and reveals its central claim to narrative authority to be founded on a self-delusion.

This paradoxical delusion of independence from his material condition is what places De Quincey's *Confessions* within the problematic form of the nervous narrative. Like Godwin in *Caleb Williams* and Hays in *Emma Courtney,* De Quincey describes a condition in which his triumphant moment of rational self-possession is subsequently revealed as a moment of complete self-delusion. In each case, the narrator describes a two-stage process. First he or she discovers a freedom from the body and its distorting passions and diseases and uses that freedom as the basis for independent speech. In the second stage, there is a recognition of that apparent freedom as a product of self-delusion. As such, the assertion of independence is recontained as a sign of the narrator's continued immanence within the body rather than an escape from it. Thus the narrator's "independent" speech loses its fundamental claim to authority, for it expresses—through its central assertion of self-possession—the narrator's *lack* of self-possession, becoming instead evidence of the speaker's unwarranted faith in his or her own transcendence.

These two stages interact with one another. They form a dialectical pattern, producing a third stage, in which a new narrative authorization arises out of the conflict between the escape from the body and its recontainment as an illusion of escape. Caleb Williams responds by disowning his past narrative and asserting a negative agency. Similarly, Emma Courtney denounces her prior actions, disavowing her words as, in effect, not hers but products of her body. Unlike these speakers, De Quincey continues to own his narrative after recognizing his earlier self-delusion. It is the uniqueness of the *Confessions* that its narrator never adopts the humbled, sadder-but-wiser tone of his predecessors. Instead, he stands behind it as written and uses his new authority in the Appendix—after further trials he at last has succeeded where all others have failed—to attest to the fundamental accuracy of his prior writing. He reauthorizes it, so that narrative authority in the *Confessions* comes retrospectively. It flows not from the narrating voice itself—which, like the other personal narrators, was, in the end, deluded in believing it had the authority to speak—but from a later voice that looks back on the narrative with the necessary detachment.

This retrospective approach to the problem of agency, however, does not eliminate the problem of authority so much as it holds it perpetually at bay. For De Quincey's second claim to independence invites the same question of self-delusion as his first. The second time around, his claim does not possess the absolute authority it had in the first case. His Appendix suggests an unending sequence in which the sense of freedom from the material is always going to be illusory when considered in retrospect; the only question is *how much* one is trapped within that illusion of freedom. It is, however, a pragmatic strategy that can be used to reauthorize his writing—as long as he maintains it as the outermost framing device. So he maintains and perpetuates this illusion of agency, one that is always going to have within it a hint of self-delusion, and this becomes the source of his discursive authority.

Later years would modify De Quincey's solution to the problem of agency in the *Confessions,* culminating in a complete restructuring of the issue within the 1856 revision. But prior to that, in his 1838

"Recollections of Charles Lamb," he published a remarkable description of how he had written his narrative in 1821. He explains that opium addiction made it nearly impossible for him and for Coleridge to write. But he discovered that "when I . . . had armed myself by a sudden increase of the opium for a few days running, I recovered, at times, a remarkable glow of jovial spirits. In some such artificial respites it was from my usual state of distress . . . that I wrote the greater part of the Opium Confessions in the autumn of 1821" (*Writings*, 3:75). Far from being "almost" free of his chains, let alone having "triumphed," De Quincey now claims that he developed a conscious strategy of bingeing on opium in order to write the *Confessions*. This admission reframes his narrative as an unambiguous product of his material condition rather than of the transcendent intellect. As he points out, opium disturbs "the intellectual system, as well as the animal, the functions of the will also no less than those of the intellect" (*Writings*, 3:77), and it was only by prostrating himself before this Circean enchantment that he was able to produce the story of his liberation.

Though he finally abandons any claims to an intellectual independence for the narrating voice, De Quincey still does not necessarily abandon his newly defined narrative, despite its dependence on his material condition. He leaves the problem overtly unaddressed in the essay on Lamb, but he turns immediately to a suggestive anecdote on the nature of bodily speech and the relationship between a speaker and his unwilled utterances. He tells us that at the time he was writing the *Confessions* he labored under two burdens. "Pecuniary embarrassments" dictated that he remain in London, unhappily separated from his family and engaged in loathsome "literary toils" (*Writings*, 3:71). Combined with this bleak social predicament was a separate, physical condition: His opium use had damaged his liver, the organ of the body he identified as the source of all despair and madness.[52] His dire social circumstance "strongly cooperated with the mere physical despondency arising out of the liver" to produce a particularly deceptive type of speech, one that mirrors the dependent speech of the *Confessions*:

> [T]his state of partial unhappiness, amongst other outward indications, expressed itself by one mark, which some people are apt greatly to misapprehend, as if it were some result of a sentimental

turn of feeling—I mean perpetual sighs. But medical men must very well know that a certain state of the liver, *mechanically,* and without any co-operation of the will, expresses itself in sighs. I was much too firm-minded, and too reasonable, to murmur or complain. I certainly suffered deeply, as one who finds himself a banished man from all that he loves. . . . But still I endured in silence. The mechanical sighs, however, revealed, or seemed to reveal, what was present in my thoughts.

(*Writings,* 3:77–78)

Entirely disconnected from his will, De Quincey's *suspiria de machina* represents a purely mechanical form of discourse, one that, because it comes from the materiality of the body, is gendered female.[53] Thus, the image of De Quincey wandering behind Charles and Mary Lamb sighing over and over again is a feminized representation, not a masculinized one. Furthermore, these sighs evoke the Lambs' sympathy by drawing attention to De Quincey's suffering, and so they epitomize that particular form of feminized speech that constitutes the nervous narrative. Propriety demands that De Quincey demonstrate an intellectual detachment from his body's "physical despondency" by not referring to it in company. Instead, he must display his disregard for his body's sensations, and the only masculine alternative, as the episode indicates, is to endure "in silence." Within these gendered terms, the expression of despair will always be gendered female, and so it is *prima facie* deprived of its claim to narrative authority.

De Quincey disclaims any willful authority over his *suspiria de machina.* This same distancing between the speaker and the act of speaking is the outcome of his redefinition of the *Confessions* as a product of his material, rather than intellectual, condition. The *Confessions* is ultimately as improper as the sighs themselves, and for the same reason. However, De Quincey asserts an ambivalent relationship to these sighs and, by implication, to his earlier narrative, for he does not entirely disown them. Instead, he points out that he was indeed suffering and that he was grateful for the sympathetic treatment he received from the Lambs, who responded kindly to his sighs. As his audience, the Lambs reacted as he seems to suggest that his readers ought to react to the redefined *Confessions.* For although he acknowledges the impropriety of the expression, and although he maintains the masculine standard of virtuous silence, he allows the sighs to function as a viable representation of his intellectual condition, which, though it could not will them, was nonetheless filled with the despair they imply. Within the dictates of the situation he describes, these alienated signs of the body become the only form of nonincriminating self-expression open to De Quincey. This is how his readers are to view the similar self-expression of the *Confessions*.

De Quincey finally abandoned this ambivalent posture toward narrative authority in his 1856 revision. As his career as a writer and as an addict grew long in the tooth together, his representation of addiction as an all-consuming ascendance of the material over the independent intellect grew untenable. Indeed, after his comments in the essay on Lamb, the whole fictional structure of authority in the *Confessions* threatened to collapse, for there was no longer even the "decent drapery" of a claim to self-delusion that he could hide behind, and the integrity of his text as a philosophical autobiography was permanently damaged. It could stand as a brilliant work of fiction, but it ceased to have any viable referentiality to the writer's life.

In his final revision De Quincey addresses this problem in dramatic fashion by completely severing the link between addiction and agency, thereby putting a period to the entire issue. In doing so, he also removes his narrative from the paradox of the nervous narrative form, for there ceases to be any connection between body and speaker. In a new, lengthy apostrophe introducing "The Pains of Opium" section, he explains that he was mistaken when, in the first edition of the *Confessions*, he attributed his sense of helpless immobility to his opium addiction. In fact, he was simply in need of physical stimulation:

all was due to my own ignorance, to neglect of cautionary measures, or to gross mismanagement of my health. . . . I sank under the lulling seductions of opium into total sedentariness. . . . The account of my depression, and almost of my helplessness, in [The Pains of Opium], is faithful as a description to the real case. But, in ascribing that case to opium, as any transcendent and overmastering agency, I was thoroughly wrong. Twenty days of exercise . . . would have sent me . . . into regions of natural and healthy excitement, where dejection is an impossible phenomenon.

(*Writings*, 3:416)

He compares his earlier belief in opium's "overmastering" power to the exaggerated fears produced by fairy tales, and so the Circean spell becomes a mere childish fantasy, which the mature man has now put aside. After a lengthy clarification of the medical properties of opium, he concludes, "The reader will infer, from what I have now said, that all passages, written at an earlier period under cloudy and uncorrected views of the evil agencies presumable in opium, stand retracted; although, shrinking from the labour of altering an error diffused so widely under my own early misconceptions of the truth, I have suffered them to remain as they were" (*Writings*, 3:429). De Quincey thus jettisons his earlier view of addiction based on the colonial model, for there are no "evil agencies" in opium. At last he has embraced the milder British domestic model of a benign dependency with few serious effects.[54] Because of this change, the basic difference between the two versions of the *Confessions* lies in their opposite approaches to the narrator's delusions about his own agency. In 1822 he suffers from a delusion of freedom while still enslaved to his material condition. But in 1856 the reverse is true: Instead of a delusion of freedom, he suffers a delusion of imprisonment. He has always been free of his material condition; he just did not know it in 1822. And he has never been trapped in an effeminized body; this was just a childish fear.

By severing the link between addiction and agency, De Quincey diminishes opium's significance to the narrative. No longer is breaking the chains essential to the act of writing. Instead, it becomes an adjunct to writing by palliating the lifelong sufferings the narrator feels as a result of his "boyish follies" (*Writings*, 3:413). Drawing on the basic model of sensationalism, he writes that the impressions of starvation and exposure are permanently etched into his nervous fibers and manifest themselves in his ongoing stomach complaint. The moral of the 1856 version is a warning to "fear and tremble" against the youthful excesses that caused his lifelong suffering, not against the "evil agency" of opium. A graphic consequence of this shift in perspective is his drastically altered description of his escape from the Manchester Grammar School, the original moment when he embarked on his youthful journey. No longer does the incident express his self-reliant independence from the tyranny of an outmoded social authority. Instead, the schoolmaster is rewritten as a sympathetic and benevolent man, and the young De Quincey is given "every possible indulgence" (*Writings*, 3:270). His elopement becomes an "*inexplicable*" and "fatal error," which he attributes to the madness produced, like the mechanical sighs, by a disordered liver (*Writings*, 3:271).[55] Perhaps the clearest demonstration of the reduced significance of opium and the increased significance of his youthful impetuosity lies in the revision's new proportions. As Ian Jack points out, opium becomes the focal point of the narrative before the middle of the book in the 1822 version.[56] In the 1856 rendition, the section on De Quincey's early life is expanded to four times its original length, and more than two-thirds of the narrative elapses before opium comes onto the stage.

Because addiction loses its connection to agency and to writing, the issue of breaking the chains becomes part of an inconsequential sidelight to the more conventional story of the narrator's life. The emancipation from addiction is subordinated to De Quincey's new posture as an expert on opium who, after "something more than half-a-century" of habitual use, is issuing his "final report" on its "good and evil results" (*Writings*, 3:414–15). Whereas his narrative authority in 1822 is based on his freedom from opium, in 1856 it is based on the expertise accumulated by his continued use. The issue of breaking the chains is thus merely a residual one, although De Quincey does maintain his expertise on that subject as well. After all, he has done it more than once. Admittedly, each time he has "returned, upon deliberate choice (after weighing all the consequences on this side and on that), to the daily use of opium" (*Writings*, 3:414 n. 1). The fact that this admission seems rather to testify against itself no longer really matters, for the whole claim has become an insignificant addition to his knowledge of opium, a subject that is itself superfluous to the main theme of his history. Having lost their structural function, De Quincey's new and expanded lectures on the physical properties of opium form a separate medical discourse interspersed within the autobiography, and so De Quincey's two discursive genres—the literature of knowledge and the literature of power—coexist within the 1856 *Confessions* without effectually intersecting, as they did in 1822.

Ultimately, De Quincey's solution to the problem of agency and the body in the *Confessions* returns to that familiar strategy adopted by Caleb Williams so many years before. For by arguing that he was originally in error when he thought opium had robbed him of agency, he is in effect disowning the earlier narrative as a product of his misconception. His new narrative is now meant to take its place.

But we can also see a second consequence of his revision, one that is far more original and suggestive of the broader evolution of narrative strategies for overcoming the restrictions of material determinism in the relation of personal narratives. This second approach hinges on the one part of the narrative that De Quincey must leave substantially untouched, the representations of his dreams. He prefaces the explanation of his "error" to the segment of the narrative describing those dreams and points out that this error is so diffuse that it remains uncorrected. Of course, that error involves a misinterpretation of the tortures inflicted on him as he lay helpless on his bed. In effect, his error was in ever having imagined himself to have been effeminized, and in no place is this error so widespread as within that final section, all of which is predicated on his sensation of immobility and immersion within his own materiality. There is no longer a place for this segment, with its feminized narrator suffering under the pains of opium, when De Quincey has reverted to a model of addiction that has no pains, has no Circean spell, and does not destroy agency.

What, then, to do with those familiar dream sequences, so well known and so wrong, in which his helplessness is most forcefully expressed? De Quincey cuts them off from their reference to his body and allows them to flow forth as purely imaginative products of his intellectual sensibility. He aestheticizes them by retaining the dreams but denuding them of their connection to the effeminized body of the dreamer. Their primary interest thus comes to rest in their status as independent products of the Romantic imagination, not in the materiality of the body or in the social experiences impressed upon it. Thus, his dreams at last float free from the materiality of the body. With this change, they also become the centerpiece of the new narrative, for he now revises his rationale for the work and explains that the dreams are "the true objects—first and last—contemplated in these Confessions" (*Writings,* 3:233). And so, in De Quincey, the aesthetic comes into being out of the compelling force for personal narrative to disavow its connection to the materiality of the body.

5

Harrington's Last Shudder

Maria Edgeworth and the Popular Fear of the Nervous Body

The circumstance that gave rise to *Harrington* (1817) is one of the more well-known facts about one of Maria Edgeworth's least-known tales.[1] In a "Note to the Reader" prefacing the story, her father, Richard Lovell Edgeworth, explains that it "was occasioned by an extremely well-written letter, which Miss Edgeworth received from America, from a Jewish lady, complaining of the illiberality with which the Jewish nation had been treated in some of Miss Edgeworth's works" (*TN*, 9:iii).[2] In response, Edgeworth composed a tale about prejudice against Jews that features an idealized Jewish gentleman, Mr. Montenero, and a narrator who must overcome his childhood anti-Semitism.

The tale is also a nervous narrative. Harrington tells the story of "the strange nervous fits I had when a boy" (*TN*, 9:197) and their repercussions in his adult body. His nervous fits are specifically anti-Semitic. They originate in the misguided actions of his childhood nurse, Fowler, who instills in him such a pronounced fear of an old-clothes seller, Simon the Jew, that as an adult he retains an unfortunate and uncontrollable tendency to faint at the recollection of Simon's stereotyped Jewish face. And so he refers to his own narrative as a study of "the affair with my nerves and the Jews" (*TN*, 9:7–8).

This is an affair that he necessarily overcomes. His last fit occurs, fittingly, in the last scene of the tale. The acutely perceptive Montenero intentionally provokes it by uttering the magic word, "Fowler!" (*TN*, 9:207). The name of the maid who threatened to give him to Simon the Jew causes a predictable, outwardly visible reflexive action in Harrington's body: "I shuddered and started back" (*TN*, 9:207). This shudder is one in a long series of such shudders in the adult

Harrington. When he earlier encounters a face reminiscent of Simon the Jew's, he reacts similarly: "[A] nervous tremor seized me in every limb. I let the purse, which I had in my hand, fall upon the ground" (*TN*, 9:132). At another moment, he is made speechless in mid-sentence by an "involuntary shudder" at the sight of a face identical to Fowler's (*TN*, 9:182).³ In these incidents, although he says he does "my utmost to suppress my feelings" (*TN*, 9:131), he finds that he cannot.

The last shudder matters because it is the *last* shudder—that is, his final nervous response. Montenero provokes it to make a point, using the shudder to insist that Harrington take the final step in exerting the "power over yourself" that has progressively cured him of the residual effects of his childhood nervous fits (*TN*, 9:208). "[Y]ou have given proofs that your matured reason and your humanity have been able to control and master your imagination and your antipathies," Montenero points out (*TN*, 9:208). It is because of these proofs that Montenero has finally welcomed a marriage between Harrington and his only daughter, Berenice. Told to master this last somatic response, Harrington determines, "I will conquer myself." (*TN*, 9:208). And so he does, not just in learning to forgive the maid Fowler but in becoming the self-controlled, authoritative voice that narrates his own nervous past from the subject-position of a detached natural historian. His shudder at the mention of Fowler is the dying gasp of a nervous inscription that he completely erases. Harrington's is thus the nervous body that is now no longer nervous.

Because Harrington tells the story of how he gradually overcomes his disorder rather than dwelling on its sequential creation, his narrative departs significantly from the pattern of the nervous narrative. Both Godwin's *Caleb Williams* and Hays's *Emma Courtney* utilize an abject narrator, one who continues to be defined by the nervous condition he or she describes. *Harrington* is told through a wholly authoritative narrator who has escaped from the condition and so has no need to appeal to the reader's sympathy. Instead, he presents "this history of the mental and corporeal ills of my childhood" (*TN*, 9:8) for their scientific value, as "experiments" (*TN*, 9:9) that can illuminate the hidden mechanisms of the mind. The stance is comparable to De Quincey's opening narrative strategy, but *Harrington* is more consistent in its construction of a subject-position identified with narrative objectivity, one that has no need for the kind of subsequent rene-gotiations that characterize De Quincey's *Confessions*. *Harrington* is an unambivalent representation of escape from the constitutive nervous effects of early experiences. As a direct result, the nervous body is redefined as more resilient than had been previously thought. The tale describes the same nervous mechanism with remarkable preci-sion, using the same physiological psychology found in Thomas Trotter's work.[4] This body remains highly susceptible to being writ-ten on, but it is now capable of being unwritten, too. Freed of his so-maticized past, this narrator not only theorizes Caleb Williams's "manly tale," he also tells it.

Maria Edgeworth originally wrote a different passage for Monte-nero in the episode of the last shudder. In the 1817 edition, the fo-cus is not on Harrington's capacity for self-control but on the un-forgivable nature of Fowler's interference in the course of true love between Harrington and Berenice, Montenero's daughter. "Con-spiring against more than my life—my love," Harrington cries.[5] In removing such references, Edgeworth shifts the emphasis away from the sanctity of romantic love to the overriding importance of rational self-control, which becomes the subject of Montenero's new speech. Edgeworth's late effort to buttress the tale's emphasis on self-mastery—that is, on Harrington's capacity for being cured—sug-gests a perceived need to clarify her representation of Harrington's escape from his nervous body. Her revisions imply an awareness of and an anxiety about how internal inconsistencies—such as the final, conventional speech elevating the passion of love above life it-self—might weaken the clarity of Harrington's escape from a body ruled by its passions.

Nonetheless, in the revised tale, reinforced and more consistent in its valorization of reason than the first edition, there remains a trend that works against the tale's claims for Harrington's escape and that Edgeworth does not eliminate. That trend flows from the precision with which *Harrington* defines the nervous body and the redefinition that body undergoes late in the narrative in order to produce the narrator's cure. By considering that disorder, we can see that the cure has two contradictory effects: It produces the nar-rator's rationality, but only by sacrificing the foundation on which the tale's concept of rationality is based. Harrington's narrative objectivity, though apparently more stable than that of the other nervous narrators discussed here, is ultimately the least stable of them all.

Harrington describes the origin of his disorder in the first chapter, using the language of physiological psychology.[6] In the tale's opening scene, he is six years old, an age of delicacy and impressionability because of the small size of nervous fibers in the child's body. It is 1761, the end of his first day in London, and he observes that his "senses had been excited, and almost exhausted, by the vast variety of objects that were new to me" (*TN*, 9:1); his body has overaccumulated stimulating impressions. In such a state, it requires a strong new stimulus to arrest his attention, and this is provided by the inexplicable appearance of "star after star of light" approaching. When he finally perceives the nearing lamplighter, he reacts as a child-scientist, experiencing "as much delight as philosopher ever enjoyed in discovering the cause of a new and general phenomenon" (*TN*, 9:1). His attention is then arrested by an even stronger novelty when the lamplighter's torch "flared on the face and figure of an old man with a long white beard and a dark visage, who, holding a great bag slung over one shoulder, walked slowly on, repeating in a low, abrupt, mysterious tone, the cry of 'Old clothes! Old clothes! Old clothes!'" (*TN*, 9:1–2). When the peddler, Simon the Jew, looks back at Harrington, the narrator receives the impression that becomes the focal point of his hysteria.

That face, initially perceived by Harrington as "good-natured," is redefined by the maid Fowler as a threat in order to compel the child's obedience.[7] "If you don't come quietly this minute . . . I'll call Simon the Jew there . . . and he shall come up and carry you away in his great bag" (*TN*, 9:2). This redefinition produces instant obedience, but the terror it causes in the enervated and vulnerable child's body has long-term consequences. Beginning that night, he suffers the pains of excessive sensibility as the face of "Simon the Jew and his bag, who had come to carry me away in the height of my joys" (*TN*, 9:2), appears and reappears to him. In the following weeks, Fowler repeats the threat, having discovered its efficacy. However, in the standard pattern of excess sensibility, the stimulus needs to be continually escalated in order to have the same effect. When "by frequent repetition this threat had lost somewhat of its power" (*TN*, 9:2), she adds increasingly gruesome details to the story of Simon and his bag, until it is fully revealed as a variant of the ancient anti-Semitic blood libel.[8]

> Above all others, there was one story—horrible! most horrible!— which she used to tell at midnight, about a Jew who lived in Paris in a dark alley, and who professed to sell pork pies; but it was found out at last that the pies were not pork—they were made of the flesh of little children. His wife used to stand at the door of her den to watch for little children, and, as they were passing, would tempt them in with cakes and sweetmeats. There was a trap-door in the cellar, and the children were dragged down; and—Oh! how my blood ran cold when we came to the terrible trap-door. Were there, I asked, such things in London now?
>
> Oh, yes! In dark narrow lanes there were Jews now living, and watching always for such little children as me.
>
> (*TN*, 9:2–3)

This escalation writes a mechanical response into Harrington's young body that causes him to suffer an "evening attack of nerves" (*TN*, 9:10) each time he hears the peddler's nightly cry.

Harrington's symptoms respond to the content of this blood-libel narrative. Every night for the next year and a half, he explains, "I lay in an indescribable agony of terror; my head under the bedclothes, my knees drawn up, in a cold perspiration. I saw faces around me grinning, glaring, receding, advancing, all turning at last into the same face of the Jew with the long beard and the terrible eyes: and that bag, in which I fancied were mangled limbs of children—it opened to receive me, or fell upon my bed, and lay heavy on my breast, so that I could neither stir nor scream" (*TN*, 9:3–4). The dark maw of the trapdoor, in Fowler's narrative, and Simon's bag, in Harrington's imagination, become synonymous, both functioning as great orifices in which the body of the child is contained and transformed. He imagines this bag as a weight pressing on his breast, a symptom that reproduces the "globus" associated with hysteria, and the effect of this weight is a bodily paralysis and an inability to speak. What Harrington experiences, in his hysterical moments, then, is his own containment within the bag, a sensation that manifests itself in his adult fits as a sense of suffocation, speechlessness, and immobility. His body responds as if it were literally confined, and thus his symptoms are consistent with the content of his fear.

Once written into his body, however, this hysterical condition persists long after its rational basis is removed. Fowler, who soon tires of tending to the hysteric she has invented, tries to undo the damage by confessing her fabrication to Harrington, explaining that the bag contained only clothes. But "to undo her work was beyond her power" (*TN*, 9:4). As an empirical proof, she brings Simon into the house to open his bag, but Harrington's "imagination was by this time proof against ocular demonstration" (*TN*, 9:5). Instead of curing his disorder, the meeting produces a new instance of it. This gulf between rational understanding and hysterical response grows during the narrative, as he retains traces of this response even as he acquires an adult sympathy for Jewish characters. He develops a friendship with Jacob, the son of Simon the peddler, and is introduced by him to a group of highly educated Jews, including a scholar he studies with at Cambridge, the art collector Montenero, and his daughter, Berenice, with whom Harrington falls in love. Yet whenever he encounters an image reminiscent of Simon the Jew, he grows faint.

Edgeworth is positing a particular theory of hysteria, one that is characterized by a slippage between signifier and signified of the sign "Jew." Initially, the content associated with this sign is threatening, and it produces a response in the body that is linked to this content. As Harrington matures, the content of the sign "Jew" changes from foe to friend, but his body continues to respond to the signifier as if it possessed the earlier meaning. Harrington's body is thus a hostage to the letter, as the signifier persists in its mechanical effects long after the signified that initially accounted for those effects has disappeared. The conflict is between Harrington's autonomy, as a rational subject, and his body's unwilled and uncontainable response to the sign "Jew."

Because the tale treats anti-Semitism as a social phenomenon, Harrington's disorder is one example of a generalized problem, a collective disorder that is represented as endemic to British social life. In the tale's thematization of group behaviors, which she calls "party spirit," Edgeworth articulates the mechanism by which disorders such as Harrington's are communicated and even come to dominate entire societies.[9] Edgeworth wrote about "party spirit" before the modern concept of a mass psychology had been formulated. Contemporary ideas about crowd behavior developed in the later nineteenth century and were most fully articulated by the French natural historian Gustave LeBon, who developed a theory in which political leaders could control populations through a form of mass hypnotism.[10] Edgeworth's ideas about crowds belong to an earlier paradigm of crowd behavior, one that has roots in Renaissance ideas about sympathetic imagination and its communication between individuals. Harrington names those sources in the opening of the tale following his description of the origin of his Jewish "antipathy," when he connects his own "history of the mental and corporeal ills of my childhood" (*TN*, 9:8) with the natural histories of Francis Bacon and the lesser-known Kenelm Digby, a seventeenth-century natural philosopher and gentleman scientist who wrote on the powers of sympathy and antipathy. Harrington defines his "experiments" as a continuation of studies begun by Bacon (who was "successfully followed" by Digby), studies that are "equally necessary to the science of morals and of medicine" (*TN*, 9:8). He adopts the anachronistic language of Bacon's *Sylva Sylvarum; or, A Natural History* when he defines his narrative as "my experiments, *solitary and in concert, touching fear* and *of and concerning sympathies and antipathies*" (*TN*, 9:9).[11] "Solitary and in concert" is an adaptation of Bacon's two most frequent phrases in *Sylva Sylvarum*, "experiment solitary" and "experiments in consort," used to differentiate singular from multiple observations on a stated topic.[12] And he returns to the language of Bacon to state the fundamental topic of his narration as " 'the history of the power and influence of the imagination, not only upon the mind and body of the imaginant, but upon those of other people'" (*TN*, 9:8–9).[13] His narrative, then, is not only about his individual experience but also about the communication of "imaginary" objects between minds and the consequences that follow.

Kenelm Digby calls this process of communication the "unpleasing contagion of the imagination," and he explains it through the mechanism of sympathetic imitation.[14] Discussed in the works of both Bacon and Digby, the concept was still in circulation in the late eighteenth century. In 1779 it appeared, for example, in the first sustained entry on sympathy in the *Encyclopaedia Britannica:*

> Sympathy, too, is often an imitative faculty, sometimes involuntary,
> frequently without consciousness: thus we yawn when we see others
> yawn, and are made to laugh by the laughing of another.
>
> (2d ed., s.v. "sympathy")

This imitative act is based on the idea of an exchange, but one that operates without any rational activity, occurring instead as a purely mechanistic imitation. According to Digby's early description of contagious laughter, in *Two Treatises* (1644), the laughing of one man will set another laughing, "though he know not the cause why the first man laugheth."[15] Digby draws a clear distinction between the first man, who knows the joke, and the second, whose laughter is a mechanical imitation of the first, distinct in that it is devoid of any ideational content. The second man's laughter is more reflexive than reflective. Digby illustrates this same mechanical imitation in reporting the case of a hapless roofer, which is today cited as the first known description of "echopraxia," the disease of compulsive imitation:[16] "I have heard of a man . . . that when he saw any man make a certain motion with his hand, could not choose but he must make the same: so that, being a tyler by his trade, and having one hand imployed with holding his tooles, whiles he held himself with the other upon the eaves of a house he was mending, a man standing below on the ground, made that signe or motion to him; whereupon he quited his holdfast to imitate that motion, and fell downe, in danger of breaking his necke" (*Two Treatises*, 335).

Digby's report expands the concept of sympathetic imitation from the commonplace to the pathological. In this example, it overwhelms any willful attempt at self-restraint, despite the immediate danger involved. This action takes place independently of the reason or will of the subject. An example of the power of sympathy, from Francis Bacon's *Sylva Sylvarum*, illustrates the complete disjunction between this category of bodily response and the subject, as it records evidence of sympathetic reaction in a corpse: "It is an usual observation, that if the body of one murthered be brought before the murtherer, the wounds will bleed afresh. Some do affirm, that the dead body, upon the presence of the murtherer, hath opened the eyes."[17]

Digby explains the psychophysiology in living bodies of this extrarational mechanism as follows: "All these effects, do proceed out of the action of the seen object upon the fantasy of the looker on: which making the picture or likenesse of its owne action in the others fantasy, maketh his spirits runne to the same parts; and consequently, move the same members, that is, do the same actions" (*Two Treatises*, 335). Based on this imitative model, Digby explains how a speaker can exert a persuasive influence over the audience through sympathetic imitation: "And hence it is that . . . whatsoever a good oratour delivereth well, (that is, with a semblance of passion agreeable to his wordes) rayseth of its own natur like affection in the hearers" (*Two Treatises*, 335). In both cases, the key element is the effect the "fantasy" has on the body of "the looker on" or "the hearers." What appears in the imagination, whether seen or orally represented, has a mimetic consequence in the body.

These consequences can be permanent, as is graphically illustrated in the 1797 edition of the *Encyclopaedia Britannica*. The *Encyclopaedia* appeals to sympathetic imitation as the explanatory principle for the presence of human bodily deformity in the world.[18] In its description of the process by which "monsters"—defined as people with bizarre or deformed limbs—come into being, the *Encyclopaedia* uses an incident from Paris, originally described in Malebranche, to illustrate how sympathetic imitation in the body of a pregnant woman can produce monstrosity in the child (3d ed., s.v. "monster"). Observing that "the view of a wound . . . wounds the person who views it," *Britannica* differentiates between the effects of viewing a public execution on "vigorous men" with firm fibers and on the more "weak and delicate" fibers of women. *Britannica* extends the scale of vulnerability to "children still in their mother's womb," whose fibers are "incomparably finer than those in women." Thus, the child's body becomes the most sensitive register of effects that are present in varying degrees in all bodies. In the specific example cited, a pregnant French woman views a criminal's limbs being individually broken, and "every stroke given to the poor man, struck forcibly the imagination of the woman. . . . [T]he violent course of the animal spirits was directed forcibly from the brain to all those parts of the body corresponding to the suffering parts of the criminal." Through the same echopraxic mechanism described by Digby, the woman's body mimics the scene before it. Whereas "the bones of the mother were strong enough" to sustain the impression, the child's body is more vulnerable. The "spirits" follow the identical course in the fetal body, whose fragile bones and nervous system are both destroyed. Its limbs are snapped by the contractions, and its brain is "quite ruined" by the "shock of those spirits . . . enough to deprive him of reason all his lifetime." The child is born "a fool, and with all its legs and arms broke in the same manner as those of criminals." And thus, concludes the *Encyclopaedia,* can "the phenomena of monsters be easily accounted for."

Within this example, when the mother's body mimics the body of the criminal, it responds to the image of pain as if it were its own. The material effects of this sympathetic mimesis are dramatized in the body of the child, who is born a copy of the broken body of the criminal. The larger danger represented by the ontological novelty of the monster's body, however, is not that it reproduces the body of the criminal but rather that it embodies—it literally gives a body to—the mother's imagined experience. The monster is the realization, in material fact, of the "fantasy of the looker on," not of the viewed execution. Any occasion that were to present this image forcefully enough to her mind would produce the same consequence. The "looker on" does not have to be witnessing an external event. Similar effects can follow from a later recollection of the execution, reading an account of an execution, or even fantasizing such an execution, as long as the idea of the execution is vividly present. Within such a scheme, any distinction between realities and representations is lost, as representations have the ability to cross over into the status of realities.[19]

In Alexander Crichton's *An Inquiry into the Nature and Origin of Mental Derangement* (1798), the central assumption of the physician's study of the physiology of delirium is that the body does not distinguish between impressions from actual objects and impressions from imaginary ones.[20] He claims that the "sensorial impressions" of fictional representations "pervade our frame in the same manner as the impressions of the objects themselves, had they been real, would have done; the only difference being in degree" (*Inquiry,* 2:149). He illustrates this claim by asserting that "Homer's description of the girdle of Venus, and of the Elysian fields; Milton's description of Eve; Spenser's description of the residence of Acrasy . . . gratify the senses" as if the reader experienced the fictional objects as fact (2:149). Such ideas tend to produce the same physiological actions in the body as the things they represent. Thus, "if an absent person imagines himself engaged in controversy, his lips move as if in conversation; if his subject of thought be an object of any passions, as anger, jealousy, envy, hatred, or love, his countenance and gestures betray the emotions natural to these passions" (2:6). Crichton explains this phenomenon in a manner similar to Digby, asserting that mental impressions are "conveyed to the extremities of those nerves of external sense by which the object, had it been a real one, would have been naturally received" (2:37–38). In this way internal impressions reproduce, in their physiology, the effects of external impressions. This physiology provides an explanatory underpinning for the belief that the physical effect of an idea is identical in kind to the physical effect of the thing for which it substitutes. This long-standing belief contributes to the climate of fear about the effects of fictional representations, such as those in novels, on younger, impressionable readers.[21]

Whereas ideas have "corporeal effects . . . that are exactly similar in kind to what the real object would have," these effects are normally "weaker in degree" (2:112). However, under certain circumstances this difference in degree disappears, and ideas can have a corporeal effect even greater than that of objects. Chief among these circumstances is repetition. "Representations of the mind," Crichton claims, "when frequently renewed by acts of the imagination, at last acquire a degree of vividness which surpasses those derived from external objects" (2:65). Brooding over an idea—as Harrington does late in the tale, when he fears he will lose Berenice and secludes himself "[t]o feed upon my thoughts in solitude" (*TN*, 9:178)—threatens the subject's health, because mental impressions grow in strength through repetition. Lingering repeatedly over the memorized images of a novel or romance poses a real danger, because the visitor to an immaterial adventure may return with a very material disorder. As Crichton observes, in pleading for a more compassionate attitude toward suicides, "Once an idea, by its being often presented to the mind, has gained such a degree of force and vividness as to command belief, it is of no consequence as to its effects, whether it originated in a real or an imaginary cause" (*Inquiry*, 2:197).[22]

Edgeworth represents this transition from imaginary to real in the character of Mrs. Harrington. In her youth, we learn, she affected a belief in "*presentiments* and presages, omens and dreams" as a fashionable snare "to interest her admirers" (*TN*, 9:37). Repeating the ruse for years, she eventually became in earnest the nervous victim in earnest of the excess sensibility she had imitated, "so that what in the beginning might have been affectation, was in the end reality" (*TN*, 9:37). Harrington's own disorder makes the identical transition. As his childhood fits in response to Simon the Jew become more pronounced, he becomes an object of popular curiosity, and there is public debate over whether or not his fits prove the existence in the Christian body of a natural racial "antipathy" to Jews.[23] As he explains in retrospect, this popular interest exacerbates his condition: "Between the effects of real fear, and the exaggerated expression of it to which I had been encouraged, I was now seriously ill. It is well known that persons have brought on fits by pretending to have them; and by yielding to feelings, at first slight and perfectly within the command of the will, have at last acquired habits beyond the power of their reason, or of their most strenuous voluntary exertion to control. Such was my pitiable case" (*TN*, 9:8). In both Harrington and his mother, the illness has finally been inscribed on the body and now exists outside the reach of "reason" and "voluntary exertion"—that is, beyond any possibility of self-mastery.

Sympathetic imitation was further used to explain why individuals exhibited behaviors in large groups that they would never exhibit singly. The leading lecturer on crowd phenomena was the Scottish empirical philosopher Dugald Stewart, a professor at the University of Edinburgh, and Edgeworth was in an excellent position to become familiar with his ideas. Stewart was a family friend of the Edgeworths and the tutor of two of Maria's brothers.[24] Even before meeting him, she sketched Stewart as Dr. Campbell, the tutor for the protagonist, in *Forester,* a novella-length story Edgeworth published as part of her *Moral Tales* (1801). She stayed with the Stewarts during her visit to Edinburgh in 1803. Afterward, she wrote of him, "I never conversed with any one with whom I was more at ease," and she expressed an interest in his ideas when she complained about not being allowed to hear his lectures because of her sex.[25] She corresponded for many years with Mrs. Stewart and last visited the family in 1823, when Dugald Stewart was quite elderly.

Stewart uses the "contagion of sympathetic imitation" to explain the unique behavior of crowds (*Works*, 3:147).[26] He specifies, in introducing the concept, that he is not interested in "any instinctive or mysterious process"(*Works*, 3:108), nor in the kind of willful imitation that occurs when one author forms his taste in writing by imitating another. "The Imitation of which I am here to treat, and which I have distinguished by the title of *Sympathetic*, is that chiefly which depends on the mimical powers connected with our *bodily frame*; and which, in certain combinations of circumstances, seems to result, with little intervention of our will, from a sympathy between the bodily organizations of different individuals" (*Works*, 3:108–9). He argues that emotions are spread from one person to another through the same "irresistible tendency to imitation" as yawns or laughter (*Works*, 3:136). As an example, he hypothesizes someone who imitates exactly the external stance, gestures, and expression of someone else in an extreme emotional state. The mimic, he claims, will internally reproduce the same feelings exhibited by the original. Because of the natural tendency to imitation, everyone is like this mimic to varying degrees, and so "something of the same kind happens to every man, more or less, when he sees any passion strongly marked in the countenance of another" (*Works*, 3:136). When a group of like-minded people come together for a common purpose—he gives the example of attendees at either a carnival or funeral—their sense of shared purpose creates a special social environment in which individuals express their emotions more freely than when alone. These strongly marked external displays combine with the bodily tendency to sympathetic imitation, resulting in a rapid escalation of emotionality: "[T]he effect is likely to be incalculably great; the mind at once acting on the body, and the body reacting on the mind, while the influence of each is manifested by the inexplicable contagion of sympathetic imitation" (*Works*, 3:147). An individual's feeling of grief is increased by a reflexive imitation of the signs of grief in another, and this produces stronger grief in others of the crowd, so that the group produces a unique and "greatly augmented" emotionality (*Works*, 3:147), which is felt by each member as his or her own but which cannot exist apart from the membership in the crowd. Stewart thus provides an explanation for a specifically crowd psychology—that is, for a new kind of psychological state that is qualitatively different than the sum of its individual parts. The group emotion is felt by all, "even among characters whom the event in question would, in their solitary hours, have scarcely affected with any emotion whatsoever" (*Works*, 3:147). Thus, individual subjectivity becomes subordinated to the new crowd subjectivity, which pushes it aside and occupies the space of the subject in each member.

In *Harrington*, Edgeworth's exploration of party spirit uses assumptions similar to those of Stewart, in particular the assumption of a direct relationship between crowd formation and a contagious imitation that overwhelms the rational autonomy of the subject. Numerous incidents in the tale—the dinner party organized by Harrington's father, the schoolboy dispute, the riot of soldiers at Gibraltar, the later Gordon riots—are thematically related as explorations of the mechanism of party spirit. The first incident defines the basic terms that the rest will utilize. Harrington's father, a Member of Parliament, hosts a dinner party to lobby the local gentry against the pending Jewish Naturalization Bill of 1753.[27] Harrington notes that his father attempts "to convince them, that they were, or ought to be, of my father's opinion, and that they had better all join him in the toast of 'The Jews are down, and keep 'em down'" (*TN*, 9:15). The room divides into opposite parties. Because "[t]he feeling of party spirit . . . is caught by children as quickly as it is revealed by men" (*TN*, 9:15), young Harrington takes a side, but he is "incapable of comprehending their arguments" on the topic (*TN*, 9:15). His response is specifically divorced from a rational engagement with the issue, a fact made explicit when his interest, unusual for a child, is questioned by the adults.

> "And what reasons did you hear?" said a gentleman in company.
> "Reasons!" interrupted my father; "oh! sir, to call upon the boy for all the reasons he has heard—But you'll not pose him: speak up, speak up, Harrington, my boy!"
> "I've nothing to say about reasons, sir."
> "No! that was not a fair question," said my father; "but, my boy, you know on which side you are, don't you?"
> "To be sure—on your side, father."
> "That's right—bravo! To know on which side one is, is one great point in life."
> "And I can tell on which side every one here is." Then going

round the table, I touched the shoulder of each of the company, saying, "A Jew!—No Jew!" and bursts of applause ensued.

(*TN*, 9:16)

Because he does not comprehend the pros and cons of the naturalization bill, taking a side, regardless of content, is the only issue. His
attention is solely focused on the signifier, "A Jew!—No Jew!" apart
from its signified. Harrington's act of labeling the guests is ap-
plauded because it so perfectly embodies the essence of party spirit:
a perfect lack of comprehension of the signified combined with a
perfect loyalty to the signifier.

Harrington's father, the principal exemplar of party spirit in the
tale, further illustrates this principle:[28] "My father was a great stick-
ler for parliamentary consistency, and moreover he was of an obsti-
nate temper. Ten years could make no change in his opinions, as he
was proud to declare" (*TN*, 9:14). In this inflexibility, Mr. Harrington offers a related example of action divorced from reason. He sus-
pends autonomous judgment in favor of a rote "consistency," and
thus his definitive feature is an "adhesion to a preconceived notion
or purpose" that reduces his actions to blind repetitions of earlier
judgments (*TN*, 9:35). Such is the pattern for his most singular
characteristic: "Now it was well known in our house, that a sentence
of my father's beginning and ending 'by Jupiter Ammon' admitted
of no reply from any mortal—it was the stamp of fate; no hope of
any reversion of the decree: it seemed to bind even him who uttered
the oath beyond his own power of revocation" (*TN*, 9:17). His trade-
mark oath transforms him into a prisoner of his own once-rational
decisions, so that what begins as purposeful ends up as mindless
repetition. The leading example is his oath that his son shall be dis-
inherited if he marries a Jew. By the narrative's end Mr. Harrington's
attitude toward Montenero and his daughter Berenice is completely
altered, yet he finds himself unable to release himself from his prior
decision.

Mr. Harrington's oath operates in the same manner as the son's
nervous shudder. In their first use, the words "by Jupiter Ammon"
refer to an explicit meaning; the signifier has a strong relationship to
its signified. But subsequently that relationship becomes secondary
in importance to the speaker's consistency. One whose oaths bind
him "beyond his own power of revocation" is one who is bound by

a signifier that has been divorced from its signified, so that the power of the letter takes precedence over the thing for which it stands. Ultimately, the juvenile Harrington perfectly embodies party spirit precisely because he has "nothing to say about reasons." This absence of reason raises the question of why Harrington, or anybody, chooses one party over another. At the dinner party, it appears his choice is an expression of loyalty to his father. But filial loyalty does not account for his basic fascination with the discussion itself, a fascination so unusual it attracts the notice of the adults (particularly after his boyhood friend, Lord Mowbray, grows fidgety and leaves). As he explains, "[a] subject apparently less liable to interest a child of my age could hardly be imagined; but from my peculiar associations it did attract my attention" (*TN*, 9:14). His fascination stems from that prior anti-Semitic condition whose social origin Edgeworth has carefully defined. The debate touches a chord in him; it moves him because of his disorder. He catches the spirit—whereas Mowbray does not—because he is predisposed to catch it. Within the mechanism of party spirit, then, the tale questions whether the choice of sides is freely made. In this opening example, Harrington's choice is no more rational or autonomous a judgment than his nervous shudders because it is predicated on an extra-rational, embodied response, one that resembles nothing so much as the man noted by Digby who, without knowing the joke, nonetheless feels moved to laugh.

The subsequent incident of the Gibraltar riot works in an identical fashion.[29] The story is told to Harrington by Jacob, the son of Simon the Jew, who is employed by a Jewish merchant supplying provisions to the garrison during the siege. Jacob's description of the initially peaceful and profitable enterprise is part of a pattern in the tale in which Jewish characters describe scenes of unprejudiced societies where Jews and Christians live in harmony. The most notable example of this utopian vision is Montenero and Berenice's America, but this harmonious utopia is not limited to place, appearing as well in repeated references to the liberal-minded English upper class. The Gibraltar peace is destroyed by Lord Mowbray, who is posted to the garrison as an army officer and raises a party against Jacob and his employers. Just as Harrington "caught" party spirit, Mowbray's subordinates catch his anti-Semitic labels for Jacob: " 'Lord Mowbray's servants heard, and caught their lord's witticism: the serjeants and soldiers repeated the colonel's words, and the nicknames spread through the regiment, and through the garrison; wherever I turned, I heard them echoed: poor Jacob was called *young Shylock* by some, and by others the *Wandering Jew*. It was a bitter jest, and soon became bitter earnest'" (*TN*, 9:76). Jacob is already known to this community, and yet the repetition of these words, as they echo through the garrison, have the power to remake him, in their eyes, as rational social relations are transformed into extraordinary fear: "'The common people felt a superstitious dread of me: the mothers charged their children to keep out of my way; and if I met them in the streets, they ran away and hid themselves'" (*TN*, 9:76). These mothers, in assuming that Jacob threatens their Christian children, are reenacting the same blood libel narrative with which the tale opens. Jacob is thus placed in the same position as his father, Simon, with his bag. This connection to the archetypal opening scene is an important part of the Gibraltar episode's rhetorical force. Because Jacob is the one telling the story, structurally it is as if the tale returned to the archetypal scene and allowed Simon to speak about the injustice of it. The "common people" of the garrison similarly substitute for the young Harrington; his individual history is simply generalized to society as a body. Every body has previously been written on by the narrative of blood libel, and they respond with the same kind of extrarational reflex as young Harrington at the dinner party.

Edgeworth's most extreme representation of party spirit in action is the Gordon riots. They begin in a manner resembling Mowbray's manipulation of the crowd at Gibraltar or Mr. Harrington's lobbying efforts at the dinner party, but they make a qualitative leap to raise the spectre of a party spirit that has escaped the control of its leader. It begins, like the other incidents, with a group of loyal partisans ready to accept anything that fits within their prior assumptions, no matter how irrational: "[T]hey were ready to believe any thing against the ministry, and some who, for party purposes, desired to influence the minds of the people, circulated the most ridiculous reports, and excited the most absurd terrors" (*TN*, 9:148). The riot begins with an incident of anti-Catholicism rather than anti-Semitism, one taken directly from an example in Bacon:[30] "It was confidently affirmed that the Pope would soon be in London, he having been seen in disguise in a gold-flowered nightgown on St. James's parade at Bath. A poor gentleman, who appeared at his door in his nightgown, had been actually taken by the Bath mob for the Pope; and they had pursued him with shouts, and hunted him, till he was forced to scramble over a wall to escape from his pursuers" (*TN*, 9:148).

It is along equally implausible lines that Edgeworth builds a bridge between the historically anti-Catholic Gordon riots and the anti-Semitism of her tale. Thomas Holcroft's widely read account of the riots, written at the time, includes only a single mention of Jews in London, but there is no crowd sentiment against Jews. Instead, Holcroft reports that Jewish families, along with all the other Londoners, were so terrified of the rioters that they wrote "this house is a true Protestant" on their shutters so that their homes would not be thought to belong to Catholics.[31] Edgeworth, normally attentive to exactly this kind of historical detail, is unusually inventive in this case: "[W]ithout any conceivable reason, suddenly a cry was raised against the Jews: unfortunately, Jews rhymed to shoes: these words were hitched into a rhyme, and the cry was, 'No Jews, no wooden shoes!' Thus, without any natural, civil, religious, moral, or political connexion, the poor Jews came in remainder to the ancient anti-Gallican antipathy felt by English feet and English fancies against the French wooden shoes" (*TN*, 9:149). Edgeworth's episode is remarkable in that, for all the detail provided on how and why the anti-Catholic cry could become anti-Semitic, the antagonism to Jews and the slogan itself serve no plot function in the narrative. The mob that descends on Montenero's house is not after him because he is Jewish. In fact, they are not after him at all; they are pursuing Mowbray's relations, Lady de Brantefield and Anne, whom they mistakenly identify as Catholics in the company of an imaginary priest. Thus, the entire assault on Montenero's home leaves the question of his Jewishness and the crowd's anti-Semitism beside the point. We are left to wonder why Edgeworth bothered to incorporate such an apparently unnecessary, convoluted, and implausible rationale into the narrative.

This anti-Jewish cry arises "without any conceivable reason," a consistent element in the party spirit mechanism. But in the earlier incidents of party spirit, the crowd is always influenced by a named leader, who introduces ideas for his own purposes. Young Harrington follows his father; the soldiers follow Mowbray. Even the initial fears of the Gordon mob about the Pope are instigated by specific leaders who have something to gain. This new cry against Jews is qualitatively different. It comes into being "without any natural, civil, religious, moral, or political" rationale, independently of any leader. The distinction between this cry and the earlier ones is that, rather than being an echo of a leader, as at Gibraltar, it arises from within the crowd as a direct manifestation of the crowd's enthusiasm, and in this the crowd takes on the quality of an independent mind.[32] The cry, "No Jews, no wooden shoes," signifies the point at which the crowd assumes a life of its own, with its own voice, its own rules, and its own slogans. This slogan, though marked by an absence of any association at the level of its content, works through the association at the level of its sound, by rhyming "Jews" with "shoes." Thus, the defining characteristic of this crowd mind is that it generates its own truths through the materiality of language. For Edgeworth, the problem posed by the crowd mind is that, like Harrington's shudder, it operates entirely through this logic of the signifier rather than the signified.

To the person within the crowd, however, such associations appear perfectly reasonable. Harrington, in recollecting his subjective experience of party spirit, explains that he was "carried away in the tide of popular enthusiasm" (*TN*, 9:20). Though in retrospect he wonders how he "could be so inhuman," then he had no doubts: [A]t the time it all appeared to me quite natural and proper; a just and necessary war" (*TN*, 9:20). There is thus no clear dividing line for the subject between participation in the crowd and the stance outside of it. Although each member of the crowd, by definition, has surrendered the ability to exercise an independent judgment, the crowd's members believe themselves to be freely engaged in making precisely those judgments. Harrington's participation is predicated on his extra-rational antipathy to the sign "Jew," but his experience of participation is accompanied by a sense of rationality, in which his actions are "proper," "just," and "necessary." Although he responds to the signifier, he believes himself to be evaluating the signified. One final and inescapable element of party spirit thus is a collective delusion of rationality, one Harrington once participated in but has since overcome.

Edgeworth's crowd psychology is not limited to scenes of party politics and violent riots. These are the most clearly labeled moments in a phenomenon that extends to all instances of group behavior. Lady Anne's devotion to fashion and to the tastes of the fashionable crowd represent an enslavement to signifiers, as her paean to the virtues of the French "pouf" illustrates (*TN*, 9:46). Fashionability itself is a type of party spirit, in which Lady Anne takes the opinions of the group for her own autonomous judgments. Similarly, Lady de Brantefield's rigid adherence to a family past is a counterpart to Mr. Harrington's adherence to his own past doctrines. The tale reserves its most systematic exploration of party spirit, however, for the variety it locates in the relationship between art and its audience. In a series of scenes including a painting exhibition, an art auction, and a performance of *The Merchant of Venice*, the tale explores the reactions of spectators to the manipulation of artists in terms that evoke the relationship between a party and its leader.

The parallel treatment of crowds and audiences can be seen by comparing two related incidents: a school yard assembly, in which Mowbray raises an anti-Semitic party, and the staging of Shakespeare's play. In the grammar school incident, Mowbray is the leader of a party raised against the Jewish vendor Jacob. As leader, his job is to create the crowd as a crowd, rather than a group of individuals. Edgeworth represents this process as a theatrical one. Mowbray asks the boys to assemble and promises to "show them some good sport," so the crowd is immediately defined as the audience to an organized spectacle (*TN*, 9:23). The schoolboys form a ring, and there is an upper gallery of boys looking on, reproducing the physical space of a theatre: "[T]hey had by this time gathered in a circle at the outside of that which we had made round Jacob, and many had brought benches, and were mounted upon them, looking over our heads to see what was going on" (*TN*, 9:25). On the stage created by this circle, Mowbray represents Jacob as an outsider against whom the schoolboys can identify as a group. He insists that, as a Jew, Jacob cannot possibly possess the feelings of love for his Jewish father that the Christian schoolboys feel for their fathers, and the boys cohere into a group, insulted by the comparison.[33] Mowbray's job, as author of the crowd, is to identify the outsider that constitutes the crowd through its difference, and Edgeworth represents this process as a performative staging of the Other. In this particular instance, Mowbray's staging is amateurish. He displays a juvenile cruelty that transforms Jacob into a sentimental icon of the victimized Man of

Feeling, making him someone to be sympathetically identified with rather than antipathetically rejected.[34] But Mowbray's technique improves with experience, and by the time of his posting to Gibraltar, he is clearly more adept at managing his audience through the same anti-Semitic performance.

The result of a more skillful staging of the Jew as Other, in the presentation of *The Merchant of Venice* before an adult audience, is less equivocal. In the central role of the Jewish Other is Charles Macklin, the eighteenth-century actor who rose to fame through his performance of Shylock. Prior to the performance, the audience is atomized and chaotic; Harrington's aristocratic companions are irritated by the middle-class vulgarians in the next box, so that the theatre is initially a setting for the reinforcement of social distinctions. But by the end of the first act, this conflicted crowd is transformed into a fascinated body with a unified voice that breaks out in sudden "thunders of applause" (*TN*, 9:59).

Harrington is a representative member of the audience, and his reaction explains this transformation. After the curtain lifts, he explains, "the Jew fixed and kept possession of my attention. . . . I forgot it was Macklin, I thought only of Shylock. In my enthusiasm I stood up, I pressed forward, I leaned far over towards the stage, that I might not lose a word" (*TN*, 9:59). His initial "enthusiasm" raises a question because it directly contradicts his character development. He has already learned to sympathize with Jewish characters, yet his reaction embraces the stereotype of Jewish villainy. The incident is structured as a contest between two extremes. The quintessential art object—the performance unites the greatest writer's drama with the world's greatest actor—competes with the matured reason of Harrington, now enlightened and apparently rid of his childhood antipathy. In the contest, his shudder resurfaces as enthusiasm, and he becomes fascinated precisely as he was fascinated at his father's dinner party, temporarily unable to recognize the anti-Semitic content of the stereotype on stage.

The mechanism by which this art object moves Harrington and, by extension, the rest of the audience follows the same logic as Harrington's nervous shudder. In a subsequent discussion of the play between Harrington and Montenero, Harrington argues that Shakespeare did not realize what he was doing; he gives a "general apology for Shakspeare's severity, by adverting to the time when he wrote, and the prejudices which then prevailed" (*TN*, 9:66).[35] But Montenero disagrees. "[A]s a dramatic poet, it was his business . . . to take advantage of the popular prejudice as a *power*—as a means of dramatic pathos and effect" (*TN*, 9:66). Montenero's Shakespeare is a more self-conscious artist than Harrington's. Far from being controlled by the prejudice of his day, his artistic "business" is manipulating the prior beliefs of his audience, and it is on this manipulation that aesthetic effect depends. To Montenero, the critic, Shakespeare is "the greatest poet that ever wrote," but he draws a clear distinction between "power" and "truth" (*TN*, 9:65). Shakespeare, he argues, reversed the characters in the original story, where a Christian demanded his pound of flesh from a Jew. Montenero notes that "we Jews must feel it peculiarly hard, that the truth of the story . . . should have been completely sacrificed to fiction" (*TN*, 9:66). Nonetheless, he concludes that "Shakspeare was right, as a dramatic poet, in reversing the characters" (*TN*, 9:66). Montenero, then, judges the play in two distinct ways: in terms of purely rhetorical artistic criteria, in which case the play is "right," and in terms of factual content, in which case it is wrong. This distinction is a consistent part of Montenero's critical commentaries on art; it recurs in his discussion of the Spanish paintings, which he collects, and again in evaluating the crude painting of torture, "The Dentition of the Jew," which he destroys. It is exactly this distinction between aesthetic effect and content that is lacking in the popular response to the play, as well as in the other moments of crowd behavior. This implication is present within Montenero's comment that "we poor Jews have felt your Shakspeare's power to our cost" (*TN*, 9:66). The sense of "power" in this phrase is distinct from the "dramatic pathos and effect" of the play. It refers to the way Jews become defined in social life as Shylocks through the fictional representation on the stage, as the riot at Gibraltar illustrated. Whereas Montenero differentiates dramatic "power" from factual "truth," society in general does not. When moved by dramatic power, society elevates representation to the status of truth.

This aesthetic theory operates through a conservative logic, for if art works through its appeal to prior beliefs, it reinforces ideas to which the spectator already subscribes. Rather than convincing the audience of a new idea, it brings out what is already present, convincing spectators of the justness of what they already feel. Art that appeals to emotions activates previously inscribed social attitudes, rather than natural or universal feelings, and so perpetuates the "prejudice" of party spirit.

This conservative model of art also appears in *Ormond*, the tale Edgeworth published together with *Harrington*, but there it is illustrated with the novel reader rather than the playgoer. Like Harrington, Ormond experiences the dramatic power of art first as an arrested attention.[36] A good-hearted young Irishman but lacking a formal education, Ormond idly opens a copy of *Tom Jones*. Though not much of a reader, he finds he "could not shut it," and "he read on, standing for a quarter of an hour, fixed in the same position" (*TN*, 9:286). His experience of reading, and that of his friend Corny, is called an "enthusiasm," in which the power of art overcomes the reader's ability to differentiate between representation and factuality (*TN*, 9:295). Ormond "believed the story to be true, for it was constructed with unparalleled ingenuity, and developed with consummate art" (*TN*, 9:287). When he next takes up *Sir Charles Grandison*, the same thing happens: "Indeed, to him it appeared no fiction, while he was reading it" (*TN*, 9:294). Corny's experience as a reader is similar: "Fictions, if they touched him at all, struck him with all the force of reality; and he never spoke of the characters as in a book, but as if they had lived and acted" (*TN*, 9:295).

To be "touched" and "struck" in this manner is literally to experience art through the body, and it is this somatic experience that generates an intellectual belief in its truth as a representation. Ormond believes "the story to be true" and Corny that the characters "lived" for the same reason that Harrington forgets Macklin is an actor. Harrington's momentary enthusiasm is explained by a susceptibility within his body, and a similar explanation is given for the novel readers in *Ormond*. Though the young Ormond attributes his experience to qualities in the art object—*Tom Jones* and *Clarissa* are both examples of novelistic "ingenuity" and "consummate art"—the narrator uses the incident to illustrate a kind of readerly naïveté and points instead to qualities within the reader that produce this susceptibility. Ormond identifies with the two different protagonists because, like him, each has a basically "generous" nature, and the narrator explains that "young readers readily assimilate and identify themselves with any character, the leading points of which resemble their own, and in whose general feelings they sympathize" (*TN*, 9:287). The difference between Ormond's experience and Harrington's is the difference between sympathy and antipathy, two closely related variants on the same bodily phenomenon. As Montenero connects dramatic power with the exploitation of a preexisting antipathy, the narrator of *Ormond* connects it with a preexisting sympathy. The underlying mechanism is the same. Ormond and Corny's convictions of the truth of art place them in the same position as the audience at the *Merchant of Venice,* and so their enthusiasm can be seen as a version of Harrington's nervous shudder. Like him, they become convinced of the justness of their own extra-rational beliefs.

This body-based model of art is one of two competing aesthetic models in *Harrington.* The other, represented by Montenero, is a critical model that exists outside the dynamics of party spirit. Montenero's ability to differentiate "dramatic pathos" from "truth," or experience from fact, allows him to evaluate art without becoming subservient to its dramatic power, and so Montenero is the only character in the tale entirely outside the rule of the letter. Called a man of "calm and proud independence" (*TN*, 9:81), he controls his acute sensibility with philosophy, and so he stands for a detached, analytical consciousness. "[C]alm had become the unvarying temper of his mind" (*TN*, 9:82), and thus he is able to interpret representations as personally repellent as *The Merchant of Venice* and *The Dentition of the Jew* with an unimpaired judgment. "[M]orbid sensibility . . . incapacitates . . . the exercise of independent virtue" (*TN*, 9:83), he lectures Berenice, complaining of her sensitivity to expressions of anti-Semitism. He himself has no such morbidity. He is the most idealized character in the tale, and his idealization lies in the way he eludes the paradox of sensibility. He is represented as capable of great sensitivity; small slights, such as the polite refusal of Mrs. Harrington to enter his house, "hurt his feelings much" (*TN*, 9:81). The detail is significant because it is represented as commonplace in the life of a Jew, being to Montenero one more in a long series of slights. Yet, unlike Godwin's characters in *Caleb Williams,* he becomes neither inured to the slight nor constituted by it. He retains his vulnerability to the world without being written upon by it, and so he escapes the pattern of prejudice and enthusiasm that leads to the larger crowd's immersion in party spirit. Though the crowd believes itself to be judging for itself, it is always imprisoned within the prejudice written on its body by prior representations; the crowd is always the prisoner of representation rather than its critic. Montenero's critical ability is what sets him apart from the crowd; his judgment is "independent." He represents the same subject-position that Harrington occupies after his last shudder, when he begins to tell the story of his emergence out of the crowd and into the space of the independent critic, able at last to narrate his body's past without becoming implicated in it.

This independence also characterizes the implied audience of *Harrington*. The narrator addresses an enlightened reader who, like him, is wholly free of prejudice and enthusiasm. "We all know," he tells the reader (*TN*, 9:148). His narrative presumes a wise, rather than a naive, reader, one distinctly different from the kind of reader illustrated by Corny and the young Ormond. "In our enlightened days," Harrington apostrophizes, it "may appear incredible" that a child could be taken in by a story like Fowler's (*TN*, 9:3). Though he speaks only of his own childhood, a period twenty years previous to the narrating present, he describes those unenlightened days as part of an earlier developmental stage in English social life, when it was still ruled by stories like Fowler's: "I am speaking of what happened many years ago: nursery-maids and children, I believe, are very different now from what they were then; and in further proof of the progress of human knowledge and reason, we may recollect that many of these very stories of the Jews, which we now hold too preposterous for the infant and the nursery-maid to credit, were some centuries ago universally believed by the English nation, and had furnished more than one of our kings with pretexts for extortion and massacres" (*TN*, 9:3).

Like the infant Harrington, the social body of this early era was "[c]harmed by the effect" of anti-Semitic narratives (*TN*, 9:3), and leaders took advantage of the public prejudice. Being "charmed" in this context suggests the experience of being placed under a spell rather than merely being entertained. Harrington defines "the effect" of these narratives on him as a deprivation of agency, claiming that Fowler repeats her story "to reduce me to passive obedience" (*TN*, 9:2). In the same manner, this charming effect was used by "kings" in the past to control the nation. Harrington's individual development is thus paralleled by a progressive social development that moves through these same stages from readerly naïveté to critical distance. *Harrington* describes a past era in which all of society functioned through party spirit, as an all-encompassing crowd, deprived of agency yet "universally" believing in the justness of its irrational beliefs. But the age of the crowd is gone, and in the narrating present the new, enlightened audience belongs more to the utopian communities described by Montenero—free from all prejudice, ruled by independent merit—than to the audience shaped by *The Merchant of Venice*. This narrative addresses a reader who, like Harrington, has already found a way to escape the crowd and become like Montenero.

Harrington tells the story, then, of how he escaped the nervous body and its socially constructed responses to become objective. Thus, his cure—the process he follows, the regimen he adopts, the mode of getting from inside to outside the nervous body and its confinement—promises to have instructive merit. That cure is as central to the logic of *Harrington* as De Quincey's cure is to his *Confessions*. But the claims in Harrington are far greater, for it is not only Harrington's escape that is being narrated but the transformation of an entire society from one ruled by the nervous body of a mobbish past to an enlightened utopia ruled by objectivity. Because of the precision with which the tale defines the nervous body, Harrington's escape has a heroic quality to it, as it is a virtually impossible act. His nervous shudder is "involuntary" (*TN*, 9:182). His condition is "beyond the power" of his "most strenuous voluntary exertion, to control" (*TN*, 9:8). Montenero himself claims the condition is "difficult, scarcely possible, completely to conquer," and he fears throughout the tale that it "might recur" (*TN*, 9:81). Thus, the method that Edgeworth devises to extract Harrington from this tenacious body merits serious attention. On that method the narrator's voice depends, as does the community of enlightened readers it presupposes.

Given what is at stake and the represented difficulty of attaining it, the cure is decidedly anticlimactic. After proposing to Berenice, Harrington receives an ultimatum from Montenero. He has discovered an unnamed "obstacle" to the union (*TN*, 9:142), and he insists that Harrington's only hope is to demonstrate a thorough ability to control himself and his emotions, without knowing the nature of the obstacle. Should he prove incapable "of this necessary self-control" (*TN*, 9:143), he will never see Berenice again. That night, says Harrington, "I felt the nervous oppression, the dreadful weight upon my chest" (*TN*, 9:145), and he is visited by the figure of Simon the Jew, who has the voice of Montenero. "My early prepossessions and *antipathies*, my mother's *presentiments*, and prophecies of evil from the connexion with the Monteneros, the prejudices which had so long, so universally prevailed against the Jews, occurred to me. I know all this was unreasonable, but still the thoughts obtruded themselves" (*TN*, 9:145, emphasis original). To gain control over precisely such hysterical thoughts, Harrington finally adopts a tried and true course the next morning: "to take strong bodily exercise, and totally to change the course of my daily occupations" (*TN*, 9:145). Through horse riding and an all-male fishing expedition to the country, he explains, "my ideas were forced into new channels" (*TN*, 9:147), and the old ideas are suspended. "I thus disciplined my imagination at the time when I seemed only to be disciplining an Arabian horse" (*TN* 9:146). In this manner, "I . . . *medicined* my mind" (*TN*, 9:146, emphasis original). Though he faces subsequent trials and several dangerous moments of isolation at which his hysterical thoughts recur, this incident is the turning point; by practicing a sustained antidote of bodily exercise and outward-directed activity, he grows increasingly like Montenero and less like his younger, impressionable self. Rather than an actual cure of the nervous body, this narrative redefines it. Edgeworth's illustration of the consequences of representations for the nervous body are extreme, as we have seen. And so this cure poses a new problem. Harrington's hysteria is initially defined as a permanent inscription on the body, one that constitutes him in the same way that Mrs. Harrington's excess sensibility has come to constitute her. Thus, although he describes a condition that is beyond self-control, that condition ultimately proves not to be so. He masters his nervous shudder through a simple exercise of self-will and without any of the dramatics described by De Quincey. In consequence, the initial attitude toward his hysteria and its permanence is called into question. Harrington believed his twitch to be "involuntary," but it never really was; his disorder was not, in fact, permanent.

Because of this redefinition, the problem represented by the tale is not ultimately Harrington's nervous shudder, which is always containable. Instead, the problem lies in the popular assumptions about nerves, the ones that led Harrington and everyone around him to assume that his shudder was "involuntary" when in fact it was within his power of self-control. In retrospect, those initial assumptions are recontained as unwarranted fears, for Harrington's body proves far more resilient that anyone believes possible. Many popular prejudices are relegated to the unenlightened past by *Harrington*. The most prominent is the myth of the nervous body that, once written on, is never free of its nervous inscription. Edgeworth cures the nervous body by situating the theory of nervous inscription as one of the leading examples of crowd delusion.

This redefinition of the nervous body as itself a popular delusion is the centerpiece in the tale's hidden plot. Many apparent coincidences in the narrative turn out to have been manipulated by Lord Mowbray. He reveals, in a deathbed confession, that he has staged his most elaborate performance, and in it he has positioned Harrington as the Other. In this drama, Mowbray manufactures an extensive sequence of events designed to convince Montenero and Berenice that her young suitor still suffers from his childhood affliction. Among other stage devices, he encourages in Harrington an appearance of excess sensibility in a visit with the Monteneros to the Tower of London, and he arranges to have Fowler dress up as Simon the Jew to induce an apparent nervous fit during the visit to the synagogue. Harrington's fits have been reactions to the sight not of actual Jews but of actors made up to appear like his image of Simon and thrown in his way at strategic points.[37] In his most convincing scene, Mowbray arranges for Montenero and Berenice to overhear a staged conversation in which Harrington's childhood apothecary confides his knowledge of the boy's ineradicable insanity and mentions the family's efforts to hide it from the public. Harrington's disorder thus constitutes the hidden obstacle to marriage raised by Montenero. It is, of course, one of two such "obstacles"; the other is Mr. Harrington's empty objection to his son's marrying a Jew. The resolution of these obstacles is frequently mentioned as an avoidance of the conflict rather than an engagement with it. Berenice is unmasked at the last moment as a Christian, and so the marriage can proceed.[38] The other obstacle is removed in identical fashion. As Montenero concludes, the marriage can go forward because Harrington does not have a hidden "Jewish insanity"; instead, he has only had an "apparent insanity" (*TN* 9:202). Harrington's cure is therefore never itself at issue, for he is never really sick. His disorder is misconstrued by a public that is overly willing to believe in the anachronistic fiction of the nervous body.

Although this solution to the problem of Harrington's cure solves one obstacle to his emergence into the space of objectivity, it creates a new problem. By recontaining the nervous body, Edgeworth compromises the opposite position of critical objectivity. The two positions exist in the tale as interdependent binary opposites, so that one is either a "nervous" embodiment of socially constructed subjectivity or objective and outside the reach of social constructs. This idea of the nervous subject is essential to the idea of an exterior position, because the nervous body, through its definition, brings into being the space of objectivity that it delimits as its non-nervous opposite. For example, Simon's bag operates throughout the tale as a metaphor for the imprisonment of the socially constructed body. Harrington's confinement in the bag is figured as both bodily antipathies and uncontrolled sympathies, and it is structured in a binary relationship with a position of nonconfinement, a stance outside the now delimited sphere of socially constituted perceptions. Harrington's confinement in the bag brings into being a space outside the bag, a space of objectivity in which the subject is free from the constitutive force of representations and thus free of the crowd. Without Harrington's clearly defined hysteria, Montenero's objectivity is vulnerable to collapse, which is exactly what the narrator describes.

Montenero's character as the ideal critic is based on his ability to differentiate the real from the represented, the historical fact from the rhetorical effect. His astuteness is indispensable in the criticism of art. But Montenero is also the central example in the tale of the "fear" that Harrington's hysteria "might recur." His astuteness fails when he confronts the enigma of Harrington's body, and this is a failure of singular magnitude, for on this one critical evaluation rests the future of his only child.

The enigma of Harrington's insanity—the confusion over whether it is real or staged—needs to be seen as the object of an interpretive competition between the dramatist Mowbray and the art critic Montenero, who are engaged in a fight for control over the text of Harrington's body. In the contest, the critic discovers only after the fact that "he had been strangely imposed upon" by "Mowbray's artifices" (*TN*, 9:201), as a result of which he is taken in, finally succumbing to the dramatic power of the performance. Though he is represented as the one character who stands outside the crowd, in misreading Harrington's body he yields to the crowd's fear of hysteria, and so his stance of objectivity is undermined at the end.[39]

Indeed, his imminent departure for America with Berenice, to escape Harrington, is itself a perfect example of crowd psychology in action: an hysterical act performed by one who mistakes his own capitulation to popular fear for reason. By failing to see through the artifice of Mowbray's performance and being moved instead to confuse its dramatic power with factual truth, Montenero is finally defined as one of the crowd at Mowbray's final play, the staging of Harrington's insanity. The ideal critic is repositioned in that schoolboy gallery or at a seat in the theatre along with the rest of the audience.

Because the tale undermines the nervous premise for objectivity, Harrington's status as narrator needs to be reevaluated. His narrative insists on its own objectivity, even as it undermines the nervous body that defines its borders. Thus, there is no stable ground on which his narrative authority can rest. This instability surfaces in the contradiction between the narrative's construction of his cure and his position as the narrator. As the narrative nears its close and the moment of Harrington's formal ascendance to the throne of the narrator, he grows increasingly reticent to discuss his subjective state. "My heart did certainly beat violently; but I must not stop to describe, if I could, my various sensations" (*TN*, 9:200). Up to this point, his narrative has been devoted to exactly that kind of description and the minute details of the consequences of his sensations. "I must add a few lines more—not about myself" (*TN*, 9:207), he claims very near the end. The surest narrative sign of his cure is precisely this new attitude, and that is why his narrative is at its end. For the narrator has learned to stop talking about himself and to take other objects for his subject. But this concluding narrative stance is not the one that opens the story of Harrington's nervous body. It is as if the narrator is emerging out of his condition even as he tells the story of that emergence, and being cured only through the act of describing his cure. The post-cure narrator hurries himself off stage, too focused on the demands of events outside himself to talk any longer about those within. Because this is the tale's concluding sign of narrative health, the opening narrator's interest in his own sensations, his insistence on their narrative value as scientific "experiments," is problematic. For although he insists on his objectivity, that claim itself is also characteristic of the victims of party spirit, most notably the narrator's mentor, Montenero. The narrator's claim to objectivity is being recontained through the events he describes, and ultimately his narrative act can never be differentiated from the nervous shudder itself. Of course, those shudders no longer matter. Through an act of will, they can be overcome. And they are overcome—but only by Harrington's hurrying himself off the narrative stage and calling an end to his earlier nervous narrative.

PART THREE

VICTORIAN BODIES

6

The Body in Need of Nerves

Working-Class Insensibility and Victorian Sanitation

In 1793 Godwin believed that a novel could permanently transform the reader. But when he described that belief in 1832 he was skeptical of it, as if discarding the delusion of a youthful enthusiast for a novel that was in fact only a "mighty trifle" (*Fleetwood*, xiii). This transformation in attitude toward fiction was characteristic of the period. His early belief in the shaping power of fiction was shared by the popular opposition to the novel, an opposition that continued throughout Edgeworth's years of dominance as a writer. The campaign against novel reading began during the eighteenth century with the publication of *Pamela*, climaxed during the counterrevolution of 1790–1820, and had disappeared by 1830. Godwin's later tone was characteristic of changed views on the power of the novel.[1] An internalist approach to literary history might explain this disappearance of opposition to the novel by pointing to the success of fiction writers at the end of the period—Maria Edgeworth, Walter Scott, Hannah More—in soothing the fears of the evangelical opposition by producing morally instructive fiction, and this opened the door for Dickens's remarkable rise in the 1830s. The problem with this account is that there were comparable "moral" novelists in earlier periods—Samuel Richardson, Sarah Fielding, Fanny Burney—yet there was no comparable decline in opposition to the novel.[2]

Only with a decline of concern about the impressionability of the nervous body could widespread social opposition to the novel finally disappear. Readers had to be redefined in a way that made them safe for the consumption of fiction before fiction could assume the place of cultural importance that it did in the Victorian period. In the Regency fiction of Maria Edgeworth, the nervous body has significantly changed. The defining characteristic of that body, I have argued, was its inability to resist being written upon by the world around it. This made it particularly vulnerable to the shaping power of fiction, whether for social change in the hands of the English Jacobin novelists or for social danger in the view of the evangelicals. But in *Harrington,* the effects of education and broader social experience enable middle-class characters such as the narrator and the Monteneros to recover from the same experiences that lead to abjection in the novels of the 1790s. These are more resilient bodies, in which impressions have a less constitutive effect. The woman who wrote to Edgeworth complaining of anti-Semitism in Edgeworth's earlier works represented this new resilience.[3] Rachel Mordecai, who became a lifelong correspondent of Edgeworth, demonstrated an ability to feel the "dramatic power" of fiction without confusing that power with the "truth." Her critical skepticism makes her a less vulnerable reader than the young Harrington, Corny, or Ormond. For this reason, Mordecai is the new reader for whom fiction is finally safe.

The most dramatic factor in the decline of concern about the middle-class nervous body was the rise of concern about a new body that appeared at this same time, one also marked by its extreme impressionability: the body of the urban working class. As represented in the social investigation literature of the 1830s and 1840s by reformers such as Southwood Smith, Peter Gaskell, and Edwin Chadwick, this body is a pure product of its environment, shaped and molded in the same determinist fashion that Godwin had described in the 1790s. Relative to the impressionability that was attributed to this new body, the impressionability of the educated middle class began to take on a less threatening quality. Edgeworth's *Harrington* contains an early and concise formulation of this contrast and its consequences. The tale begins with the familiar danger of Harrington's nervous impressionability, a disorder produced through fiction. It then presents the imminent danger of mass hysteria within the working-class mob of the Gordon riots. And against that volatile mob, Harrington's nervousness is redefined as a puerile fear that he can and does overcome.

By looking at the representation of the working class in the early Victorian period, we can see how the problem of extreme inscribability became identified, in the minds of the middle class, as the central problem of the working-class body. We can also see that it became less significant as a problem within the self-image of the middle class.

In 1842, when Edwin Chadwick published his *Report on the Sanitary Condition of the Labouring Population of Great Britain*, he finally put an end to his reputation as a stone-hearted victimizer of the poor. As the Benthamite architect of the 1834 New Poor Law—he had been Jeremy Bentham's secretary—and as the appointed secretary for the Poor Law Commission, the lawyer Chadwick had borne much of the criticism for the hardships imposed by the new minimalist system of relief.[4] His role in writing the 1837 *Police Report* that resulted in the Rural Constabulary Act furthered his identification with repressive social measures.[5] In the *Sanitary Report*, however, he became reinvented as a champion of the poor. He advocated large-scale social intervention to improve the physical conditions in the worst working-class neighborhoods. Those improvements, for all their apparent self-evidence today, were not givens at the time, and he was careful to define them clearly. "The primary and most important measures" to be taken were "drainage, the removal of all refuse of habitations, streets, and roads, and the improvement of the supplies of water."[6] He concluded by recommending the formation of a new state bureaucracy to take control over the inadequate drainage, ventilation, and building design thought to generate epidemic diseases such as cholera and typhus in the slums. Because of his *Sanitary Report* and the subsequent sanitary reform movement, today Chadwick is primarily remembered as the founder of the public health movement.[7]

Interest in the *Report* was widespread, and its images of working-class bodies will appear familiar to present-day readers of the Victorian novel. Elizabeth Gaskell inserted parts of it as a realistic description of a street scene and the interior of the Davenport's home in *Mary Barton* (1848). Charles Kingsley also used it in his representation of rural laborers in his 1848 novel *Yeast* and of London sweatshops in *Alton Locke, Tailor and Poet* (1850). By that date, Chadwick's reformist zeal was so culturally familiar it had become linked to youthful idealism. Kingsley's hero in *Yeast* sees an "unspoken poetry" in sanitary reform as "the great fact of the age" and then proposes a future epic poem on the matter, to be called "the *Chad-wickiad*" and beginning, "Smells and the Man I sing" (*Yeast*, 103).[8] Harriet Martineau read the *Report* all in one sitting, and Dickens thought highly of it and mentioned it in *American Notes*.[9] When published in 1842, the *Report* caused enough comment that it sold seven times more copies than any previous parliamentary report. In all, 30,000 copies were printed, of which Chadwick had 10,000 copies distributed free. It was reviewed in *The Times*, the *Morning Chronicle*, *Blackwood's Magazine*, the *Quarterly Review*, and, of course, the *Westminster Review*, where his associate J. S. Mill was the editor. As Mary Poovey notes, it "was probably the most widely read government document of the Victorian period," and thus Chadwick's representation of the working-class body holds a central place in defining the middle-class Victorian interpretation of working-class life, and it needs to be seen within that larger cultural context.[10]

Despite the apparent distance between the lawyer Chadwick's *Sanitary Report* and Thomas Trotter's 1805 medical text, *A View of the Nervous Temperament,* the two publications have a strong conceptual relationship. Like Trotter, Chadwick uses a scheme of environmental determinism to define the effects of an unhealthy environment on the body. He also warns that these conditions are producing a newly diseased population, one that poses a threat to the nation as a whole. And he focuses exclusively on the disorder of one class. Chadwick is describing epidemic disorders in a generic sense, eliding differences between types of fevers, cholera, consumption, and so forth as insignificant and so defining, in essence, a single disorder requiring a single preventive remedy. Where Trotter describes the paradigmatic disorder of the middle class, Chadwick describes that of the working class.

For that reason, Chadwick's text could never have been written in Trotter's day. Trotter, like his predecessors George Cheyne and John Burton, subscribed to the belief that the laborer's body was less susceptible to disease by virtue of its insensibility. As Trotter pointed out, the illnesses of poverty and deprivation were far less serious and long-lasting than the illnesses of wealth and luxury. He represented the prevailing wisdom in 1805 when he thought that the laborer's coarse nerves precluded nervous disorder. By 1853, the physician Robert Brudenell Carter was more representative of the changed wisdom when, in his full-length study of hysteria, he devoted a separate chapter to "Hysteria Among the Poor" and asserted plainly, "All the varieties of hysteria, are of frequent occurrence among the poorer classes."[11]

Chadwick's *Sanitary Report*, as a specialty text on the disorders of laborers, was part of a paradigm shift in thinking about the working class that took place in the early nineteenth century. In response to the new conditions of industrialism, the emergence of the trades union movement, and the Chartist demonstrations, the working class became an object of a new and intensive scrutiny in government reports and surveys of factories. Parliamentary reports, or "blue books," on working-class life increased markedly after 1830. The *Sanitary Report* was preceded by the 1833 *Report on the Employment of Children in Factories*, the 1839 *Factory Inspector's Report*, and the 1841 *Report on Handloom Weavers*, among many others. James Phillips Kay's 1832 study, *The Moral and Physical Condition of the Working Classes*, and Peter Gaskell's 1836 *Artisans and Machinery* were two of a number of private social investigations under way.[12] By 1840, the working-class body had an apparent need for sustained professional attention that it did not have in 1800, when its disorders were of little concern to emerging middle-class professionals like Trotter. The new discipline of public health specifically arose as the medicine for the diseases of the urban working class, and it was therefore the discursive practice in which the materiality of this class-specific body was most intensively scrutinized.[13]

Chadwick's assumptions about the laboring body differ from those of his predecessors in a particularly significant way. Whereas insensibility protects the laborer from disease in 1805, in 1842 it becomes the cause of the laborer's endangerment. To move from Trotter's text to Chadwick's is to move between two opposite cultural focal points for middle-class anxiety. Unlike the middle class, the Victorian working class is a body in need of sensibility. Thus, the new interest in the social problem posed by the industrial working class needs to be seen as a shift of focus away from the danger posed by too much sensibility, as in the late Georgian period, to the danger of too little. Chadwick identifies that danger as a medicalized resistance to culture, so that the unsanitary working class exists in a pathological condition, reduced to a pure physicality marked by riotous behavior and anomic desire.[14]

The writing of the *Report* was initiated by the House of Lords, which requested a report from the Poor Law Commission on the relationship between poverty and unhealthy living conditions in the nation outside of the metropolis. As secretary to the commission, Chadwick was given full responsibility for compiling and authoring the *Report*, and he developed methods that made the final product a uniquely compelling piece of Victorian social investigation. Approximately half of the *Report* consists of quotations from questionnaires Chadwick circulated to the Poor Law assistant commissioners and union medical officers throughout England and Scotland—2,000 correspondents in all.[15] He asked all to do firsthand investigations of the poorest neighborhoods in their respective regions and to send him the results. He offered them concrete suggestions on how to proceed; for example, if the assistant commissioner did not know where to find the worst neighborhoods, he should look for sickly children on the street and wait to follow them home.[16] Chadwick requested specific information on the number of inhabitants, building design, width of streets, drainage, and ventilation. When interested by a particular response, he wrote back with additional questions. His procedure generated a massive base of reports, which he then compiled and edited. Because of the nature of his questions, the local reports tend to mirror his own assumptions. Though the final *Report* has the appearance of independent voices, it is in fact a well-orchestrated chorus reciting Chadwick's libretto.[17] The other half of the work is taken up with his analysis of the evidence and recommendations, written in a journalistic style and supported with tables from the new science of statistics.[18] He distributed an early draft of it to select friends for comments, and J. S. Mill suggested revisions to unify its argument further, which Chadwick followed.[19]

When published, the *Report* shocked readers with its repetitious litany of poverty, feces, and miasmatic effluvia.[20] It constructed a blunt portrait of the working class as mired in their own refuse, and its quoted reports focused on the most intimate particulars:

> I found the whole area of the cellars of both houses were full of night-soil, to the depth of three feet, which had been permitted for years to accumulate from the overflow of the cesspools. . . . I found the yard covered with night-soil, from the overflowing of the privy, to the depth of nearly six inches, and bricks were placed to enable the inmates to get across dry shod; in addition to this, there was an accumulation of filth piled up against the walls, of the most

objectionable nature . . . I am constantly shocked almost beyond endurance at the filth and misery in which a large part of our population are permitted to drag on a diseased and miserable existence.

(*SR*, 117–18)

These, of course, were precisely the conditions Chadwick wanted to create a state bureaucracy to eliminate. However, convincing upper- and middle-class Victorians of the need to clean up the working-class areas was not as easy as it might seem. One of Chadwick's principal obstacles was the fear of overpopulation through working-class fecundity, which was tied to the Malthusian interpretation of disease as a natural and necessary restraint on population growth. He also had to convince his readers that there existed a causal association between mounds of putrefying waste and outbreaks of disease in nearby living quarters, an association not at all settled in the medical community.[21] Even if he could prove this and claim that, therefore, the accumulation of refuse was a literally "removable cause" of epidemics, he still had to argue for the basic desirability of removing it, and to do this he had to show that Thomas Malthus had been wrong. Disease did not, in fact, inhibit population growth. With this basic premise, Chadwick became engaged in the much larger argument on the problematic nature of the social body, which, because it was healthy, was seen to be breeding itself into sickness through overpopulation.[22]

He addressed the Malthusian issue directly in the *Report* as a source of inaction on the dismaying conditions described within: "An impression of an undefined optimism is frequently entertained by persons who are aware of the wretched condition of a large portion of the labouring population; and this impression is more frequently entertained than expressed, as the ground of inaction for the relief of the prevalent misery from disease, that its ravages form the natural or positive check . . . to the pressure of population on the means of subsistence" (*SR*, 242).

This opinion originated in Malthus's 1798 *Essay on the Principle of Population*. Malthus argued that society, under optimal conditions, always reproduces faster than it can feed itself because population "increases in a geometrical ratio," whereas the production of food only increases "arithmetically" (*Essay*, 20). Thus, in the social body the potential for reproduction always exceeds the capacity for

production. Starvation is averted only by different checks on population growth to correct this imbalance. The "preventive check"
refers to the social and economic factors that tend to restrain reproduction—education, for example, or cultural conventions that encourage later marriages and thus lower rates of reproduction. The
"positive check," however, "represses an increase which is already
begun" by raising the death rate (*Essay*, 36). Epidemic disease and
unhealthy conditions, by causing early deaths, balance the burgeon-
ing population with the limits of production. Malthus noted that
the positive check is "confined chiefly . . . to the lowest orders of society" (*Essay*, 36). Thus, in the Malthusian scheme, disease reduces
the threat to the social body by restraining a specifically working-
class fecundity.

Chadwick calls the theory of the positive check a "dreadful fal-
lacy" (*SR*, 270) and insists that "pestilence does not check the progress of population" (*SR*, 246). Quite on the contrary, he writes, "the
ravages of epidemics and other diseases do not diminish but tend to
increase the pressure of population" (*SR*, 423). He assembles a mass
of statistics to show a contemporary correlation between high mortality and high birth rates. In the poorest districts of the country,
where disease and bad conditions prevail, births are double the national average (*SR*, 248–49).

He explains this anomaly by articulating a theory of moral contagion, which he links to epidemic contagion. In the conservative
miasmatic theory to which Chadwick subscribed, disease is caused
by gases generated within all decaying organic matter: feces, plants,
and animal products.[23] Foul breath, sweat, and human gas are also
dangerous and produce the same miasmatic effluvia.[24] Accordingly,
dampness and ventilation are particular concerns for health, in that
the first hastens decay and the other disperses the "noxious effluvium," or "miasmatic gas," generated by decay. Chadwick extends
this logic of miasmatic contagion to moral decay. He argues that the
same unhealthy environment that leads to disease also destroys social morality. "Thus tenements of an inferior construction had man-
ifestly an injurious operation on the moral as well as on the sanitary
condition, independently of any overcrowding" (*SR*, 194). Damp
and dirty dwellings, for instance, "form a strong barrier against personal cleanliness and the use of decent clothes" (*SR*, 196). Expanding
his arguments, residents soon become "of a piece" with their dwell-

ing (*SR*, 194). People who are subjected to damp walls, stuffy rooms, or the stench of refuse are rapidly forced into intemperance to medicate the colds and rheumatism caused by the miasmatic gases in their dwellings. Each of these environmental conditions, he declares, "has an effect on the moral habits by acting as a strong and often irresistible provocative" to drink, uncleanness, and sexual promiscuity (*SR*, 197).

Chadwick defines this working-class body in precise terms: "These adverse circumstances tend to produce an adult population short-lived, improvident, reckless, and intemperate, and with habitual avidity for sensual gratification" (*SR*, 423). Each of these terms is linked conceptually. Working-class improvidence and sensuality stem from an inability to see beyond the immediacy of the moment and its present, palpable sensations. Chadwick explains this pattern, and its resultant sensuality, by describing a sense of insecurity for residents of high-mortality districts: "Seeing the apparent uncertainty of the morrow, the inhabitants really take no heed of it, and abandon themselves with the recklessness and avidity of common soldiers in a war to whatever gross enjoyment comes within their reach" (*SR*, 198). Thus, one representative neighborhood is characterized by five times as many "whiskey-shops" as bakeries (*SR*, 198). Disease is always accompanied in the social body by an unbridled sexuality, which is represented by the high rate of reproduction. So although Chadwick allows that the poor are reproducing at a frightening rate, he argues that they reproduce because they are diseased. Instead of acting as positive checks on population growth, he explains, dirt and disease actually "create the evils" that, in the Malthusian view, they are supposed to correct (*SR*, 269). Thus, ameliorating conditions in the slums will actually decrease working-class reproduction. Sanitation, then, is a far richer sign than basic cleanliness; in the *Sanitary Report*, it becomes the means for a moral reinvention of the working class.

Chadwick's economy of birth and death reverses the traditional view that rapid reproduction indicates a healthy social body. Population growth for centuries was interpreted as a sign of social prosperity; it signified freedom from disease and the presence of adequate food and shelter. Malthus, of course, accepted this view. But he argued that, paradoxically, this same population growth would eventually destroy the very prosperity that brought it into being.[25]

Prosperity today inevitably leads to starvation tomorrow, and so the social body becomes redefined in Malthus as constitutively unstable across time. Chadwick responds to this instability by upending the basic assumption that population growth is related to social prosperity. To Chadwick, a high birth rate indicates a weak social organism, for it always accompanies disease and moral decay. As such, it signifies the absence of prosperity rather than its presence. By this argument Chadwick extricates the issue of public health from the problem of overpopulation.

As a rhetorical strategy for inventing a national bureaucracy (with Chadwick at its head) to control drainage, sewer construction, and building inspection, this association of dirt with population growth is essential to the *Report*. Chadwick reinforces it with eyewitness accounts from local correspondents in which dirt and population growth are causally linked through a form of diseased sexuality represented as endemic among the poor. "[I]n the most crowded districts," he insists, "the fact is observable, that where the mortality is the highest, the number of births are more than sufficient to replace the deaths, however numerous they may be" (*SR*, 243). He also shows this to be a universal phenomenon by drawing examples from Europe and the New World. The most extreme example is his description of the "inferior Mexican population" (*SR*, 246), borrowed from the 1831 *Bibliothèque Universelle*. Set in a distant land, the example takes on the freak-show quality of a colonial travel narrative. The population is described as "half clothed, idle, stained all over with vices; in a word, hideous and known under the name of *leperos*, lepers, on account of the malady to which their filth and bad diet subjects them" (*SR*, 246). Not in the least deterred, these lepers spend their days in idle sensuality, enjoying the natural abundance of their tropical environment. Using Mexican vital statistics, Chadwick is able to conclude that the "fecundity of this population, sunk in the lowest vice and misery amidst the means of the highest abundance, was greater than amidst any other whole population in Christendom" (*SR*, 247).[26] This hideously diseased population, then, combines an unthinkable fecundity with grotesque disfigurement. The image of these sexualized lepers, furiously reproducing despite their deformed and perhaps absent limbs, suggests a structural absurdity within his linkage of disease and reproduction. The report on the lepers takes the association to its logical extreme, at which point it threatens to collapse. Nonetheless, Chadwick insists that these mythic lepers pose a real threat in industrialized England: "They are much mistaken who imagine that a similarly conditioned population is not to be found in this country; it is found in parts of the population of every large town; the description of the Mexican populace will recall features characteristic of the wretched population in the worst parts of Glasgow, Edinburgh, London, and Bath, and the lodging-houses throughout the country" (*SR*, 247).

Though Chadwick's diseased lepers are highly reproductive, constantly generating more mouths to feed, they do not produce any food themselves, living entirely off the natural bounty of the land. Noting that these are no debilitated laborers or tillers of the soil, the *Bibliothèque* observes that they convert "the gifts of heaven to the sustenance of disgusting misery" (*SR*, 246). These indolent bodies combine an extreme capacity for reproduction with an equally extreme incapacity for productive labor. Their nonproductive nature is part of Chadwick's answer to the Malthusian paradox, in which production and reproduction are irreconcilable antagonists within the social body. Rather than confront the instability such a combination necessarily entails, Chadwick divides the two elements into two distinct working-class bodies, each defined by its dominant characteristic, productive or reproductive. His treatment of disease reinforces this binary opposition, because the same diseased condition that, Chadwick insists, increases fertility is readily associated with a decreased productivity caused by the physically weakened body and its muscular atrophy.

Chadwick assembles more statistics to demonstrate that this working-class body has literally shrunk under the influence of England's new unsanitary conditions, suggesting that the working class is becoming less productive at the same time that it becomes more reproductive. He asserts that "weavers, though not originally a large race . . . have become still more diminutive under the noxious influences to which they are subject" (*SR*, 251). And he quotes another physician, who states, "They are decayed in their bodies; the whole race of them is rapidly descending to the size of Lilliputians" (*SR*, 251). Of factory workers, Chadwick reports, "the sons who are employed at the same work are generally inferior in stature to their parents" (*SR*, 251). Evidence from military recruiting offices shows that "fewer recruits of the proper strength and stature . . . are obtainable now than heretofore" (*SR*, 251), and the French army has dropped its standard height from 5' 4" to 5' 1½". Chadwick sums up the diminishing evidence by emphasizing that he is speaking of a measurable difference in the space of a single generation: "Mr. Duce concurs in the fact of the deterioration of their size and appearance within the last 30 years, and attributes it to bad air, bad lodging, bad food, 'which causes the children to grow up an enfeebled and diminutive race of men'" (*SR*, 252).

Thus, the binary counterpart to the reproductive body of the Mexican leper and the modern worker is an older body, the healthy, physically strong body of the previous generation, whose size and stamina allowed it to work longer and more productively than its descendants. This productive body is disappearing from the modern British landscape; like Trotter's mythic past and Godwin's future, it is an absent ideal but one that is more liminal, as it continues to exist in the memories of living men, in the records of the heights of army recruits, and even in the disappearing regional pockets of older populations. It needs to be seen as part of a larger historical narrative Chadwick produces, one that tells the story of the rise of the unhealthy reproductive body and the decline of the healthy productive body under the influence of industrial Britain's unsanitary conditions. This is also a strongly gendered narrative and similar to Trotter's in describing the transition from a healthier, masculinized past body to a sick and effeminized one that threatens the national future.

Chadwick's effort to keep the reproductive and productive bodies distinct moves through the *Report* in a broad undercurrent that informs his treatment of virtually every individual description. Yet the harder he tries to divorce images of physical health and strength from images of sexuality, the more he creates monstrous images—represented as scientific fact—of either a sexualized debility, like that of the Mexican lepers, or its productive opposite, a combination of physical strength with impotence or infertility.

In his description of a Manchester trades union riot, the two bodies are shown in direct conflict. Chadwick analyzes the physical conditions in the area and claims that there actually are two distinct working-class populations to consider. The first, representing the "physically depressed district," is "a young and comparatively weak population" (*SR*, 265). The population is young because unsanitary conditions shorten the average life span; the older workers are all dead. Thus, representations of young bodies are paradoxically equated with disease and weakness in the *Report,* because the individual body stands as representative of its general population rather than being significant in its particularity. The second, healthier district has a higher life expectancy and thus is characterized by what he calls "a comparatively mature and strong population," so that age and physical strength are combined (*SR,* 265). Chadwick describes the torchlight meetings of the union members with these two populations in mind: "It was reported to us, on close observation by peace-officers, that there were scarcely any men of mature age to be seen amongst them. Those of mature age . . . were generally described as being above the influence of the anarchical fallacies which appeared to sway those wild and really dangerous assemblages" (*SR,* 266).

Thus, the young and diseased individuals, rather than their stronger elders, are solely responsible for the strikes and protests in this incident. Chadwick, of course, is not just describing one strike here but is making a structural connection between the issue of sanitation and the problem of working-class unrest, a topic much on the minds of the British middle class in 1842, at the tail end of the 1837–1842 depression and the year the second Chartist petition was presented to Parliament. He describes London mobs in similar terms, asserting they are all from "the most depressed districts" and very young. Juvenile delinquents in the metropolis are "conspicuously under size" (*SR,* 267). This observation is then extended to all criminals. "An impression is often prevalent that the criminal population consists of persons of the greatest physical strength. Instances of criminals of great strength certainly do occur; but speaking from observation of the adult prisoners from the towns and the convicts in the hulks, they are in general below the average standard of height" (*SR,* 267). For Chadwick, these riots and examples of criminality are expressions of the same moral decay, the same contaminated passion, that cause the excessive reproduction and higher mortality in the diseased district.

In his representation of the relationships between the new and the traditional populations, between the reproductive and productive social bodies, Chadwick has a problem. He asks why the stronger and older men, who disapprove of such riots, do not physically prevent them and is told the older men dislike union meetings. They "would not attend to be borne down by 'mere boys,' who were furious, and knew not what they were about" (*SR*, 267). The "mere boys," diseased and debilitated as they are, clearly have the upper hand over the stronger male workers, who stand passively on the sidelines. Thus, the strong become weak, in this image, and the weak become strong. What exactly is the nature of these younger workers, who paradoxically are debilitated and overpowering? Chadwick does not really know, and the sudden tongue-twisting clumsiness of his normally clean and accessible prose reflects his discomfort as he tries to convey their combination of weakness and danger. He writes, "The mobs from such districts as Bethnal Green are proportionately conspicuous for a deficiency of bodily strength, without, however, being from that cause proportionately the less dangerously mischievous" (*SR* 267). Although he tries to brazen it out, their moral debility is crossing over into images of strength and vigor, in this case under the rubric of danger. The traditional workers are also problematic in their notable absence of the passion that Chadwick associates with working-class sexuality. Therefore, these males adopt a position of passivity as they wait helplessly on the sidelines. Whereas the new population, he tells us, is "passionate, and dangerous, having a perpetual tendency to moral as well as physical deterioration" (*SR*, 268), their opposites are neither passionate nor dangerous. They are docile, well-mannered, productive bodies, combining "thrifty poverty" with "sobriety and industry," and are infrequently seen in Chadwick's spare, marginal portraits of the insular rural poor and their one or two children (*SR*, 221, 324).

In addition to its diseased sexuality, the reproductive body suffers from a constitutional incapacity for education. Malthus had held that, in addition to epidemic diseases, cultural factors could form a "preventive check" to overpopulation by restraining promiscuity and marriages, but Chadwick insists that all efforts to reform the diseased working class based on education or moral instruction are doomed to failure: "The facts . . . show . . . that the noxious physical agencies depress the health and bodily condition of the population, and act as obstacles to education and to moral culture" (*SR*, 268).[27] A dirty environment not only obstructs new education but even undoes the effects of prior instruction. According to Captain Miller, the superintendent of police, the most unsanitary neighborhood in his district has lost all "civil or social regulation" (*SR*, 198). Yet the adults there "were intelligent and so far as could be ascertained, had received the ordinary education which should have given better tastes and led to better habits" (*SR,* 199). But such culturally refined tastes yield to the determinant influence of the district, and "better tastes" give way to filthy habits.

This incapacity for education suggests a representational deficiency in which the reproductive body is immersed within the realm of the material and incapable of symbolic activity. This is a consistent pattern in Chadwick's representation of the working class. Because the working class takes no heed of the future, its improvidence implies an inability to conceptualize a time other than the present or to see beyond the immediate moment to an imaginary future. There is a deficiency of symbolic activity in the description of the insanitary neighborhoods; Captain Miller notes that the entry to the neighborhood above is through "some nameless narrow passage" (*SR,* 111), and the neighborhoods themselves are characterized by unnamed byways. The many children inevitably found in these neighborhoods are the material consequence of the diseased resident's excessive materiality and are themselves nameless. " 'The fact is,' observed Captain Miller . . . 'they really have no names. Within the range of buildings I have no doubt I should be able to find a thousand children who have no names whatever'" (*SR,* 198–99). This incapacity for symbolic forms of activity, such as naming, is a means of representing the working class as outside the sphere of representation and thus resistant to educational attempts at improvement.[28]

Dirt eventually creates an active resistance to education. Workers develop a perverse attachment to their present mode of life and become rigidly conservative, resisting even minor changes that might preserve their own health. An employer supplies water, soap, and towels so his men can wash before eating, but they refuse to do so and sicken themselves with the lead and arsenic on their hands: "There is no persuading them to be habitually clean" (*SR,* 320), Chadwick argues. "Under the slavery of the existing habits of labourers, it is found that the faculty of perceiving the advantage of a change is so obliterated as to render them incapable of using, or indifferent to the use of, the means of improvement which may happen to come within their reach" (*SR,* 297). In this manner the reproductive body acquires an attachment to its own unsanitary environment, developing a perverse love of dirt with which it becomes reluctant to part. The active resistance to education thus takes the form of an attachment to "filthy habits." Paupers covered with dirt are washed on admission to the hospital or workhouse. They "usually manifest an extreme repugnance to the process. Their common feeling was expressed by one of them when he declared that he considered it 'equal to robbing him of a great coat which he had had for some years'" (*SR*, 316). This reproductive body does not want improvement. In building better homes, one architect notes, "It may be said that . . . we shall be furnishing them with that which they do not desire; that habitual and long acquaintance with privation has taught them to regard and to endure, without any lively distaste, much of that misery from which other, more delicately educated, would shrink with disgust" (*SR*, 334).

The working class's resistance to change and its insistent preferences and habits have the appearance of a coherent system of culture with a counteraestheticism at work. But it is more precisely termed an absence of culture in Chadwick's scheme, one that opens up a space for the emergence of atavistic traits such as unrestrained promiscuity. Working-class dislike of sanitation is itself a significant sign of its diseased state. Its love of dirt and resistance to education are not to be listened to as coherent cultural expressions any more than are the complaints of the middle-class hypochondriac. Its attachment to "filthy habits," like its incessant reproduction, is connected to a diseased sexuality founded on immediate sensual gratification without regard for future consequences. The architect's response is central to Chadwick's theory. "If these deplorable habits have really acquired so much force, it should be our part to make corresponding efforts to teach the victims of them to become more sensible of their misery . . . by affording to them facilities for providing themselves with healthier and happier abodes" (*SR*, 334). The problem with the working class, then, is that it is "insensible" of its own misery, and sanitary reform is the means to provide it with an increased sensibility. It needs to develop the sensitivity that preserves the "delicately educated" by making them intolerant of the miasmatic stench that causes epidemic disease. As Chadwick points out, "[t]he sense of smell . . . generally gives certain warning of the presence of malaria or gases noxious to the health," but this sensitivity "appears often to be obliterated in the labourer by his employment. He appears to be insensible to anything" (*SR*, 297). The reproductive body is thus a body in need of sensibility. Chadwick has transformed its insensibility from a preservative against disease, as it had been regarded in 1800, to the central cause of its disease.

Because education is ineffective, the *Sanitary Report* concerns itself solely with methods of "compulsory prevention" (*SR*, 320), in which recalcitrant laborers develop a healthy sensibility against their will. These sanitary methods are a way of making the reproductive body receptive not just to smells but to education and moral instruction in general. The older body of the idealized productive worker is one that "accumulates and preserves instruction and is steadily progressive" (*SR*, 268), whereas the body of the "ignorant, credulous" diseased worker does not. Sanitation is the material of a rudimentary cultivation in Victorian ideology. It is a means to produce a working class capable of instruction and receptive, rather than resistant, to being taught.

In the *Report*'s scheme of environmental determinism, the key to producing this educable body is architectural change: to drain and ventilate the spaces occupied by the poor, eliminating the miasmatic causes of working-class disruption. Chadwick is concerned with sanitary conditions at both workplaces and residences, but his programmatic association of reproduction with disease leads him to differentiate between his treatment of the site of reproduction, or the working-class residence, and the site of production, or the workplace. His comments on sanitation at the factory are brief and perfunctory, and they stand in stark contrast to his extended critical appraisal of the most minute details of ventilation, drainage, and refuse removal at working-class dwellings. His claim that, among weavers, "the greatest proportion of the diseases to which they are subject arise from circumstances separable from their occupation" (*SR*, 186) is a novel one at a time when the sickness of laborers was generally associated with the conditions of their labor, as the debates during the 1830s over the Ten Hours Bill and the *Report on the Employment of Children in Factories* show. However, in his system the residence is consistently associated with disease, whereas sites of production stand for health. Thus, he logically favors factory labor for children because of the greater danger the home poses to their fragile health. "That opinion is erroneous," he clarifies, "which ascribes greater sickness and mortality to the children employed in factories than amongst the children who remain in such homes as these towns afford to the labouring classes" (*SR*, 223). He argues that all factories are "drier and more equably warm than the residence of the parent; and we had proof that weakly children have been put into the better-managed factories as healthier places for them than their own homes" (*SR*, 223). This argument precisely embodies his formal solution to the underlying antagonism between production and reproduction in the social body. Factory work "cures" children of "disease" by transforming them from signs of reproduction into signs of production. They cease to represent the fecundity of the working class and become instead representatives of productive labor.

As one historian has pointed out, Chadwick had no pragmatic solution to the problem of urban sanitation because he had no workable means of disposing of all that waste.[29] The material problem of large-scale urban sanitation remained unresolved until biological sewage treatment was developed in the 1890s. However, Chadwick's solutions function efficiently as symbolic resolutions of the problem posed by working-class fecundity, as in his redefinition of the child's body, and it is at this symbolic level that the ideological work of the *Report* is carried out. An identical symbolic transformation takes place, in architectural terms, in Chadwick's endorsement of factory-owned housing, which he favors over private dwellings for the working class. "No position" in relation to the working class, he asserts, has "so extensive and certain a beneficial interest . . . as that of the capitalist who stands in the double relation of landlord and employer" (*SR*, 300). He illustrates the advantages of factory control over the workers' homes with an anecdote he heard while visiting Glasgow about an outbreak of fever among factory workers:

> I was informed there was in that city an assemblage of dwellings for their workpeople, called, from its mode of construction and the crowd collected in it, the Barracks. This building contained 500 persons; every room contained one family. The consequences of this crowding of the apartments, which were badly ventilated, and the filth were, that fever was scarcely ever absent from the building. There were sometimes as many as seven cases in one day, and in the last two months of 1831 there were 57 cases in the building. All attempts to induce the inmates to ventilate their rooms were ineffectual, and the proprietors of the work, on the recommendation of Mr. Fleming, a surgeon of the district, fixed a simple tin tube of two inches in diameter, into the ceiling of each room, and these tubes led

into one general tube, the extremity of which was inserted into the chimney of the factory furnace. By perpetual draught thus produced upon the atmosphere of each room the inmates were compelled, whether they would or not, to breathe pure air. The effect was that, during the ensuing eight years, fever was scarcely known in the place.

(*SR*, 175–76)

The surgeon Fleming, an expert on the biological body, operates on the ailing social body, a body that is ill only because it is still faintly divided between home and factory. His cure thus is to eradicate the reproductive danger within the residential space by joining it to the factory and resolving the conflicted social body into one of unambivalent productivity. The worker's domestic space thus becomes subsumed within the space of production.[30]

In Chadwick's ideology of the domestic, the Barracks can only be termed a "domestic space" at the point it comes under the middle-class control represented by the ventilation tube and its compulsory enforcement of sanitary ideals. This particular ventilation tube is the work of one enlightened factory owner, but Chadwick's larger concern is with asserting a similar right on the part of the state to regulate the internal conditions of all private residences. His *Report* includes a detailed analysis of the moment in law at which the public interest justifies intervention in the space of private property.[31] This legal concept of *"publicum in privato"* (*SR*, 362) is the technical underpinning that justifies the public control—through Chadwick's own new bureaucracy—of drainage construction in private houses so that all residences, like the Barracks, can be interconnected in the service of the public good. The demonstrable value of drains in reducing disease is of course very high, and no one suggests a need to liberate society from its sewer hookups. But Chadwick's drains remove more than organic waste; they are specifically a means of correcting "the physical causes of . . . the moral degradation of the labouring classes" (*SR*, 375). In his scheme, the private space is always morally unwholesome and needs public intervention to be made morally efficacious. Drains are thus part of an "architecture that would operate to transform individuals: to act on those it shelters, to provide a hold on their conduct" (Foucault, *Discipline and Punish*, 172).

The forms of intervention also include a medical policing of private space within the working class. When a sick laborer is attended by the medical officer of the local union created by Chadwick's revision of the Poor Laws, the officer is specifically instructed to survey "the interior of the abode of the sufferer" as a means of "carrying investigation precisely to the place where the evil is the most rife, and where the public intervention is most called for" (*SR*, 398–99). The *Report* makes medical surveillance as integral to public health and morals as drainage and ventilation.[32] His architectural schemes, for example, stress wide and open streets, both to allow ventilation that will carry away the miasma and to encourage outsiders to enter and exit. His designs for factory spaces stress the moral advantages of open, undivided rooms. Small, enclosed spaces not only allow miasmatic gases to accumulate but also encourage "bad manners and immoralities" to occur because workers are "secluded from superior inspection and from common observation" (*SR*, 306–7). Rates of illegitimacy decline in areas where factories have an open architecture because they permit a patriarchal mode of surveillance:

> But whilst employed in this one large room, the young are under the inspection of the old; the children are in many instances under the inspection of parents, and all under the observation of the whole body of workers, and under the inspection of the employer. It was observed that the moral conditions of the females in this room stood comparatively high. . . . [T]here were fewer cases of illegitimacy and less vice observable among the population engaged in this manufactory than amongst the surrounding population of the labouring class.
> (*SR*, 307)

In the *Report*, the residences of the working class become true domestic spaces only when they are ventilated, drained, and opened up to the surveillance of the middle class. In repeated examples, he shows how working-class women who are married and stay at home in a damp, unventilated cottage regularly grow derelict in their duty. Even when the cottage is physically improved, she still regularly lapses into her previous "filthy habits," neglecting sanitation because she is unable to escape the disorder that has been inscribed in her body by the prior experience. Eventually, the husband finds the public comforts of the alehouse more inviting than the private comforts of the cottage, and so the danger spirals; the constructed domestic space collapses into disorder, creating the working class's diseased sexuality. The possibility of inspection changes this predictable narrative. Chadwick writes: "The wife and family generally gain, by proximity to the employer or the employer's family, in motives to neatness and cleanliness by their being known and being under observation; as a general rule, the whole economy of the cottages in bye-lanes and out-of-the-way places appears to be below those exposed to observation" (*SR*, 299).

The domestic space for the working class, then, is never a private space but is always open, literally or figuratively, to middle-class inspection. It is through the creation of this nonprivate domestic residence that the diseased and overly reproductive body of the laboring poor is to be transformed into the productive body that Chadwick defines as natural. Thus, Victorian sanitation, with its apparatus of ventilation tubes, sewage connections, and open architecture, needs to be seen as an insistence, ultimately, on the presence within the working-class residence of the middle-class employer and the internalization of middle-class values by the no-longer-resisting worker. Sanitation holds out the promise of making the industrialized worker safe for the Victorian middle class by eliminating the long-standing difference between the material body of the laborer and that of the higher classes. This new universality comes about through the redefinition of the laborer's insensibility as a disease produced by its environment rather than a natural attribute, as it had been defined in the past. With this redefinition comes the reassuring assumption that the healthy working-class body now resembles more than it differs from the middle-class body. Chadwick's *Sanitary Report* is thus both an articulation of the specific attributes of the working-class body and a prescription for its elimination.

The reader of the *Report* plays an active role in this process, and for this reason a book overflowing with represented sewage becomes essential reading. The *Report* possesses sensationalist qualities in its insistence on exposing the hidden secrets—including the promise of diseased sexuality—within working-class neighborhoods, and it has been argued that the document "appealed to the voyeur in the reader."[33] But this appeal to sensationalism alone does not explain the popularity of the *Report*, because it accounts neither for the way surveillance is constructed nor for its centrality to the ideology of domesticity.[34] The reader's duty is illustrated within the text by the army of correspondents Chadwick organized to compile the *Report*. Each is asked to look inside the working-class home, to read its physical details, and to note its drainage and ventilation. This surveillance itself has a reforming effect because of the centrality of middle-class inspection to working-class reform. These correspondents transform the dangerous private space into an observable and hence healthy domestic space through their observation. Their act is defined as a moral necessity, one that by itself, and through the promise of further repetition, is an integral part of curing the working class of its diseased sexuality. This imperative has a paradoxical logic within it, for it assigns the highest value to the surveillance of the worst residences. The more repellent the scene, the more fetid and unbearable to the correspondent's senses, the more necessary it is that it becomes seen and smelled and thus opened up to observation. The descriptions involve a fascination with repugnance, as the correspondents are compelled by the logic of sanitation to describe ever more repellent scenes involving ever greater examples of filth and moral decay. At the extremes, description of the scene gives way to description of the correspondent's response: "In several instances I had to retreat to the door to write down my notes, as I found the stench and close atmosphere produce a sickening sensation which, on one occasion, terminated in vomiting" (SR, 282). The observer's revulsion is thus valorized as the measure of moral efficacy.

This pattern helps explain Victorians' impulse to read this unlikely study of privies and open sewers in provincial working-class neighborhoods. The reader of the *Report* who encounters, for example, the description of the family asleep on a damp mud floor, oblivious to the excrement that is oozing upward through it, is in a position similar to that of the sanitary correspondent, symbolically surveying the scene of working-class disease.[35] Reading the *Sanitary Report* is itself a sanitary act within the symbolic logic of sanitation the *Report* proposes. It becomes a moral necessity, one that holds out the promise that readers might symbolically cure the disorder it describes by reading and responding to the descriptions. The reader's surveillance of the scenes is the key to their elimination and to the elimination of the peril posed by working-class reproduction.

By this logic, it is now imperative that middle-class readers take up texts of unexpected and horrifying scenes and become increasingly able to endure the shocks entailed. It becomes an act of moral good to read of working-class promiscuity and disease. This valorization of the reader's encounter with the sensational, through the logic of domestic ideology, presupposes a new kind of reader, one no longer defined by the cultural episteme of the late Georgian nervous body. For this Victorian reader, it becomes morally necessary to read texts that in the earlier period it would have been morally necessary to avoid.

This new readerly surveillance implies a middle-class body that is more resistant to impressions than it had been previously because it has redefined itself in relation to the working-class body. Within this new construction, the realist novel is finally freed of its dangerous tendency to disturb the susceptible reader, for the danger of excess sensibility has been replaced by the danger of nervous insensibility. It thus becomes possible for novelists taking on the reformist task of representing the horrors of urban life—novelists such as those named at the beginning of this chapter—to establish a position of new moral authority for the novel, one that was never available to it within the cultural episteme of the late Georgian nervous body.

7

The Story of the Story
of the Body
Conceiving the Body in Middlemarch

The nervous body, as a medical construct, underwent a significant transformation in medical texts of the early nineteenth century. In this rewriting, the idea of the narrative in the body was multiplied. Whereas the body at the start of the century contained one story, by the mid-Victorian period it encompassed many. Throughout the eighteenth century, the nervous system was thought to have a physically centralized, hierarchical structure. All sensation flowed through the nervous fibers to the brain, or "sensorium." In *The English Malady*, George Cheyne described this process by comparing the body to a musical instrument. He likened the nerves to keys sounding in the brain or ropes running from a bell in a steeple to a crowd of people pulling on them (*English Malady*, 4). This model represented nerves as simple pathways for sensations entering the brain and for motor impulses flowing to the muscles. All bodily authority was thus centralized in a single discrete source. This was the model utilized by the physicians of the Scottish Enlightenment and their disciples, such as Thomas Trotter.

Between 1800 and 1840, this centralized structure yielded to a new structure of dispersed authority.[1] The nervous system ceased to be seen as a simple vehicle for sensations and motor impulses. Instead it became reconceived as a network of localized, semiautonomous centers spread throughout the body. The spinal column was transformed from a large bundle of connecting wires for the brain into a congress of distinct nerve centers, called ganglia, with semiautonomous control over their distinct regions of the body. The brain itself was reimagined as a group of divisible ganglionic units instead of a single, unified authority. The body in effect was thought to comprise many little "brains" dispersed throughout the cerebro-spinal axis, each with a type of regional authority. By 1840 the concept of the brain as the sole, centralized source of authority in the nervous system was dead.

Of the various forms of localized authority, the reflex was considered the most important. Marshall Hall's early Victorian investigations into reflexive mechanisms provide a significant example of how this multiplicity of narratives became incorporated in the physiology of the body. A leading physiologist of the early nineteenth century, Hall (1790–1857) was a founder of the British Medical Association and the son of a successful manufacturer. In 1833 he published a series of influential papers on the reflex system that formed the basis of his *Memoirs of the Nervous System* (1837). In it, Hall argues for the presence of two distinct nervous systems in the body, centered separately in the brain and the spine. The "Cerebral, or Sentient and Voluntary, System" is the seat of the intellect and judgment. As its name implies, it is the recipient of all perceived sensation and the source of all willful activity.[2] Unlike the cerebral system, the "True Spinal, or Excito-Motory, System" has "no sensation, no volition, no consciousness, nothing psychical."[3] This system performs in a wholly mechanistic manner that Hall christens the "reflex arc." In the spinal system he locates all of the body's digestive, respiratory, and reproductive functions, thereby replacing the eighteenth-century concept of "sympathy" between bodily organs with the reflex action in the spinal system. In addition, the spinal system is "the seat or nervous agent of the appetites and passions," controlling facial expressions, blushing, breathing, "and indeed the whole muscular system of the animal frame" (*Nervous System*, 73). Although reflexes can be manipulated by the volition present in the cerebral system, the spinal system is fundamentally independent of it. The reflex system has its own logic, which does not involve the brain.

Hall's concept of the reflex arc allows bodies to engage in unwilled forms of action. His many detailed experiments are designed to show that brainless bodies can produce coordinated motions. His fundamental rhetorical project is to convince his audience of the misleading nature of apparently voluntary activity in the body. Through a scientific freak show of encephalic infants, spineless frogs, sexually aroused quadriplegics, and an unfortunate horse he knocks unconscious with a pole ax to see if its eyelid will twitch when he brushes the lash with a feather, he proves again and again that bodies have a second form of action, one that is independent of the subject's will. Nor are these unwilled actions meaningless. Hall attributes significance to spinal reflexive action, arguing that it embodies the principle of self-preservation in the individual. The spine is also a site for actions designed to promote the preservation of the species as a whole. His separation of action from all mental involvement opens the route for new forms of meaning in the body's acts and gestures, some of which become redefined as expressions of a primitive ancestry. Hall's work is thus part of a trend toward creating a body that is capable of containing more than one narrative in its physiology. By constructing a body with two separate nervous systems, he creates a body with two distinct stories, one of voluntary action operating through the brain, and a second of the species' distant past, operating independently through the spinal system. Although the specifics of Hall's approach would not survive the end of the nineteenth century, there was no turning back from the general direction he took.[4]

The difference between the two models of the body—that is, between single and multiple narratives—helps to explain why the bodies that appear in Victorian novels function so differently from those of the early century, with which this study is primarily concerned. In the early part of the century, bodies are essentially sincere. Trotter is explicit on this point: "Many external signs correspond with our internal emotions. It is a difficult task, if at all possible, to wear the smile of gladness when the heart is sad. A nervous constitution is ill qualified to disguise its feelings" (*NT,* 81). In Elizabeth Inchbald's *A Simple Story,* Miss Milner's bodily signs are ambiguous, but the novel situates that ambiguity in the clumsy constructions of the interpreter, not in the expression of the subject, which has a definite meaning. The preoccupation with the possibility of dissemblance, embodied in the stock figure of the rake, is itself a consequence of this fundamental sincerity.[5] For it presumes that the body has an essential meaning within it, one that can be dissembled but is nonetheless there. With its centralized authority, the single-narrative model supports a strong relationship between the particular signs of the body and a larger, generalizing totality that they represent.

In the new model, the structure of meaning in the body is diffused. It becomes a group of specific signs without the earlier security of an assumed reference to a central source of significance. Whereas in the early part of the century observers face the problem of misconstruing the body's truthful signs or of being misled by deliberately false signs, in the new body they face the problem of signs that, although they have meaning, are inherently ambiguous. In one of several antiphysiognomy passages, George Eliot's narrator in *Adam Bede* comments on the problematic appearance of Hetty Sorrel: "One begins to suspect at length that there is no direct correlation between eyelashes and moral; or else, that the eyelashes express the disposition of the fair one's grandmother."[6]

Hetty's character cannot be read in her body, yet its attributes are not meaningless or random but "express" instead the character of her ancestry. This disjunction takes place passively, without the sense of willful dissemblance seen in male figures at the beginning of the century. Thus, the earlier anxiety about the ability to dissemble the prior truth hidden within the body's sensations shifts, in *Adam Bede*, to a fear of the reverse, that this truth can never *not* be dissembled: "Falsehood is so easy, truth so difficult . . . even when you have no motive to be false, it is a very hard thing to say the exact truth, even about your own immediate feelings—much harder than to say something fine about them which is not the exact truth" (*Adam Bede*, 222–23). George Eliot's bodies are unable to express the truth of their feelings because they no longer know what it is. Sensations, which in Wollstonecraft, Godwin, and Edgeworth have an oppressive clarity, in Eliot are more opaque, or elusive; it requires effort to recover their significance.

These two positions are not simply different sides of the same argument. They indicate two separate epistemologies of the body, one in which signs have a strong connection to a single central meaning, as in Cheyne, and the other in which signs have a weak connection to diffused, multiple meanings, as in Marshall Hall. These two sides suggest a realignment of terms in a larger cultural debate, a move from the question of whether the body's signs are true or false to the question of whether bodily signs have any meaning at all and, if so, of what sort. This problem in terms of the significance of external bodily signs has an internal correlative, in which the meaning of the body's sensations to the subject undergoes a similar realignment. In the early period, the questions of middle-class sensibility are whether or not to feel, how much feeling is enough, how much is too much? In the later period, it is less a question of the presence or absence of feeling than of confronting its uncertain significance. With the diffusion of its structure of meaning, the body ceases to function as a centralized reservoir of knowable truth, as it had earlier.

These two models of signification are closely related to the shift that takes place in the representational assumptions of the realist novel.[7] In both the English Jacobin novels of the 1790s and the morally efficacious novels of the Regency, realism is based on the premise that significance resides in an overarching, general design. Discrete, specific details become significant through their ability to reveal this larger order. In this essentially didactic method, realism requires presenting a careful selection of details, leaving out specifics that, although they might be accurate in terms of social experience, tend to mislead or obscure those general principles that constitute the real. In the assumed connections between specific signs and the controlling design, the didactic method resembles the centralized model of the body, in which particular signs are assumed to have a strong connection to a general meaning.

In George Eliot's writing, the strong connection between sign and meaning of the earlier didactic method is replaced with a programmatically ambiguous connection. We can see this difference even in the essentially descriptive realism of her early novels. "Nature has her language," explains the narrator of *Adam Bede*, "and she is not unveracious; but we don't know all the intricacies of her syntax just yet" (*Adam Bede*, 198). In this passage, particular details are not devoid of meaning; they retain a connection to a generalized truth that is revealed through them, but the nature of that truth is uncertain to the narrator. George Eliot's strategy for representing this uncertain reality is thus to jettison the earlier principle of selectivity used by Godwin, Hays, and Edgeworth in favor of a new emphasis on fullness of details, as if realism requires heaping ambiguous sign on top of sign, trusting that meaning will emerge in the accumulation.

George Eliot, more than any other Victorian novelist, was aware of the significant changes taking place in Victorian science, and she knew of the intrinsic redefinition that had taken place in the epistemology of nerves. Because such redefinitions created new ways of imagining the body, they also raised into high relief the changing nature of scientific explanations for what was necessarily conceptualized as the unchanging "real" body.[8] Medicine at any given moment produces an all-encompassing narrative of the body, describing its processes of growth and aging, its daily cycles and monthly rhythms. Each disease, from the onset of symptoms to termination, has its own story, case histories their own plots. Medicine, too, in its historical dimension, creates its own evolving narrative of the body, as its etiologies change and its taxonomies reconfigure. It is in this medical narrative itself, with its inescapable historical relativity, that the authority of medicine to tell the story of the body is most called into question.

In *Middlemarch*, George Eliot focuses not on the new medical narrative she knew so well but on medical history. Rather than embracing the medical story of the body, *Middlemarch* represents medicine's uncertain relationship with bodies as objects of knowledge. Thus, this novel is less concerned with representing the meaning of the body than with representing the problems involved in knowing that meaning. She does this by shifting her focus from the body to the doctor and telling the story of him telling the story of the body.

According to her partner, the philosopher and biologist George Henry Lewes, one remark pleased George Eliot above all other early comments on *Middlemarch*:[9] It "was like 'assisting at the creation— a universe formed out of nothing!'"[10] The speaker was her real-life surgeon, Sir James Paget, and he was referring to her creation of the fictional surgeon, Tertius Lydgate, one of the novel's two central protagonists.[11] Paget was astonished at George Eliot's "surprisingly deep" insights into medical life. He found it amazing that, although "she had never even known a surgeon intimately," she was able to create the ambitious, scientifically minded Lydgate, a practitioner of 1830, some forty years earlier, whose commitment to professional reform and to the new scientific medicine leads him into a losing conflict with provincial society and the local medical orthodoxy. George Eliot's pleasure at the remark, we can guess, stemmed in part—but only in part—from Paget's official endorsement of the lifelike qualities of the portrait, for the principle of historical accuracy combined with richly detailed specificity was a central component of her realistic technique. In preparation for the novel, she had read Pierre Victor Renouard's *Histoire de la Medecine*, John Thompson's *Life of William Cullen*, Southwood Smith's *Treatise on Fever*, J. Rutherford Russell's *History and Heroes of the Art of Medicine*, and other works on the history of medicine.[12] But Paget's astonishment, and George Eliot's pleasure at it, was not caused by her impressive command of historical detail, which he praised but did not express surprise at.[13]

Instead he was astonished at the wholly speculative nature of her accomplishment. Without actually knowing such a person, she was able to conceive a fictional surgeon who seemed as real to Paget as those that walked abroad. And thus he compared her achievement to "the creation." As Lewes reports, Paget "could not understand how the author had not had some direct personal experience—it seemed to him that there must have been a biographical foundation for Lydgate's career."

George Eliot had reason to be particularly pleased with this response, for it replayed one side of a debate on realism that she stages within *Middlemarch*. Appropriately, Paget played the part of the fictional surgeon he so admired. Through the particulars of Lydgate's work, his confrontation with the structure of the human body, and the epistemology of his new scientific medicine, George Eliot delineates her character's scientific strategy for representing the hidden structures of the human body. Her use of medicine in the novel thus explores a particular brand of realism, one in which the fictional Lydgate, like the science-minded Paget, insists that representation must be firmly tied to empirical experience in order to be truthful. However, George Eliot, who continued to insist on Lydgate's fictionality long after Paget made his remarks, holds that realistic representation can indeed be unanchored from actual experience.[14] In fact, as we will see, truthfulness for George Eliot depends on an imaginative freedom from immediate experience. The debate, then, centers on the reliability of empiricism and on the need for an escape from the narrowness of sensory experience. Lydgate (as well as his real-life counterpart) resists the idea that representation can be free from experience and thus "formed out of nothing," whereas from the writer's point of view it is only when representation is "formed out of nothing" that it stands a chance of becoming realistic.

As a novelist, George Eliot demonstrated a strong bond with the sciences.[15] Not only did she collaborate with Lewes on his writing, she also recognized a deep affinity between science and her own work as a novelist.[16] Thus, her delineation of competing representational strategies in the novel does not reflect a simple opposition between a materialistic "scientific" and a humanistic "literary" way of looking at the world.[17] On the contrary, through the character of Lydgate she describes a necessary role for imagination in science itself and so asserts a fundamental kinship between the projects of literary and scientific realism.

Medical issues in *Middlemarch* consist of three subjects: scientific research, professional reform, and clinical treatment. Lydgate is at the leading edge of medical research for 1830. He successfully distinguishes between typhus and "typhoid" fever, a hotly debated subject at the time. He studies pathological anatomy in Paris, the specialty that contributed more than any other to the scientific reform of medicine.[18] And he performs his own scientific research and institutes scientific procedures of observation and record-keeping at the New Hospital, which he hopes to turn into a research center for fevers. His education at Edinburgh and Paris, rather than London, further suggests that he has received the best medical training available at a time when the English schools were more interested in turning out gentlemen with broad, classical training than scientific practitioners.[19] The backward state of medical education in England—which *Middlemarch* describes in chapter 15—was due to the powerful London professional colleges, which controlled the structure and practice of medicine and resisted the introduction of new techniques. Lydgate is a partisan in the historical campaign for professional reform that sought to end the division of medical practice into the three branches of physicians, surgeons, and apothecaries. The campaign grew during the 1820s into an important force within the profession, although the London colleges maintained their division until 1858. Lydgate's opinions are based on the reformist Thomas Wakley's editorials for the time in the *Lancet,* and his decision not to profit from the sale of drugs is particularly topical.[20] However, the new scientific medicine, though it significantly improved diagnosis, did not generate effective therapies until much later in the nineteenth century, and Lydgate's cases demonstrate this.

He can recognize typhoid fever in Fred Vincy, for example, but without antibiotics he can do little actively to cure it. The public gives him credit for Vincy's recovery, but Lydgate himself is uncomfortable with the "trash talked on such occasions" (*M*, 45:440).[21] His superiority as a practitioner is that he abstains from poisoning patients with unnecessary drugs or weakening them through a ritualistic practice of venesection. Lydgate practices a form of therapeutic nihilism, relying mainly on bed rest, dietary control, and close observation. Because he assists rather than hinders the healing process, he is presented as a more effective practitioner than his rivals.

Scientific research and its insights into the body most clearly distinguish Lydgate's medicine from the heroic practice of the provincial medical men in the novel. Lydgate is interested in what is unseen, in hidden mechanisms and physical laws; he seeks a firm basis of knowledge on which to act. The older medicine concentrates on appearance, on visual, readily perceived surfaces. They practice a client-based form of treatment, catering to the whims of their often hypochondriacal patients.[22] Their medicine has an exaggerated, theatrical quality that appeals to patients. The old practitioners engage in the broad gestures of treatment, as though playing to the balconies and trying to compensate in appearance for what is lacking in substance. To the patients, those gestures are all-important. The patients of Toller, a popular surgeon-apothecary, for example, "commonly observed that Mr. Toller had lazy manners, but his treatment was as active as you could desire:—no man, said they, carried more seriousness into his profession: he was a little slow in coming, but when he came, he *did* something" (*M*, 45:438; italics original).

Stressed is the simple, reductive quality of action itself. He acted, "*did* something," something that is left undefined because it is insignificant except as a gesture. His laziness suggests an indifference to the outcome; he is "slow in coming" and thus either disinterested in the sufferer's illness or unconvinced of his own ability to ameliorate it. This implication is lost on the naive patient, who is more concerned with the dramatic surface of the "heroic" treatment than with its substance. All that matters is the degree of apparent activity, that treatment be "as active as you could desire"—that is, that it be clearly seen or felt. Patients admire the tangible, visible procedures, the "bleeding and blistering and starving," for which Toller is particularly known (*M*, 45:438). The same emphasis on visibility can be seen in the leading therapeutic, prescribed compounds. Their effectiveness, or substantive quality, is clearly subordinated to their mere tangibility. The narrator points out that "since professional practice chiefly consisted in giving a great many drugs, the public inferred that it might be better off with more drugs still, if they could only be got cheaply, and hence swallowed large cubic measures of physic" (*M,* 15:143). Undifferentiated quantity is the notable factor about these drugs, the "large cubic measure," without regard to their substantive qualities or effects. When Mrs. Mawmsey declares, "what keeps me up best is the pink mixture, not the brown" (*M,* 45:437), her attention is focused on the colorful aesthetic surface of the compound, suggesting an ignorance of its deeper characteristics. Such drugs, like the highly visible procedures of bleeding and blistering, are apparent enough in their form (though not in their effects) to constitute "active" treatment—that is, something worth paying for.

Ultimately the older medicine, with its emphasis on what is visible or tangible, on the drama of treatment, on the color and bulk of physic, is less grounded in the mechanism of the individual physical body than in the subjective and unreliable experience of the patient. Hence, George Eliot's descriptions of the older medical work focus more on the public perception of it and its practitioners than on the caricatured men themselves or their theories of treatment. As the narrator explains:

> For everybody's family doctor was remarkably clever, and was understood to have immeasurable skill in the management and training of the most skittish or vicious diseases. The evidence of his cleverness was of the higher intuitive order, lying in his lady-patients' immovable conviction, and was unassailable by any objection except that their intuitions were opposed by others equally strong; each lady who saw medical truth in Wrench and "the strengthening treatment" regarding Toller and "the lowering system" as medical perdition.
>
> (*M,* 15:139)

She claims not that the doctors have "immeasurable skill," only that they are "understood" to have it; her claim that "everybody's" doctor is "remarkably clever" is a commentary on "everybody's" judgment, not on the doctors themselves. She directly describes the *perception* of medical practice, concentrating on its visible surface and on the public response to that surface. And people's naive perceptions, which misappropriate the work of nature to the skill of the physician, are noticeably free from any connection to the reality that the treatment is at best ineffective.

Thus, in the older, client-based medicine, the doctor's practice lives and dies in the breath of popular opinion, for when effectiveness is illusory, a practitioner's "management and treatment" of his reputation is a more substantial part of his work than the management of disease. The unsolicited advice of Rosamond to Lydgate for reviving his failing practice—"It cannot answer to be eccentric; you should think what will be generally liked" (*M*, 64:637)—merely reflects the social context for medical practice in Middlemarch. At the same time, although it cannot be ignored, public opinion is notoriously inaccurate. Describing the various reactions to the new doctor in town, the narrator points out: "For surely all must admit that a man may be puffed and belauded, envied, ridiculed, counted upon as a tool and fallen in love with, or at least selected as a future husband, and yet remain virtually unknown—known merely as a cluster of signs for his neighbors' false suppositions" (*M*, 15:139). Reputation thus is a distorted product of the public's mind, not a reflection of deeper qualities within the object itself. It is within these fickle waters of social prejudice that the older medicine swims. This narrative emphasis on the falsity of public opinion and on the lack of correspondence between popular belief and reality suggests that the older medicine is Sir James Paget's worst nightmare, for it floats, free of any material referent, in the fancy of its patients. Instead of medicine as science, the older practitioners perform medicine as theater.

Whereas the older practitioners can only gesture wildly over the body's surface, Lydgate is able to penetrate that surface and perceive the "finely-adjusted mechanism in the human frame" (*M*, 15:141).[23] Underscoring this difference is the fact that he corrects the mistakes of the other practitioners: He correctly diagnoses typhoid fever in Fred Vincy after the surgeon Wrench sends "just the wrong medicines" (*M*, 26:255), and he sees in the charwoman Nancy Nash a cramp that Dr. Minchin has mistakenly perceived as a tumor (*M*, 45:441).[24] The older practitioners equate Lydgate's medicine with charlatanism precisely because it dives beneath that visible surface, leading to new forms of treatment.[25] The surgeon Wrench, for example, denounces Lydgate's "flighty, foreign notions" and calls his new treatments "worthy only of a quack." "That cant about cures," he concludes, "was never got up by sound practitioners" (*M,* 26:257). Toller clarifies the definition of charlatanism at work among the provincial practitioners when one of his simpleminded patients recollects a wonder worker who, she believes, was a charlatan like Lydgate:

> "There are so many of that sort. I remember Mr. Cheshire, with his irons, trying to make people straight when the Almighty had made them crooked."
> "No, no," said Mr. Toller, "Cheshire was all right—all fair and above board."
>
> (*M,* 45:446)

Indeed Cheshire's treatment is literally "above board," consisting entirely of observable surface activity, and it is for this reason, and this reason alone, that it is "all right." The true charlatan, Toller explains, advertises "cures in ways nobody knows anything about: a fellow who wants to make a noise by pretending to go deeper than other people." Because it literally goes "deeper," Lydgate's medicine epitomizes "the essence of the charlatan" in the eyes of the older practitioners (*M,* 45:446).

Lydgate's ability to "go deeper," to penetrate the sentient body's surface, can be divided into two categories. The first includes various forms of *sensory* penetration, such as listening through a stethoscope. Second, by means of a specifically *imaginative* penetration, Lydgate draws on his conceptual understanding of the body to infer its interior condition. Each of these forms of penetration, sensory and imaginative, needs to be considered separately.

Although the senses are barred from the interior of another's body by its surface, Lydgate is able to "see" further into the body's interior than others by extending the range of these senses with the recently improved microscope and newly invented stethoscope and thermometer.[26] His attendance on Borthrop Trumbull, for example, consists wholly of sensory penetration; he monitors Trumbull's body, and it becomes "a beautiful example of a disease with all its phases seen in clear delineation" (*M,* 45:443). The body "furnished objects for the microscope," which gives Trumbull a sense of "the dignity of his secretions," as they are transformed by Lydgate into scientific evidence of the body's interior state.

Each of these forms of sensory penetration, though challenging the body's physical boundary, nonetheless leaves it intact. The sounds Lydgate hears with his stethoscope, though originating in the interior, are heard at the surface of the skin; the "secretions" are, by definition, already part of the exterior world at the moment they are secreted. Thus, although calling these procedures a form of penetration, in fact each of them respects the material integrity of the body's shell. Each is a mediated form of reaching into the body, so that Lydgate is inevitably stationed at one remove from the interior.

The shell of the body preserves its biological life by keeping the interior hidden, inaccessible and safe from the external world. In *Middlemarch*, the sentient body cannot be physically opened without destroying the life that resides inside it. Although the modern context of safe, effective surgery makes it difficult to imagine the skin as an impassable boundary, this was still the reigning view in George Eliot's time. Anesthesia was not introduced until 1846, fifteen years after the novel's historical setting, when Eliot was in her late twenties. By 1870 it was still rudimentary, commonly consisting of chloroform on a rag. Though anesthesia greatly increased the use of some surgical procedures at mid-century, the unsolved danger of septic infection meant that open surgery—"cutting" operations in which the protective skin is broken—remained a course of last resort.[27] It was not until 1872, the same year *Middlemarch* was published, that Joseph Lister introduced the use of carbolic acid spray to produce an aseptic operating field. His ideas, however, were embroiled in the controversy over Pasteur's germ theory, on which they depended, and it was 1886 before the more advanced German surgeons, who accepted Pasteur's theory, began the antiseptic procedures of washing their hands and sterilizing their instruments. During World War I, aseptic procedures finally met with widespread acceptance. But during George Eliot's lifetime, open surgery was a perilous procedure, and the skin constituted a significantly more impermeable boundary than it does today. By looking at the two separate instances in the text—each crucial in Lydgate's development—where the boundary of the body is physically pierced, the impassability of the sentient body's surface, and the paradox it poses for scientific medicine, can be more clearly seen.

Lydgate's love of medicine begins "under the head of Anatomy" when, as a boy, he discovers the passage in the *Cyclopaedia* on "the valves of the heart" (*M*, 15:141).[28] The two major medical figures in Lydgate's personal hierarchy, his "patron saints," are Vesalius and Bichat, both important anatomists (*M*, 45:448).[29] But even though anatomy penetrates the surface of the body, a corpse can only indirectly represent the sentient body. Between the two lies a temporal boundary that parallels the impassable spatial boundary of the skin and keeps the practitioner, again, at one remove from the processes of the sentient body. Popular objections to Lydgate's practice of pathology are rooted in the idea that he allows patients to die so that he can open the body when it is as temporally close to life as possible. The vociferous landlady of the Tankard, Mrs. Dollop, suggests that he does not quite wait for the patient's death; she refers to him as "this Dr Lydgate that's been for cutting up everybody before the breath was well out o' their body" (*M*, 71:712).[30] Certainly erroneous as a statement of fact, her observation nonetheless possesses an ironic truth (as does much of *Middlemarch* gossip). Because Lydgate's object of interest is not the corpse but the still breathing body which it imperfectly represents, he is in fact trying to look inside the living body.[31] That he cannot is a testament to the physically impassable nature of the sentient body's boundary at that stage in medical history.

Yet in one crucial instance the novel does indeed represent the physical penetration of the living body. This unique image is carefully bracketed at several removes from the ongoing action of the story. It takes place in the past, far away in another country, framed as the action of a play. The story of Lydgate's first romance, in Paris with Laure, is itself a digression from the main action in *Middlemarch*, and the story of the play is a digression within the digression. Further attention is drawn to this elaborate framework (if any were needed) by the introduction to the chapter in which it occurs; the narrator distinguishes her concise narrative project from the "copious remarks and digressions" of her predecessor, Henry Fielding. "All the light I can command must be concentrated on this particular web, and not dispersed," she says (*M*, 15:139). The doubly digressive nature of the episode of Laure thus indicates its importance, for the narrator must make a major effort to weave this distant event into her purposeful "web."

Laure is "the actress whose part it was to stab her lover" (*M*, 15:148). Nightly assuming her role in the melodrama, Laure on stage is an emblem of penetration to which Lydgate repeatedly returns. Thus, the young student's first experience with love is coupled with the image of opening the boundary of the skin. As a young medical student pursuing anatomical studies at the Paris school, Lydgate also experiments with animal bodies, subjecting "frogs and rabbits" to galvanic shocks, experiments that are "over and above his other work." [32] He works at a grueling pace and some nights becomes frustrated. "Tired with his experimenting, and not being able to elicit the facts he needed" from the intellectually impenetrable bodies of his animal subjects, he returns again and again to Laure and her representation of direct penetration. This idealized image of the woman who succeeds where he fails rejuvenates his flagging spirits. As we are told, the interlude is "without prejudice to his galvanism, to which he would presently return." Thus the play has a beneficial effect on Lydgate, for it rekindles his enthusiasm, inspiring him to continue in his scientific pursuit. But the image remains positive only as long as it remains idealized—that is, as long as Laure remains "a woman with whom he never expects to speak." As will be considered later, this restorative dynamic reverses after the old drama's "new catastrophe," in which Laure "veritably stabbed her husband." Laure's motives are famously enigmatic.[33] But Lydgate's response is quickly summarized. He falls immediately in love with the actress and, in the pandemonium at the theatre, rushes to the stage, takes her in his arms, and begins a lone crusade to defend her against charges of murder. This personal obsession temporarily destroys his medical studies.

In the story of Lydgate's love for the actress, then, the penetration of the body benefits Lydgate's science as long as it remains idealized. But, as in the practice of anatomy, at the moment it becomes real the work of science ceases and the question of murder emerges. In both cases, the boundary of the skin cannot be physically crossed without transforming the object of study, the sentient body, into an insentient corpse. By definition, then, the skin of the sentient body must remain inviolate, for once it is broached the body loses its sentience. This categorical impermeability poses the central epistemological problem for Lydgate's scientific medicine. The interior of the living body, by its very nature, is necessarily hidden. The body's life—which is the source of the body's meaning to the physician, who seeks to preserve it—depends absolutely upon the boundary's integrity. But, paradoxically, that same boundary prevents the physician from knowing that meaning, for the skin bars him from access to the body's interior, where its meaning resides. Thus, although the work of medicine requires the penetration of the body's surface, the goal of medicine is to preserve the very surface that prevents this penetration.[34]

Because of this paradox, the most significant aspect of Lydgate's penetration of the body is imaginative rather than sensory. The impassable physical boundary that intervenes between the medical laborer and the object of his labor determines that medicine will be primarily a "labour of the imagination" (*M*, 16:161), for the object of work can never be directly reached nor directly observed. Lydgate's "daily work," George Eliot writes, consists of "careful observation and inference" (*M*, 15:144). His essential task is the "observation" of the surface, which leads to his "inference" about the interior. Because that interior is inaccessible, he correlates the surface signs with an imagined interior. The interior is the "living structure" that he seeks to represent with his "anatomical conception" (*M*, 15:146, 144). Thus, his intellectual penetration, his "insight" into the hidden interior, depends upon that profoundly creative act of conceptualization. He describes this act as "the imagination that reveals subtle actions inaccessible by any sort of lens, but tracked in that outer darkness through long pathways of necessary sequence by the inward light which is the last refinement of Energy, capable of bathing even the ethereal atoms in its ideally illuminated space" (*M*, 16:161–62). Through this use of the imagination he hopes "to pierce the obscurity of those minute processes" that lay hidden in the body and thus to create his image of its living interior.

This argument on the central role of imagination in the scientific project was not original to George Eliot. It was shared within the scientific circle to which she and Lewes belonged.[35] Among her favorite visitors at the Priory was the physicist John Tyndall, a respected scientist and popular lecturer, whose ideas Lydgate embodies.[36] Tyndall's 1870 lecture, "Scientific Use of the Imagination," asks: "How, for example, are we to lay hold of the physical basis of light, since, like that of life itself, it lies entirely without the domain of the senses? . . . We are gifted with the power of Imagination . . . and by this power we can lighten the darkness which surrounds the world of the senses."[37] The new tools, such as the microscope, that extend the range of the senses present a dilemma for the empiricist. For as they reveal a new world to the observer, and thereby prove the fallibility of the unaided senses, so too they suggest the unseen presence of more minute structures. Hence, Tyndall notes, "beyond the present outposts of microscopic enquiry lies an immense field for the exercise of the speculative power" because the material world possesses "infinite permutations and combinations" (*Imagination in Science*, 40–41). It is only through such imaginative activities as hypothesizing that one can hope to comprehend the mechanisms for the transmission of light and sound. Thus, for Tyndall imagination is an essential element of scientific inquiry, for it takes the scientist "behind the drop-scene of the senses" (*Imagination in Science*, 15). In Tyndall, the "real" becomes located in this extra-sensible universe of atomic structure, and so the imagination becomes the essential tool for perceiving reality.[38]

Lydgate's research is thus primarily a representational project, one in which he works to construct a model of the body's unseen interior. The representational nature of this project has invited frequent comparison with the author's own representational project. In a famous passage, George Eliot's narrator comments on that project and on the difficulty of penetrating a different sort of barrier to perceive the material world beyond, and in it Lydgate's representational problems reappear:[39]

> [W]e do not expect people to be deeply moved by what is not unusual. That element of tragedy which lies in the very fact of frequency, has not yet wrought itself into the coarse emotion of mankind; and perhaps our frames could hardly bear much of it. If we had a keen vision and feeling of all ordinary human life, it would be like hearing the grass grow and the squirrel's heart beat, and we should die of that roar which lies on the other side of silence. As it is, the quickest of us walk about well wadded with stupidity.
>
> (*M*, 20:189)

The narrator characterizes the external world as a world of excess meaning; there are simply too many facts, all with their own significance, to comprehend. The human subject defends against this life-threatening "roar" of unlimited meaning by perceptual "stupidity," by an absence of "keen vision and feeling." She reiterates Wordsworth's complaint against overstimulation, reducing one's sensitivity to a state of mental torpor.[40] But instead of limiting the complaint to the hurried pace of urban life, she uses the inescapable, sheer presence of an external world to account for the same insensibility. Silence in this passage is thus a perceptual threshold that protects the subject from the overwhelming presence of the external world (represented here in terms of sound, but impinging equally on all the senses).[41] This threshold of perceptual "stupidity," like the body's skin, separates the human subject from the excess of meaning in the material world. It becomes a metaphorical extension of the skin, protecting the life that resides "inside" from the threat that exists "outside." Lydgate seeks to penetrate the skin to understand better the unknown yet real structure of the body; similarly, George Eliot's narrator recognizes the presence of a perceptual threshold intervening between herself and an equally unknown yet real external world. As Lydgate finds a hidden realm of signification in the body's interior, so too the narrator sees a veiled significance in ordinary life. What unites these two views is the assertion of a threshold for the empirical powers of the observer beyond which significance resides.

It becomes, then, the task of the realistic novelist to penetrate this empirical boundary, much as the scientist must penetrate the skin. The duty of the novelist, in George Eliot's view, is specifically to overcome this perceptual "stupidity" and to represent for others the existence of those ordinary, unnoticed tragedies as a means of furthering the understanding between individuals and social classes.[42] "The greatest benefit we owe to the artist, whether painter, poet, or novelist, is the extension of our sympathies," she wrote at the beginning of her novelistic career.[43] "Art is the nearest thing to life; it is a mode of amplifying experience and extending our contact with our fellowmen beyond the bounds of our personal lot" (*Essays*, 271). The realistic artist must thus penetrate the drop-scene of the senses in order to expand the phenomenon of sympathy within society. This social responsibility places severe demands on the truthfulness of the writer's representation of everyday experience. Misrepresentation, she claims, is "a grave evil" in the realistic novel because it claims to represent "people as they are" (*Essays*, 270). The sympathy of the believing reader becomes "perverted, and turned towards a false object instead of a true one. . . . We want to be taught to feel, not for the heroic artisan or the sentimental peasant, but for the peasant in all his coarse apathy, and the artisan in all his suspicious selfishness" (*Essays*, 271). To avoid this danger, the novelist must become in a very real sense a scientist. Forgoing customary ideas or sentimental doctrines, the writer must study the social body with the same sort of direct observation and attention to detail that Lydgate practices on the physical body. "[A] real knowledge of the People" is needed to "guide our sympathies rightly," and this knowledge requires "a thorough study of their habits, their ideas, their motives" (*Essays*, 272). George Eliot sees this immersion in the concrete, particular details of everyday experience as a corrective to the tendency to interpret the real through the lens of generalized theories or systems of thought. Early influenced by Comtian positivism, she decries the vitiating effects of *à priori* knowledge and stresses reliance on gradually amassed observations.[44] "The abstract is derived from the concrete," she held, rather than the reverse (*Essays*, 150).[45] She calls this form of intimate social study the natural history of social bodies, and her description of what such a science would look like bears a close resemblance to her own novels:[46]

> If any man of sufficient moral and intellectual breadth, whose observations would not be vitiated by a foregone conclusion, or by a professional point of view, would devote himself to studying the natural history of our social classes, especially of the small shopkeepers, artisans, and peasantry,—the degree in which they are influenced by local conditions, their maxims and habits, the points of view from which they regard their religious teachers, and the degree in which they are influenced by religious doctrines, the interaction of the various classes on each other, and what are the tendencies in their position towards disintegration or towards development,—and if, after all this study, he would give us the result of his observations in a book well nourished with specific facts, his work would be a valuable aid to the social and political reformer.
>
> (*Essays*, 272–3)

In the attention to detailed observation and the avoidance of prior systematized beliefs, in the attempt to improve society by representing its hidden processes, the project of the realistic novelist resembles that of the Victorian scientist.[47]

George Eliot's later ideas about realism were deeply influenced by Matthew Arnold's concept of the role of culture and the problem of expanding social sympathy.[48] Her notion of a perceptual threshold—the "drop-scene of the senses"—is closely related to Arnold's idea of the "ordinary self ."[49] The primary restraint, as Arnold sees it, on the development of social sympathy is the tyranny of self-interest. The actions of individuals and social classes are determined by their material self-interests; there is no recognition of the needs of other classes or competing individuals. The "ordinary self" perceives the world in terms of its limited, day-to-day experience, mistaking this narrow and distorted vision for the larger social reality. The expansion of social sympathy depends on the development, in the individual, of an altruistic identity that can see beyond the threshold of the individual's social experience. In their "best self," individuals can escape the self-interests of their class, parochial interests that blind them to the common good. Thus, for Arnold, the perceptions of the "ordinary self" are bounded by a form of social relativism, whereas the "best self" penetrates the blindness of daily experience and perceives the larger set of social relations that constitutes reality.

George Eliot transcribes Arnold's vision of culture note for note in her handling of Lydgate's science. The ordinary self is above all the individual as determined by empirical experience and operating on the partial information available to the senses. It sees the surface of the body or admires the drama of treatment but never understands the natural laws at work. It is because Lydgate, unlike the older practitioners, is able to transcend these empirical limits, through Tyndall's scientific imagination, that he resembles the Arnoldian intellectual, escaping the distortion of immediate experience to recognize the real presence of a deeper set of unapparent relations.

His outsider status further marks him as a representative of Arnoldian culture. Lydgate comes to Middlemarch to avoid being hampered in his scientific research by the London professional colleges that represent, in the very worst sense, the pursuit of narrow self-interest at the expense of the larger social good. Thus, Lydgate asserts his independence from the social determinants of the "ordinary," and this independence is the necessary condition for the unimpeded pursuit of knowledge. Similarly, he resolves to stay disengaged from all provincial entanglements, political, social, or otherwise. His independence marks him as one of Arnold's cultural intellectuals, and it points to the central element of Arnold's thought. For "objective" thought depends on independence. In order to represent a social group, either politically or as an intellectual object of study, the individual cannot belong to the group but must be what Arnold terms an "alien." Thus, Lydgate's disinterestedness and aloofness are an attempt to keep his research uncontaminated by the social and material determinants that make up Arnold's "ordinary self."

Although George Eliot recognized a strong kinship between aesthetic and scientific realism, her medical protagonist anxiously avoids any such connection. Lydgate, like Sir James Paget, wants his science to be more "real" than "fictional," and this anxiety about the representational status of his work leads him to disassociate himself, both in his personal tastes and in his research, from artistry. Thus, he introduces his encomium on the scientific imagination with a harsh denigration of aesthetic creativity: "Many men have been praised as vividly imaginative on the strength of their profuseness in indifferent drawing or cheap narration" (*M*, 16:161). Lydgate seems to use *Paradise Lost* as an example of "cheap inventions where ignorance finds itself able and at ease." He rejects aesthetic representation in general as an excessive or inaccurate portrayal of the real, one that seems "to reflect life in a diseased dream." He does not restrict his objection to what George Eliot classed as "bad" art, such as the hackneyed sentimentality of the *Keepsake* album that Rosamond Vincy and her suitor read.[50] Instead, as he admits to Rosamond, Lydgate has simply given up on the whole puerile business of aesthetic representation: "Oh, I read no literature now. . . . I read so much when I was a lad, that I suppose it will last me all my life" (*M*, 27:265). Behind this disdain for artistic creativity lies a denial of his own immersion in fictionality, a denial that his reliance on the "labour of the imagination" has anything in common with aesthetic representation (*M*, 16:161). That is, he tries to place science essentially outside of representation, outside the arbitrariness of language, and thus to deny that his imaginative reaching beyond the boundary of empiricism has any hermeneutic difficulties. Rather than an exposition on George Eliot's own self-conscious practice of realism, Lydgate's science is a case study in the limitations and dangers of naive realism—that is, of representation that denies its own status as representation.[51]

Lydgate's naive stance is not limited to his medical labors. The man who determines to "take a strictly scientific view of woman" does not confine his denial of the problematics of scientific representation to scientific research (*M*, 15:151). It is a global part of his personality, as he generally insists on a strong correspondence between sign and meaning. This can be seen in his contempt for the disingenuous posturing of politicians, in his dislike of wealthy patients who expect him to feign respect and "listen more deferentially to nonsense" (*M*, 31:287), and in his general disdain for the hollow forms of conventionality. In each case, Lydgate expects that what people say, do, or otherwise signify will accurately reflect what they mean. Because he dislikes slippage between signifier and signified, he declines to participate even in innocent forms of activity involving dissemblance, such as the after-dinner games at the Vincy's house. As the narrator succinctly explains, "Lydgate was no Puritan, but he did not care for play" (*M*, 18:174). Similarly, he wants to succeed based on the substantive merits of his own work, on what he perceives as its meaning and value, rather than on supposedly superficial characteristics, such as the network of friendship and political alliance that characterizes the existing system of medical patronage. "[H]e would keep away from the range of London intrigues, jealousies, and social truckling, and win celebrity, however slowly, as Jenner had done, by the independent value of his work" (*M*, 15:143). Indeed, his support of professional reform in medicine, of stricter licensing requirements and the transformation of the profession into a meritocracy, is an insistence on stricter correspondence between title and training, signifier and signified, so that there is a greater stability of meaning within the profession itself.[52]

Middlemarch provides no clearer answer to Lydgate's naive representational assumptions than his infatuation with Rosamond Vincy. She perfectly epitomizes the disjunction between sign and signification that Lydgate refuses to acknowledge. In judging her inner character, he employs his "scientific view of woman," reading her bodily signs much as he reads the bodies of his patients. He operates on precisely the same assumption of a strong, one-to-one correspondence between representation and meaning when he argues that her physical mannerisms and poise—her bodily signs—adequately convey the truth about her identity: "Miss Vincy . . . had just the kind of intelligence one would desire in a woman—polished, refined, docile, lending itself to finish in all the delicacies of life, and

enshrined in a body which expressed this with a force of demonstration that excluded the need for other evidence" (*M*, 16:161). Lydgate
draws his conclusions from the evidence, ignoring the possibility
that this sentient body is less legible than he assumes. And this assumption that her body is sincere, that her character is unmistakably
"enshrined in" and "expressed" by her appearance, is his central
error. With her practiced manners, self-serving deceptions, and intractable will, Rosamond is the perfect foil to Lydgate's underesti-
mation of the problems of representation: "Every nerve and muscle
in Rosamond was adjusted to the consciousness that she was being
looked at. She was by nature an actress of parts that entered into her
physique: she even acted her own character, and so well, that she did
not know it to be precisely her own" (*M*, 12:114).

In direct contradiction to Lydgate's view, her body enshrines
idealized roles, not a fixed identity. The most notable aspect of her
character is in fact the absence of any fixed meaning; "she did not
know" her own character but "acted" it, inseparable in her mind
from her varied roles. She is a dreamer who resides perpetually in
the "thoughtwoven 'might-be' such as she was in the habit of oppos-
ing to the actual" (*M*, 12:115). With no identity outside of the imaginary and so "by nature an actress," Rosamond stands for a weak
correspondence between sign and meaning. The marriage between
her and Lydgate thus unites the problematics of pure representation
with the naive realism of the scientist who will not acknowledge its
existence. Because of her character's limitations, she is an unlikely
and even an objectionable heroine. Yet by defeating Lydgate's sim-
plistic determination to "take a strictly scientific view of woman,"
she becomes a heroine nonetheless.[53]

Lydgate's effectiveness as a practitioner—or at least the greater
accuracy of his diagnosis—seems to justify his faith in the referentiality of scientific language, as opposed to the nonreferentiality of
aesthetic representation. But his new scientific ideas raise the very
problem of referentiality he tries to erase. Lydgate's concept of the
body comes from that of his hero, Bichat, the Romantic-era surgeon,
physiologist, and anatomist who died at the age of thirty-one.[54]
Bichat's new conception of the body, Lydgate cautions, "must be
taken into account in considering the symptoms of maladies and the
action of medicaments" (*M*, 15:145). Whereas Lydgate's rivals are
still "shambling along the old paths," viewing the physical body in

the old way, Lydgate follows Bichat's new physiological concept, one that describes a body different from any previously seen: "That great Frenchman first carried out the conception that living bodies, fundamentally considered, are not associations of organs which can be understood by studying them first apart, and then as it were federally; but must be regarded as consisting of certain primary webs or tissues, out of which the various organs—brain, heart, lungs, and so on—are compacted, as the various accommodations of a house are built up in various proportions of wood, iron, stone, brick, zinc, and the rest" (*M*, 15:145–46).

George Eliot's repeated use of the word "conception" in connection with Bichat's idea is carefully chosen. It suggests that Bichat has given birth to a new body, one that consists of "primary webs or tissues" and thus differs fundamentally from the old body of "associations of organs." This new body seems not merely verified but actually reified by Lydgate's success, as though the "conception wrought out by Bichat," to use George Eliot's remarkable phrase, were the imagination made flesh. The idea has not only been "conceived" but "wrought" as well, and by this double language of reproduction and production, George Eliot stresses the absolute materiality of Bichat's intellectual construction. In this vision of science, the one-to-one relationship between idea and thing becomes so absolute that ideas seem even to slip over the line from representations to constructions, remaking their referents in their own image, so that the imagined body gives rise to the material body and not the reverse.

Yet the apparent referentiality of Bichat's conception raises the very problem of referentiality that Lydgate wants to deny.[55] Because it gives rise to a "new" body and asserts that the "old" body was a misrepresentation, Bichat's idea implies a disjunction between the shifting, historically relative nature of medical concepts and their unchanging referent in the material world. As Will Ladislaw explains elsewhere in the novel, "new discoveries are constantly making new points of view" (*M*, 22:217), and this continual reconceptualization emphasizes the distance between idea and referent about which Lydgate is so anxious. [56] Lydgate's dedication to discovering a new "anatomical conception" exacerbates the problem, for his revision of Bichat's theory suggests yet another sequence of new bodies defined by their increasingly minute structural units: "This great seer did not go beyond the consideration of the tissues as ultimate facts in the living organism, marking the limit of anatomical analysis; but it was open to another mind to say, have not these structures some common basis from which they have all started, as your sarsnet, gauze, net, satin and velvet from the raw cocoon? Here would be another light, as of oxy-hydrogen, showing the very grain of things, and revising all former explanations" (*M*, 15:146).

Lydgate's proposed revision mirrors Bichat's; his textiles (gauze, satin, velvet) mimic Bichat's building materials (wood, iron, stone). But in the progression between the two schemes, the originary structure of the body is pushed back—from organ to Bichat's "primary tissue" to Lydgate's "primitive tissue"—and each explanation creates a new image of the body, overturning "all former explanations." As Lydgate's science continually uncovers new horizons of knowledge, the stable significance of the body remains a distant goal, always chased and always receding into more minute units, creating an endless proliferation of meaning. The sequence suggests an inescapable disjunction between the conceptualized body and the infinitely complex material body it seeks to represent. His "conception" is not, in fact, the word made flesh but the word endlessly seeking to represent the flesh, whereas the flesh always exceeds its representation in the word. The body is not merely unknown in *Middlemarch* but unknowable as well.

Lydgate's strong correlation of facts with significance is an attempt to tame the excesses of fancy with the principle of scientific verifiability. Like Sir James Paget, he insists that ideas have a "foundation." For Lydgate, scientific representation differs from aesthetic because it is "not mere arbitrariness, but the exercise of disciplined power"—that is, it is rooted in empirical verification, which brings scientific representations into "more and more exactness of relation" (*M*, 16:161–62). In this, Lydgate again reproduces the arguments of the eloquent scientist John Tyndall. Tyndall reassured those "tories in science" who were afraid of the arbitrariness of the imagination that verification could elevate imaginative concepts to the same degree of certainty as empirical evidence:

> [If a concept] has actually forced upon our attention phenomena which no eye had previously seen, and which no mind had previously imagined, such a conception, which never disappoints us, but always lands us on the solid shores of fact, must, we think, be something more than a mere figment of the scientific fancy. In forming it

that composite and creative unity in which reason and imagination
are together blent, has, we believe, led us into a world not less real
than that of the senses, and of which the world of sense itself is the
suggestion and justification.

(Imagination in Science, 19–20)

However, in George Eliot's view, relying on the senses to establish
the referentiality of ideas has, as we have seen, significant difficulties. For it reintroduces the same problematic misperception that
characterizes the day-to-day experience of the "ordinary self." It
thus complicates the original question of referentiality without completely eliminating it. Because the realist's project is to escape from
the relativism of social experience and see behind the "drop-scene of
the senses," Tyndall's attempt to elevate representation to the level
of empiricism—by turning it into "a world not less real than that of
the senses"—also has the opposite effect. It recontains the truer perception of the "best self" within the relativistic framework of the
"ordinary self." Similarly, Lydgate's denial of the fundamentally
representational nature of his work, although intended as a reinforcement of his work's claim to referentiality, carries with it a danger of entrapment within the narrow relativism that characterizes
day-to-day experience.

George Eliot's treatment of Lydgate suggests that, by trying to ig-
nore the hermeneutic problems of realism, he becomes their prisoner. The scientist who, in the desire to avoid the contamination of
fictionality and to strengthen science's claim to referentiality, denies
the representational nature of science loses sight of the *essentially*
fictional condition of science, thereby becoming less objective than
ever. Instead of acknowledging the contingent nature of scientific
knowledge, such a scientist becomes an unwitting participant in a
representational project that is no longer recognized as representation. By seeking to distance itself from imagination, science becomes
increasingly blinded by an excessive faith in its own idealized concept of the material and thus, ironically, grows more distant from the
referentiality it claims to possess.

George Eliot illustrates the mechanics of precisely this problem in
the conclusion of that distant but crucial narrative about Laure, the
emblematic actress who represents, as we have seen, the penetration
through the empirical boundary to the realm of significance beyond.
As long as Lydgate recognizes the representational nature of the act,

his science proceeds admirably. But when Laure "veritably stabbed her husband" on stage (*M*, 15:148), the necessary distinction between representation and reality dissolves. What was first purely a representation suddenly becomes real. But what is real—or, more to the point, what is now seen to be real—takes place on a stage, so that the real and the represented become intractably confused. The immediate consequence of this conflation is that the orderly distinction between observer and observed is erased as illustrated when Laure's audience rushes onto the stage. The scientist who denies the representational status of science and believes in its direct referentiality behaves as Lydgate does, leaving his distant seat in the audience ("he hardly knew how") to embrace his emblem of penetration. But he does so only by placing himself on stage. The observer thus becomes an actor in a representation that is no longer recognized as representation. The consequence for Lydgate is straightforward: "all science" we are told, "had come to a standstill" (*M*, 15:150). The subsequent affair with Laure is characterized by the total loss of objectivity that leads Lydgate, and Lydgate alone, to maintain her innocence. His response afterward, the naive and persistent belief that now "illusions were at an end for him," that as a result he "had more reason than ever for trusting his judgment, now that it was so experienced" (*M*, 15:151), further suggests an ongoing and deeply pervasive self-deception about his own ability to be objective.

Despite his claims to a disinterested science, Lydgate is unable to rise above the social determinants that make up the "ordinary" self. By placing him and his research in a remarkably specific, historically conditioned environment, George Eliot historicizes him, making the social context a member of the dramatis personae, influencing the direction and progress his research takes. His research is influenced by a vast array of social forces, including the vulgar prejudice against anatomy and his professional rivalries with the older practitioners. George Eliot explores the political issues involved in Lydgate's appointment to the New Hospital for fevers, where his research takes place, and keeps his work there in a highly politicized context, as his fortunes are tied to those of the power-broker responsible for the appointment, Mr. Bulstrode. In his discussion with the evangelical banker over the new chaplain for the hospital, Lydgate is shown participating in a localized boundary dispute with the clergy over hospital authority. Even in his own appointment, Lydgate is an instrument in a struggle for provincial power between Bulstrode, whose goal is "to gain as much power as possible" (*M*, 16:152), and the local opposition to his rule. There is a competition with the old infirmary for patients, a campaign against the New Hospital by the rest of the medical profession (which refuses to participate and tries to hinder subscriptions), and a financial crisis that threatens to sink the hospital following Bulstrode's public disgrace. Lydgate's research is finally halted by the press of financial problems, which forces him to seek a more lucrative practice curing gout in wealthy patients. His research thus takes place within a series of negotiations between multifarious social forces, not in isolation from them. Rather than a mythologized scientist locked within a sealed laboratory of pure ideas, Lydgate is a particular individual working within a historically defined medical tradition in a particular time and place. From the wiser and more objective perspective of the narrator, Lydgate's knowledge is limited and his assumptions are flawed; he poses his fundamental questions "not quite in the way required by the awaiting answer" (*M*, 15:146). His scientific ideas are not, then, abstractly "pure" or objective but are part of a historically determined group of ideas and assumptions—such as that of the "primitive tissue"—that were unique to a brief span of time in the early part of the nineteenth century. His medicine is not simply a prescient version of the future; it includes medical dead ends, notably Bichat's tissue theory. Consequently, Lydgate—despite his romantic enthusiasm and altruistic dreams—remains a product of his own profoundly historicized culture. His refusal to acknowledge these necessary limitations on the pursuit of pure science, on the embrace of the ideal as reality, leaves him trapped within them. Thus, on a grand scale, he continues to act out the scene with Laure.

For George Eliot, naive realism manifests a state of unreflective and premature faith in the abilities of language to refer truthfully to material reality and of the scientist, armed with his belief in scientific verification, to comprehend it. Her critique of Lydgate's science, however, does not suggest a fundamental division between science and literature, nor does it imply a superiority of aesthetic over scientific realism. The two share an essential kinship in *Middlemarch*, one Lydgate's naiveté does not eradicate but only emphasizes. Thus, her exploration of science can be seen as a cautionary tale against a form of naive science that, overconfident in its methodology and in the referentiality of its concepts, turns back on itself and comes full circle. With the sort of blind faith in the scientific method that Lydgate exhibits, concepts prematurely receive the status of truth. Thus, the whole positivist project of building a firm basis of knowledge becomes contaminated with naive conclusions, presenting the same obstacle to conceiving the real as that raised by the orthodox knowledge that the scientific method was meant to overturn. What matters to George Eliot is that the body can *only* be conceived, and so to underestimate the conceptual nature of science is to pervert its greatest asset.

Unlike her medical protagonist, George Eliot's narrators consistently insist on the tentativeness of the connection between representation and referent. The *Middlemarch* narrator, using a microscope analogy reminiscent of Tyndall's lectures, points to the essential relativity of perception: "Even with a microscope directed on a water-drop we find ourselves making interpretations which turn out to be rather coarse; for whereas under a weak lens you may seem to see a creature exhibiting an active voracity into which other small creatures actively play . . . a stronger lens reveals to you certain tiniest hairlets which make vortices for these victims while the swallower waits passively at his receipt of custom" (*M*, 6:58–59). As in the historical relativity of Bichat's concept, referentiality is never assured in the stepwise progression from one level of signification to the other. The observer is always in the position of not knowing, of needing that "stronger lens" to overcome the misrepresentation of an "interpretation," which is inevitably "rather coarse."[57] *Middlemarch* implies a far weaker and more problematic correspondence between idea and referent than Lydgate allows, and it is a problem that even empirical verification does not entirely overcome.

George Eliot's novels, particularly the later ones, are emphatic about pointing to their own status as representations and to their necessarily imperfect ability to represent the everyday experience they so painstakingly describe. But they use this same arbitrariness, which so troubles Lydgate, as a sign of their own authority to speak about the world.[58] For this weak correspondence of idea to thing makes it possible to imagine a world that is other than it seems. The same autonomy of representation that creates the problem of misrepresentation and that leads to necessarily "coarse" interpretations also makes possible the independent perception of the "best self." For it is only through the independence of ideas from the tyranny of individual social experience that the larger vision of relations that constitutes the real becomes possible.

Middlemarch as a whole celebrates the freedom from the ordinary that representation allows. Though she exposes the hypocrisy and ineffectiveness of the older practitioners, George Eliot also has a keen perception of the wit and humor of their theatrical medicine and the almost random generation of narratives it inspires, with its conspiracy of ignorance between doctor, patient, and the gossip-riddled community. The charwoman Nancy Nash, for example, "became a subject of compassionate conversation" because of her tumor, which was "at first declared to be as large and hard as a duck's egg, but later in the day to be about the size of 'your fist'" (*M*, 45: 441). After treatment, it "wandered to another region with angrier pain." Nancy Nash's tumor "of the wandering sort" (*M*, 45:442) has a wondrous quality in its extraordinary transformations and migrations; it transfigures the ordinary body of the simple charwoman into a region of mystery bordering on the magical.[59]

The purpose of George Eliot's realism, as we have seen, is to point beyond the relativistic perceptions of everyday experience to a realm of signification that is free from the limitations of individual experience. But a simple description of "things as they are"—theoretically impossible, in any event—by itself cannot accomplish this goal, for it simply reproduces those same facts that already determine the distorted perceptions of the "ordinary self." Simple description of everyday life leads to the same inescapable but erroneous conclusions that everyday life produces. Realism for George Eliot always demands the wider, unconfined vision of social relations that defines the "best self," the perspective that floats free from all social determinants, existing in an Arnoldian realm of pure representation. The acknowledgment, then, of realism's representational nature becomes indicative of its freedom from "things as they are." Like Lydgate's early independence from the politics of his profession, this narrative independence becomes a condition of the authority to speak because it represents the wider perspective of the "best self." By pointing to the boundaries and to the fallibility of even her own interpretation, the narrator distances herself from the central element of the socially determined perspective: the characteristic inability to differentiate what one knows from what is real.

Because the "best self" floats free from "things as they are," it is synonymous with the ability to conceptualize, to penetrate beyond the surface and escape the prisonhouse of the everyday. The realist project, then, as a representation of the "best self," centers on these moments of penetration, conceptualization, and imagination, in addition to its concrete description of facts and events. *Middlemarch* combines, as we have seen, the dense texture of dates, places, and meticulous particularity with the ongoing efforts—of Dorothea, Casaubon, and Ladislaw as well as of Lydgate—to look beyond these specifics for their general significance. This act of looking beyond the surface, so paradigmatic in Lydgate's medicine, is nothing more nor less than the act of representation. Thus, in a perfect circularity, realism comes to hinge on the representation of representation.[60] Thus George Eliot's exploration of Lydgate, both in his conception of the body and in his scientific view of women, is a central expression of this realist impulse.

So when Sir James Paget, in his unguarded astonishment, describes her creation of Lydgate as "a whole universe formed out of nothing," his remark underscores the remarkable success of the author's project even as it acknowledges the basis for it. That "nothing" acknowledges the same independence of representation that she proposes in the novel. Because Paget plays the role of Lydgate, it is as if, for one brief moment, her fictional surgeon has come alive in Paget and, instead of denying the potentials of representation along with its problems, has marveled even briefly at its possibilities. To George Eliot's way of thinking, Paget's astonishment represented a hope for the project of Victorian science, because it meant that Lydgate's fate was not necessarily the fate of a social enterprise to which she was, herself, deeply committed.

Notes

INTRODUCTION

1. The proportion is cited by Thomas Trotter and is taken up in chapter 1 of this study. My use of it is conservative, for after William Cullen's redefinition of nerves, no disorders remained unaffected. As the *Encyclopaedia Britannica* notes in 1779, "the distinguishing characteristic of [Cullen's] pathology will be, that almost all diseases are the consequence of an affection of the nervous system" (2nd ed., s.v. "medicine"). Thomas Arnold, in his *Observations on the Nature, Kinds, Causes, and Prevention of Insanity*, 2 vols., 2nd edition (London: Richard Phillips, 1806), defined insanity in such broad terms that virtually no one escaped its net. For a historical overview of the rise and decline of "nerves," see W. F. Bynum, "The Nervous Patient in Eighteenth- and Nineteenth-Century Britain: The Psychiatric Origins of British Neurology," in *The Anatomy of Madness: Essays in the History of Psychiatry*, ed. W. F. Bynum, Roy Porter, and Michael Shepherd (London: Tavistock, 1985), 1:89–102.

2. Roy Porter discusses Trotter and Beddoes as examples of the new medical critique of the consumption of luxuries, which he links to the rise of the theory of addiction. See Roy Porter, "Addicted to Modernity: Nervousness in the Early Consumer Society," in *Culture in History: Production, Consumption and Values in Historical Perspective*, ed. Joseph Melling and Jonathan Barry (Exeter: Exeter University Press, 1992), 180–94. For Arnold, see his *Observations*, 1:14–25.

3. On nervous conditions in the Victorian period, see Janet Oppenheim, *"Shattered Nerves": Doctors, Patients and Depression in Victorian England* (New York: Oxford University Press, 1991). See also the following anthologies: Andrew Scull, ed., *Madhouses, Mad-Doctors, and Madmen: The Social History of Psychiatry in the Victorian Era* (London: Athlone, 1981); W. F. Bynum, Roy Porter and Michael Sheperd, eds., *The Anatomy of Madness: Essays in the History of Psychiatry*, 2 vols. (London: Tavistock, 1985). On the history of asylums in the early nineteenth century, see Micheal Donnelly, *Managing the Mind: A Study of Medical Psychology in Early Nineteenth-Century Britain* (London: Tavistock, 1983).

4. Thomas Laqueur, *Making Sex: Body and Gender from the Greeks to Freud* (Cambridge, MA: Harvard University Press, 1990), 21.

5. Thomas Trotter produced his own medical analysis of society by doing precisely this kind of occupational typing; see *A View of the Nervous*

Temperament (London: Longman, 1807; reprint, New York: Arno, 1976), 37–53.

6. For an introduction to these concepts and their relevance for literature, see G. S. Rousseau's "Nerves, Spirits, and Fibres: Towards Defining the Origins of Sensibility," *Studies in the Eighteenth Century III*, ed. R. F. Brissenden and J. C. Eade (Canberra: Australian National University Press, 1976), 137–57.

7. I must admit, however, that after almost ten years of immersion in books on the nervous body, I have begun to wonder about this.

8. Edwin Clarke and L. S. Jacyna, *Nineteenth-Century Origins of Neuroscientific Concepts* (Berkeley: University of California Press, 1988), 4.

9. Helen King has challenged the idea that hysteria exists as a disease concept in the Hippocratic texts; see "Once Upon a Text: Hysteria from Hippocrates," in Sander L. Gilman, Helen King, Roy Porter, George Rousseau, and Elaine Showalter, *Hysteria Beyond Freud* (Berkeley: University of California Press, 1993), 3–89.

10. "On the Psychical Mechanism of Hysterical Phenomena: Preliminary Communication" was first published in 1893 and then included as the opening chapter of *Studies on Hysteria* in 1895. See Josef Breuer and Sigmund Freud, *Studies on Hysteria*, trans. James Strachey (New York: Basic Books, 1957).

11. Mark S. Micale describes the redistribution of previously hysterical symptoms into new clinical categories in *Approaching Hysteria: Disease and Its Interpretations* (Princeton, NJ: Princeton University Press, 1995), 292. See also Steven E. Hyler and Robert L. Spitzer, "Hysteria Split Asunder," *American Journal of Psychiatry* 135, no. 12 (December 1978): 1500–4.

12. Micale discusses the impossibility, in this day, of even attempting a positivist intellectual history of hysteria, calling its ontological status a "convenient fiction" (*Approaching Hysteria*, 115).

13. I am grateful to Jack Pressman for bringing this anomaly to my attention in a conversation in 1989. For an analysis of hysteria's disappearance as a diagnostic category, see Phillip R. Slavney, *Perspectives on "Hysteria"* (Baltimore: Johns Hopkins University Press, 1990).

14. Mary Jacobus, *Reading Woman: Essays in Feminist Criticism* (New York: Columbia University Press, 1986), 29. I use the American theorist Jacobus's *Reading Woman* as exemplary, but see also the French theorists Hélène Cixous, "Castration or Decapitation?" *Signs* 7 (1981): 36–55; Luce Irigaray, *Speculum of the Other Woman*, trans. Gillian C. Gill (Ithaca: Cornell University Press, 1985); and Julia Kristeva, "Oscillation Between Power and Denial," *New French Feminisms*, ed. Elaine Marks and Isabelle de Courtivron (New York: Schocker, 1981), 165–67. In an article critical of this body of literary criticism ("On Hysterical Narrative," *Narrative* 1 [1993]: 24–35), Elaine Showalter reviews the major theorists, French and American, and argues that the concept of "hysterical narrative has become the waste-basket term of literary criticism" ("Hysterical Narrative," 24) because of the broadness of its associations between hysteria, woman, and the failure of narrative. For an intellectual history of psychoanalytic feminism, see Martha Noel Evans,

Fits and Starts: A Genealogy of Hysteria in Modern France (Ithaca, NY: Cornell University Press, 1991). Claire Kahane, in a nuanced study of the New Woman novels and the problematics of subject position in literature of the late nineteenth century, proposes a new approace to the definition of the hysterical voice: *Passions of the Voice; Hysteria Narrative, and the Figure of the Speaking Woman, 1850–1915* (Baltimore: Johns Hopkins University Press, 1995).

15. Feminist psychoanalytic criticism has opened up new possibilities for interpretation that were simply unthinkable before. A recent example of the innovative consequences it has had in contributing to our understanding of noncanonical woman writers within the late Georgian period is Eleanor Ty's *Unsex'd Revolutionaries: Five Women Novelists of the 1790s* (Toronto: University of Toronto Press, 1993), which combines an attention to historical detail with a Lacanian feminist approach to hysteria.

16. The most comprehensive study of the various threads that Freud drew on is Henri F. Ellenberger's *The Discovery of the Unconscious: The History and Evolution of Dynamic Psychiatry* (New York: Basic Books, 1970).

17. See Ellenberger, *Discovery of the Unconscious,* 474–80.

18. Veith, *Hysteria.*

19. John E. Toews has written on Foucault's cultural critique of psychoanalysis in the 1960s and 1970s; see "Foucault and the Freudian Subject: Archaeology, Genealogy, and the Historicization of Psychoanalysis," in *Foucault and the Writing of History,* ed. Jan Goldstein (Cambridge, MA: Basil Blackwell, 1994), 116–34. Mark S. Micale has an extended discussion of "Freudocentrism" in his chapter on hysteria historiography, "Theorizing Disease Historiography," *Approaching Hysteria,* 108–75.

20. For an extended discussion of this concept, including a review of the grab bag of symptoms, see Micale, *Approaching Hysteria,* 108–75.

21. See Roger Chartier, *Cultural History: Between Practices and Representations,* trans. Lydia G. Cochrane (Ithaca, NY: Cornell University Press, 1988). For recent examples of this practice, see also Jan Goldstein's *Console and Classify: The French Psychiatric Profession in the Nineteenth-Century* (Cambridge: Cambridge University Press, 1987), and two important anthologies: *Foucault and the Writing of History,* ed. Jan Goldstein (Cambridge, MA: Basil Blackwell, 1994); and *Framing Disease: Studies in Cultural History,* ed. Charles E. Rosenberg and Janet Golden (New Brunswick, NJ: Rutgers University Press, 1992).

22. Gillian Beer, in her introduction to *Darwin's Plots: Evolutionary Narrative in Darwin, George Eliot and Nineteenth-Century Fiction* (London: Routledge, 1983), is the first critic I ever encountered who used this model, and I have never forgotten it.

CHAPTER ONE

1. His collected poems are in *Sea Weeds: Poems, Written on Various Occasions, Chiefly During a Naval Life* (London: Longman; Edinburgh: D. Lizars, 1829). Trotter also published another book of poems, *Suspiria Oceani* (London:

Hatchard, 1800), and a five-act tragedy, *The Noble Foundling; or, The Hermit of the Tweed* (1812). The introduction to *Sea Weeds* contains his most important autobiographical material. The principal biographical essays on Trotter are Humphry Rolleston, "Thomas Trotter, M.D.," in *Contributions to Medical and Biological Research Dedicated to Sir William Osler in Honour of His Seventieth Birthday, July 12, 1919, by His Pupils and Co-Workers* (New York: Hoeber, 1919), 1:153–65; Ian Alexander Porter, "Thomas Trotter, M.D., Naval Physician," *Medical History* 7 (1963): 155–64; and Christopher Lloyd's brief introduction to *The Health of Seamen: Selections from the Works of Dr. James Lind, Sir Gilbert Blane and Dr. Thomas Trotter* (London: Navy Records Society, 1965). Roy Porter discusses Trotter's life and work in two detailed articles: his introduction to Trotter's *An Essay, Medical, Philosophical, and Chemical, on Drunkenness, and its Effects on the Human Body* (1804; reprint, London: Routledge, 1988), ix–xl; and "Addicted to Modernity: Nervousness in the Early Consumer Society," in *Culture in History: Production, Consumption and Values in Historical Perspective*, ed. Joseph Melling and Jonathan Barry (Exeter: Exeter University Press, 1992), 180–94.

2. Trotter's other writings are: *Observations on the Scurvy* (Edinburgh: Elliot, 1786); *Medical and Chemical Essays, Containing Additional Observations on Scurvy* (1795); *Medicina Nautica*, 3 vols. (London: Cadell, 1797–1803); *An Essay, Medical, Philosophical, and Chemical, on Drunkenness and its Effects on the Human Body* (London: Longman, 1804); *A Proposal for Destroying the Fire and Choak-Damps of Coal Mines . . . Addressed to the Agents and Owners of Coal Works* (Newcastle: J. Mitchell, 1805); *A Second Address to the Owners and Agents of Coal Mines on Destroying the Fire and Choak Damp* (1806).

3. Thomas Trotter, *A View of the Nervous Temperament* (London: Longman, 1807; reprint, New York: Arno, 1976). Parenthetical references to this edition are abbreviated *NT*.

4. On the phenomenon of sensibility in literature, see: Janet Todd, *Sensibility: An Introduction* (London: Meuthuen, 1986); John Mullan, *Sentiment and Sociability: The Language of Feeling in the Eighteenth Century* (Oxford: Oxford University Press, 1988); and F. J. Barker-Benfield, *The Culture of Sensibility: Sex and Society in Eighteenth-Century Britain* (Chicago: University of Chicago Press, 1992).

5. On the influence of Trotter's book, see Roy Porter, "Addicted to Modernity," and Porter's *Mind-Forg'd Manacles: A History of Madness in England from the Restoration to the Regency* (Cambridge, MA: Harvard University Press, 1987), 182; Bynum, "The Nervous Patient," 92–94; and Richard Hunter and Ida Macalpine, *Three Hundred Years of Psychiatry, 1535–1860: A History Presented in Selected English Texts* (London: Oxford University Press, 1963), 588.

6. The term "hypochondriasis" was introduced by G. Smollius in 1610, who attributed hysteria-like behaviors in males to a disorder of the hypochondrium. The eighteenth-century view of hypochondria is summarized in the concise and useful book by John Hill, *Hyponchondriasis: A Practical Treatise*, intro. G. S. Rousseau (1766; reprint, Los Angeles: William Andrews

Clark Memorial Library, 1969). On the invention of hypochondria and the history of attempts to differentiate male and female hysteria, see Micale, *Approaching Hysteria*, 161–68 and passim; and Veith, *Hysteria*, 137–47, in which Veith discusses the early work of Thomas Sydenham (1624–1689), whose approach to hysteria marked the shift in historical thinking about the concept, away from an affliction of the body to one of the mind. See also R. Porter's discussion, *Mind-Forg'd Manacles*, 48–50.

7. The modern, narrow definition of the hypochondriac as a person having a morbid preoccupation with his or her own health was popularized in 1822 by Jean Pierre Falret.

8. For the intellectual history of Lacan's most famous formulation and its post-Lacanian evolution, see Evans, *Fits and Starts*.

9. Elaine Showalter discusses the association of hysteria with aphasia in psychoanalytic feminist literary criticism; see "On Hysterical Narrative."

10. The pronounced interest in hysteria and its history from the different fields of clinical psychology and psychoanalysis within the health sciences, and from intellectual history, history of medicine, legal history, women's studies, psychoanalytic studies, and literary theory within the humanities, contributes to a definable corpus of texts that Mark S. Micale terms "the new hysteria studies" (*Approaching Hysteria*, 3). His overview of the differences between the distinct disciplinary assumptions and his review of the strengths and weaknesses of the major existing histories of hysteria are much-needed starting points for new work.

11. *The Works of Robert Whytt, M.D.* (Edinburgh, 1768; reprint, Classics of Neurology and Neurosurgery Library, Birmingham, AL: Leslie B. Adams, 1984), 537.

12. William Cullen, *First Lines of the Practice of Physic* (Edinburgh, 1778–84), 2:121.

13. Richardson was also Cheyne's printer, and he printed *The English Malady*. For Cheyne's correspondence with Richardson, see *The Letters of Dr. George Cheyne to Samuel Richardson (1733–1743)*, ed. Charles F. Mullett (Columbia: University of Missouri, 1934). On the influence of Cheyne's theories on Richardson's work, see Raymond Stephanson, "Richardson's 'Nerves': The Physiology of Sensibility in *Clarissa*," *Journal of the History of Ideas* 44 (1988): 267–86. On *The English Malady*, see R. Porter, *Mind-Forg'd Manacles*, 81–89.

14. George Cheyne, *The English Malady* (London, 1733; Delmar, NY: Scholar's Facsimile, 1976). Cheyne's ideas are indebted to Sydenham; see Veith, *Hysteria*, 140–46.

15. This class distinction has a long history in theories of madness. In the Renaissance, melancholia—associated with both despair and artistic inspiration—was the exclusive province of the aristocracy, and Cheyne inherits this tradition. On melancholia in the Renaissance, see Michael MacDonald, *Mystical Bedlam: Madness, Anxiety and Healing in Seventeenth-Century England* (Cambridge: Cambridge University Press, 1981), 150–64.

16. James Boswell, for example, titled his essays, written from 1777 to

1783, "The Hypochondriack" as part of this fad, although Samuel Johnson considered it dangerous. For a discussion of the historical meanings associated with the word "nerves," see Bynum, "Nervous Patient."

17. Trotter's text is a prime example of what Michel Foucault calls the "bourgeois transposition of themes of the nobility" onto the newly sensitized body of the middle class; see his discussion of the class descent of nerves in *The History of Sexuality: Volume I*, trans. Robert Hurley (New York: Vintage, 1980), 122–27.

18. Trotter refers to Thomas Sydenham's frequently cited estimate, in 1666, that fever then constituted two-thirds of all disease.

19. Guenter Risse shows that nervous conditions among the lower class were commonly accepted in clinical practice of the late eighteenth century, in "Hysteria at the Edinburgh Infirmary: The Construction and Treatment of a Disease, 1770–1800," *Medical History* 32 (1988): 1–22. As Veith points out, Benjamin Rush made the same democratic claim in the United States as early as 1774 (*Hysteria*, 174).

20. Trotter attributes virtually every case of nerves in lower-class bodies to drunkenness. See his description of working-class conditions (*NT*, 46–49). See also his earlier *Essay on Drunkenness*.

21. Robert Burton, *The Anatomy of Melancholy*, ed. Holbrook Jackson, 3 vols. (London: Everyman's Library, 1968), 1:397.

22. On women and nervous disorders, Veith's *Hysteria* remains the fundamental text. But see Goldstein's important analysis of hysteria and the medical profession in chapter 9 of her *Console and Classify*. See also Foucault's discussion of sensibility in *Madness and Civilization: A History of Insanity in the Age of Reason*, trans. Richard Howard (New York: Vintage, 1965), 150–58, where he notes how the female body in medical literature of the period "is riddled by obscure but strangely direct paths of sympathy . . . from one extreme of its organic space to the other, it encloses a perpetual possibility of hysteria" (153–54).

23. In his discussion of nervous theories in relation to Romantic poetry and the novel, Philip W. Martin also points out Trotter's concept of female contagion in his *Mad Women in Romantic Writing* (New York: St. Martin's, 1987), 32–33.

24. Alexander Pope's "Epistle to a Lady" is a prime illustration of Enlightenment ideology on the changeability of women. Katharine M. Rogers points out that Pope's statement was reproduced by male conduct book writers of the late century; see "The Contribution of Mary Hays," *Prose Studies* 10 (1987): 134–35.

25. Gibbon discusses Tacitus in chapter 9 of *The Decline and Fall of the Roman Empire*. J.G.A. Pocock has a remarkable analysis of Gibbon's Tacitus; see *Virtue, Commerce, and History: Essays on Political Thought and History, Chiefly in the Eighteenth Century* (Cambridge: Cambridge University Press, 1985), 116–19, 143–56.

26. Pocock discusses the deployment of this historical narrative in other writing of the period in *Virtue*, 114–18.

27. On the role of social sympathy in philosophy, see Mullan, *Sentiment and Sociability.*

28. The concept of these two distinct levels of functioning is common in Romantic culture. William Godwin, for example, bases his philosophy on the distinction between "primary" pleasures, stemming from external sensations, and the more exquisite "secondary" pleasures that come from internal sensations, such as "intellectual feeling," "sympathy," and "self-approbation." See the first principle in the Summary of Principles that introduces Godwin's *Enquiry Concerning Political Justice: And Its Influence on Modern Morals and Happiness* (New York: Penguin, 1985), 75. All subsequent references in this edition are abbreviated *PJ.*

29. *Madness and Civilization*, 155–57.

30. On the importance of the national debt in eighteenth-century England, see John Brewer, *The Sinews of Power: War, Money and the English State, 1688–1783* (London: Unwin Hyman, 1989), 114–34. On the history of public credit in England, see P.G.M. Dickson, *The Financial Revolution in England: A Study in the Development of Public Credit* (New York: St. Martin's, 1967).

31. In *Virtue.* On the relationship between passion and the stock market, see Albert Hirschman, *The Passions and the Interests* (Princeton, NJ: Princeton University Press, 1976).

32. See Pocock, *Virtue*, 110–13, 122–23; and see also his earlier study, *The Machiavellian Moment: Florentine Political Thought and the Atlantic Republican Tradition* (Princeton, NJ: Princeton University Press, 1975), 432–35.

33. For biographical sources, see chapter 1, n. 1.

34. On medical education and professional organization in the early nineteenth century, see Ivan Waddington, *The Medical Profession in the Industrial Revolution* (Dublin: Gill, 1984), chapters 1–2.

35. Trotter's improvements included the regular provisioning of fresh citrus fruits to fight scurvy, mass smallpox inoculations (giving Edward Jenner his first public recognition), and closing 200 "ginshops" catering to sailors in Plymouth.

36. Despite his rhetoric of principled independence, Trotter was not always above adjusting his views to avoid offending powerful interests. His warnings against the effects of bad air and inadequate ventilation, for example, do not apply to the conditions within coal mines; he does not find "that the pitmen in the coal-mines of this district are liable to any particular diseases" (*NT*, 47). Given his extended writings on the need for ventilation in ships' holds, this position is a singular anomaly that can only be explained by reference to Trotter's residence in Newcastle, the center of Britain's coal industry, at the time. He was trying to establish a private practice and probably wished to avoid antagonizing local industrialists.

37. This was a period of mounting pressure for reform in the medical profession, and complaints by "outsiders" such as Trotter are frequent. See, for example, *Hygeia*, 3 vols. (Bristol: Mills, 1802–3), by Trotter's radical contemporary and acquaintance, Thomas Beddoes. Roy Porter discusses Beddoes and professional reform in *Doctor of Society: Thomas Beddoes and*

the Sick Trade in Late-Enlightenment England (London: Routledge, 1992), 37–53, 140–50.

38. On the practitioner/patient relationship and the system of patronage within the medical profession, see N. D. Jewson, "Medical Knowledge and the Patronage System in Eighteenth-Century England," *Sociology* 8 (1974): 369–85, and see Waddington, *Medical Profession,* 176–205.

39. The system of patronage in the practitioner/patient relationship was a characteristic of most professions at this stage. E. J. Hobsbawm, for example, refers to the professions at the turn of the century as "parasites of rural aristocratic society . . . traditional, somnolent, corrupt and . . . increasingly reactionary," in *Industry and Empire,* The Pelican Economic History of Britain, vol. 3 (New York: Pelican, 1968), 81.

40. See Waddington, *Medical Profession,* 7–28.

41. Emphasis original.

42. On monomania and hysteria, see Goldstein, *Console and Classify,* 152–96, 322–77. Freud's redefinition of the neuroses certainly had a similar effect, bringing marginal disorders that previously would not have required the treatment of the professional into the medical realm.

43. William Wordsworth, "Essay, Supplementary to the Preface" (1815).

CHAPTER TWO

1. William Godwin, *Caleb Williams,* ed. David McCracken (New York: Norton, 1977), 313. Subsequent references to this edition are abbreviated *CW.*

2. There has been a large body of recent work done on literature and nineteenth-century nervous theory. On nerves and the sensation novel, see Sally Shuttleworth, "'Preaching to the Nerves': Psychological Disorder in Sensation Fiction," in *A Question of Identity: Women, Science, and Literature,* ed. Marina Benjamin (New Brunswick, NJ: Rutgers University Press, 1993), 192–222. See also Shuttleworth's discussion of mid-Victorian nervous psychology in relation to George Eliot's *Villette,* "'The Surveillance of a Sleepless Eye': The Constitution of Neurosis in *Villette,*" in *One Culture: Essays in Science and Literature,* ed. George Levine (Madison: University of Wisconsin Press, 1987), 313–35. On the same topic, see Athena Vrettos, "From Neurosis to Narrative: The Private Life of the Nerves," in *Somatic Fictions: Imagining Illness in Victorian Culture* (Stanford: Stanford University Press, 1995), 48–180. And see D. A. Miller, "*Cage aux folles:* Sensation and Gender in Wilkie Collins's *The Woman in White,*" in *The Novel and the Police* (Berkeley: University of California Press, 1988), 146–91. Ekbert Faas outlines the influence of nineteenth-century psychological medicine on the dramatic monologue in *Retreat into the Mind: Victorian Poetry and the Rise of Psychiatry* (Princeton: Princeton University Press, 1988). For a discussion of nervous theories in relation to Romantic poetry and the novel, see Philip W. Martin, *Mad Women in Romantic Writing* (New York: St. Martin's, 1987). Janet Beizer discusses nineteenth-century theories of hysteria and French literature in *Ventriloquized Bodies: Narratives of Hysteria in Nineteenth-Century France* (Ithaca, NY: Cornell University Press, 1994). Tom Lutz discusses the Ameri-

can context in *American Nervousness, 1903: An Anecdotal History* (Ithaca, NY: Cornell University Press, 1991).

3. On the penitentiary, see Michael Ignatieff, *A Just Measure of Pain: The Penitentiary in the Industrial Revolution, 1750–1850* (London: Penguin, 1978); and see Michel Foucault, *Discipline and Punish: The Birth of the Prison*, trans. Alan Sheridan (New York: Vintage, 1979). In *Imagining the Penitentiary: Fiction and the Architecture of Mind in Eighteenth-Century England* (Chicago: University of Chicago Press, 1987), John Bender has a detailed critique of the narrative organization of this new penitentiary space and relates it to developments in the novel, which made such structures imaginable. David J. Rothman's *The Discovery of the Asylum: Social Order and Disorder in the New Republic* (Boston: Little, Brown, 1971), though a U.S. social history, is particularly useful for students of the British experience because it broadens the issue to encompass all the institutional forms this utopian impulse took.

4. On the York Retreat, see Ann Digby's full-length study *Madness, Morality and Medicine: A Study of the York Retreat, 1796–1914* (New York: Cambridge Univ. Press, 1985). On the related issue of "moral therapy" in France, see Goldstein, *Console and Classify*, 64–119.

5. On Howard, see Ignatieff, *A Just Measure of Pain*, 47–59; Ignatieff also discusses Godwin's attack on Howard's ideas, 117–18.

6. Janet Todd provides a succinct discussion of the range of political meanings given to sensibility during the period, in *Sensibility*, 10–14, 129–46. Trotter's political beliefs are most evident in his poetry, much of it a "King and Country" response to the French Revolution; see *Sea Weeds*.

7. *PJ*, 775. The Penguin edition is based on the third and final revision of *Political Justice*, published in 1798. For a useful discussion of the changes Godwin made between the first and third editions, see chapter 7 in Peter H. Marshall, *William Godwin* (New Haven: Yale University Press, 1984).

8. *Fleetwood: Or the New Man of Feeling*, Standard Novels, No. 22 (London: Bentley, 1832; reprint, New York: AMS, 1975), xi. Godwin described his composition of *Caleb Williams* in his 1832 preface to *Fleetwood*, from which this and subsequent quotations are taken. The preface is also reprinted as Appendix 2 in McCracken's edition of *Caleb Williams*.

9. Although not viewing it as a form of writing, Marilyn Butler nonetheless shares this view, arguing that Godwin was mainly interested in "the factors that shape" Caleb and Falkland, who are "not individuals but stereotypes" ("Godwin, Burke, and Caleb Williams," *Essays in Criticism* 32 [1982]: 245).

10. Thomas Malthus answers Godwin's ideas on reproduction and longevity in *An Essay on the Principle of Population* (1798).

11. I refer here to Mary Wollstonecraft's identification of woman with reproduction in the *Vindication of the Rights of Woman*, ed. Miriam Brody (New York: Penguin, 1985), not to some categorical association. See my discussion of this issue in chapter 3.

12. As McCracken points out in his Note on the Text, the word "chest" is used throughout the first edition of the novel (*CW*, xxv). Godwin changes it to "trunk" in the second edition, but both words maintain the metaphor

with the body. As I discuss later, it is only at the story's conclusion that Caleb finally reveals what he thinks was in his master's chest.

13. Thus Godwin's novelistic characters resist melodramatic simplification; even tyrants like Squire Tyrell behave within the dictates of their situation and so must also be seen as victims.

14. For an explanation of the evolution in Godwin's thought on the best way to effect social reform, concluding with his belief in small group discussions, see Marshall, *Godwin*, 113–15.

15. On the relationship between rational speech and Godwin's philosophy, see McCracken's discussion of the "plain-spoken tale" in his introduction to the novel, xvii–xx. The mistrust of rhetorical forms Godwin displays, and his insistence on a nonrhetorical form of truth-telling, is closely related to the conventional distrust of eloquent speech in sentimental literature; see G. A. Starr's discussion of eloquence and sentimentality, "'Only a Boy': Notes on Sentimental Novels," *Genre* 10 (1977): 501–27. Tilottama Rajan's discussion of the interpretive issues at stake in Godwin's use of plain speaking is directly relevant here, particularly her insight into the revised trial scene and its effect on the project of the reader; see her "Wollstonecraft and Godwin: Reading the Secrets of the Political Novel," *Studies in Romanticism* 27 (1988): 221–51.

16. On free will, see *PJ*, bk. 4, chapter 7.

17. D. Gilbert Dumas discovered the manuscript ending in 1966; see his "Things as They Were: The Original Ending of Caleb Williams," *SEL: Studies in English Literature, 1500–1900* 6 (1966): 575–97. Mitzi Myers added further details, finalizing the actual dates of composition for the printed ending; see "Godwin's Changing Conception of *Caleb Williams*," *SEL: Studies in English Literature, 1500–1900* 12 (1972): 591–628. The two essays define the opposite basic positions that continue to dominate the controversy over the ending of *Caleb Williams*. Dumas argues that the printed ending is inconsistent with the narrative that leads up to it and prefers the original ending. Myers, responding directly to Dumas, prefers the moral complexity of the revised ending and makes the case for serious inconsistencies in the original version that the revised ending reconciles.

18. Many critics assume he is inside a prison, but the presence of the nurse and Caleb's treatment suggest that Godwin is describing an eighteenth-century private madhouse.

19. Godwin tells us that he wrote the novel in reverse order; see *Fleetwood*, xii–ix.

20. The force of this dialectic is most evident in the reviews of Thomas De Quincey's *Confessions* that criticized it for enticing more people to try opium than to avoid the dangers he so eloquently warns against.

21. Gary Kelly, *The English Jacobin Novel, 1780–1805* (Oxford: Clarendon Press, 1976), 197–98. I use Kelly's formulation here as a prominent example of the prevailing attitude toward the original ending. In a more general sense, however, I need to acknowledge an indebtedness to Kelly's work and its many insights into the novels of the period.

22. See Tilottama Rajan's analysis of the "moral" and "tendency" in God-

win's literary theory, which I rely on here: "Wollstonecraft and Godwin," 167–70.

23. Gary Handwerk, in his analysis of this scene ("Of Caleb's Guilt and Godwin's Truth: Ideology and Ethics in Caleb Williams," *ELH* 60 [1993]: 939–60), provides an engaging analysis of problems in Caleb's subject position, but I disagree with his assessment that Caleb's narrative succeeds because it displays "magnanimity towards his tormentor" (p. 946).

24. Karl N. Simms, in analyzing the trope of writing in the novel, comes to a similar conclusion about the enigmatic narrative in the trunk ("Caleb Williams' Godwin: Things as They Are Written," *Studies in Romanticism* 26 [987]: 343–63). Simms notes how "truth . . . is contained not as an absolute, but as another writing, a pre-text the existence of which is only conjectural" (357–58), and he also shows how Caleb "becomes a narrative himself," one that "is the effect of which it is the cause" (p. 347).

CHAPTER THREE

1. Mary Hays, *Memoirs of Emma Courtney* (London, 1796; reprint, with an introduction by Gina Luria, New York: Garland, 1974), 1:2. Subsequent references to this two-volume facsimile edition are abbreviated *EC*.

2. Standard works on Hays are few. The main biographical sources are the two volumes of her correspondence, *The Love-Letters of Mary Hays (1779–1780)*, ed. A. F. Wedd (London: Methuen, 1925), and *Letters and Essays, Moral and Miscellaneous*, with an introduction by Gina Luria (New York: Garland, 1974). See also Gina Luria's "Mary Hays's Letters and Manuscripts," *Signs* 3 (1977): 524–30. And see Eliza Fenwick, *The Fate of the Fenwicks: Letters to Mary Hays (1798–1828)*, ed. A. F. Wedd (London: Methuen, 1927). For a reprint of her feminist philosophy, see Mary Hays, *Appeal to the Men of Great Britain in Behalf of Women*, with an introduction by Gina Luria (New York: Garland, 1974).

3. Rogers, "The Contribution of Mary Hays." On Hays's feminism, see also B. K. Pollin, "Mary Hays on Woman's Rights in the *Monthly Magazine*," *Etudes Anglaises* 24 (1971): 271–82.

4. The body of criticism on Hays is small but of high quality. There are two important earlier critical essays: J.M.S. Tompkins, "Mary Hays, Philosophess," in *The Polite Marriage* (Cambridge: Cambridge University Press, 1938), 150–90; and M. Ray Adams, "Mary Hays, Disciple of William Godwin," *PMLA* 55 (1940): 472–83. More recently, see Janet Todd, "'The Unsex'd Females': Mary Wollstonecraft and Mary Hays," in *The Sign of Angellica: Women, Writing and Fiction, 1660–1800* (New York: Columbia University Press, 1989), 236–52; Eleanor Ty, "Breaking the 'Magic Circle': From Repression to Effusion in *Memoirs of Emma Courtney*," in *Unsex'd Revolutionaries*, 46–59; Tillotama Rajan, "Autonarration and Genotext in Mary Hays's *Memoirs of Emma Courtney*," *Studies in Romanticism* 32 (1993): 149–76; and Nicola Watson, *Revolution and the Form of the British Novel, 1790–1825: Intercepted Letters, Interrupted Seductions* (Oxford: Clarendon Press, 1994), 39–49.

5. See Adams, "Mary Hays, Disciple." James R. Foster said it in such a way as to elide both Hays and Wollstonecraft simultaneously—"Mary Hays, the most faithful disciple of the Godwins"—in *History of the Pre-Romantic Novel in England*, Monograph Series of the Modern Language Association of America, vol. 12 (New York: MLA, 1949), 259. In fairness, Adams was one of the few critics of the day to take Hays's writing seriously. Adams is also sympathetic to Hays, calling her a "free-born spirit" in an oppressive age (483) and hence especially admirable for her lifelong commitment to the unpopular ideas she espoused. Published in 1940, this assessment seems particularly relevant to the year.

6. She also quotes from Helvetius, Wollstonecraft, Holcroft, Rousseau, Aiken, and Madame de Genlis.

7. This mixing of text and life, and how it constructs the real within the reader through desire, is taken up by Rajan in "Autonarration and Genotext."

8. This shocking proposal, which apparently had an autobiographical basis, led to a caricature of Hays herself as an unattractive philosophical radical hopelessly pursuing men with no interest in her. Hays is caricatured as the man-chasing Bridgetina Botherim in Elizabeth Hamilton's *Memoirs of Modern Philosophers* (1800) and also is ridiculed in Charles Lloyd's *Edmund Oliver* (1798). Maria Edgeworth's "Angelina," in her *Moral Tales* (1801), is a commentary on Hays's style of novel writing; see Marilyn Butler, *Maria Edgeworth: A Literary Biography* (Oxford: Oxford University Press, 1972), 161.

9. Mary Wollstonecraft makes a related point on relations within marriage by encouraging women to be self-reliant and make themselves "respectable," regardless of their husband's attention or lack of attention; see *Vindication of the Rights of Woman*, 111. Emma's later self-reliant behavior during her marriage to the jealous Montague directly embodies this idea.

10. In trying to bend the ideology of sentiment to the purpose of a rational feminism, both writers inevitably ended up "creating unstable stories that proclaimed and castigated women's particular sensibility, the emotional vulnerability of the superior feeling heart that twists and turns to irritate and wound itself" (*Sign of Angellica*, 238). Such insights are the beginning point for much subsequent criticism of the novel. Watson and Ty, as well as the present writer, all use this basic instability between the competing appeals to reason and passion as the starting point for modern discussion. As the exchange between Mr. Francis and Emma illustrates, the novel is also an interrogation of that self-violence, and that interrogation continues on into the framing voice.

11. The quote is taken from Madame de Genlis's gothic romance, *Tales of the Castle*.

12. See Ty's useful discussion of Emma's reading, in *Unsex'd Revolutionaries*, 52–53.

13. In his analysis of love at first sight, Alexander Crichton describes a physiological psychology that squares perfectly with Mary Hays's argument on sexuality; see *An Inquiry into the Nature and Origin of Mental Derangement*

(London: Cadell and Davies,1798; reprint, with an introduction by Robert Ellenbogen [2 vols. in 1], New York: AMS Press, 1976), 2:312–14.

14. As Rogers points out, Hays's feminism did not go as far as Wollstonecraft's in challenging sentimental ideology, and so the early moments of the marriage with Montague and the birth of the child read like an endorsement of the new domestic role.

15. Watson, *Revolution and the Form of the British Novel*, 45. Watson's is one of the best recent critical essays on the novel, but neither she nor Ty, in another high-level engagement, extends the analysis to the frame. Todd also tends to underestimate the ideological work of the frame. She is astute at identifying the same problems at work within the inner narrative, however, and my focus on self-violence is an attempt to extend those insights beyond the inner story. Rajan is the only critic I have encountered who actively engages the frame, but she also figuratively elides it by eliminating the difference between narrating past and present; she sees the narrative as operating within an eternal present, the moment of narration. I obviously agree with Rajan that the past is erupting into "the unresolved present" ("Autonarration and Genotext," 153), but I disagree on the consequence of this eruption. In a general sense, Rajan (as well as Watson) interprets physicality as immediacy, so that feeling comes at the expense of history. But in the nervous body, feeling is history, and that's the problem with it. It is when the narrator recognizes feeling as history that its cultural constructedness comes into view. Because the frame is where that historicity is most overt, my analysis emphasizes that element.

16. See Todd's comment that both Wollstonecraft and Hays "understood the imprisoning cultural construction of female sensibility" (*Sign of Angellica*, 237).

17. See Mary Poovey, *The Proper Lady and the Woman Writer* (Chicago: University of Chicago Press, 1984), 71–81.

18. Wollstonecraft's most dramatic image of the heroic mother appears at the conclusion of chapter 3 (*Vindication*, 138–39).

19. See Rajan's distinct analysis of this relationship in "Autonarration and Genotext," 153.

CHAPTER FOUR

1. References to the 1822 version of the *Confessions* are to *Confessions of an English Opium-Eater*, ed. Alethea Hayter (New York: Penguin, 1971), hereafter abbreviated as *OE*. References to the appendix are to *The Collected Writings of Thomas De Quincey*, ed. David Masson, 14 vols. (Edinburgh: Adam and Charles Black, 1889–90), 3:466–72.

2. The *British Critic* thought the work was a product of his opium use (Review of *Confessions of an English Opium-Eater*, by Thomas De Quincey, *British Critic* ns 18 [1822]: 531–34). For an overview of the contemporary reviews, see John O. Hayden, "De Quincey's Confessions and the Reviewers," *Wordsworth Circle* 6 (1975): 273–79.

3. This body of criticism is discussed in Alethea Hayter, *Opium and the Romantic Imagination: Addiction and Creativity in De Quincey, Coleridge, Baudelaire and Others* (Wellingborough, England: Crucible, 1988), 11–14. A more recent study that appeared too late for me to incorporate into my discussion is very promising; see Alina Clej, *A Geneology of the Modern Self: Thomas De Quincey and the Intoxication of Writing* (Stanford: Stanford University Press, 1995).

4. M. H. Abrams, *The Milk of Paradise: The Effect of Opium Visions on the Works of De Quincey, Crabbe, Francis Thompson, and Coleridge* (New York: Octagon Books, 1971); Elisabeth Schneider, *Coleridge, Opium and "Kubla Khan"* (Chicago: University of Chicago Press, 1953); Hayter, *Opium and the Romantic Imagination*.

5. Virginia Berridge and Griffith Edwards, *Opium and the People: Opiate Use in Nineteenth-Century England* (New Haven: Yale University Press, 1987), 37.

6. For a brief period in the late eighteenth and early nineteenth century, several entrepreneurs tried to grow opium commercially in Britain. On opium cultivation in Britain and on its widespread usage in the Fens, where growing conditions were optimal, see Berridge and Edwards, *Opium and the People*, 38–48.

7. Quoted in ibid., xxiv.

8. John Brown, *Elements of Medicine*, trans. Thomas Beddoes, 2 vols. (Portsmouth, NH: 1804), 1:244. On Brown's medical theory see Guenter B. Risse, "Brunonian Therapeutics: New Wine in Old Bottles?" *Medical History*, Supplement 8 (1988): 46–62. De Quincey, in his early years, subscribed to the Brunonian doctrine of excitability. He was also acquainted with the physician Thomas Beddoes, the leading disciple of Brown in the Romantic period and a member of Coleridge's circle. Beddoes was married to a sister of Maria Edgeworth and was the father of the poet Thomas Lovell Beddoes.

9. Berridge and Edwards. *Opium and the People*, 36; Terry M. Parssinen, *Secret Passions, Secret Remedies: Narcotic Drugs in British Society: 1820–1930* (Philadelphia: ISHI, 1983), 8; Hayden, "De Quincey's *Confessions*," 275.

10. See Parssinen, *Secret Passions*, 46, and Berridge and Edwards, *Opium and the People*, 105–9.

11. See Parssinen, *Secret Passions*, 69.

12. Ibid., 70–111.

13. John Tinnon Taylor mentions that patent medicines were sold in circulating libraries; see *Early Opposition to the English Novel* (New York: King's Crown Press, 1943), 30. Richard Altick points out that bookstores frequently sold patent medicines; see *The English Common Reader: A Social History of the Mass Reading Public 1800–1900* (Chicago: University of Chicago Press, 1957), 57.

14. Review of *Confessions of an English Opium-Eater*, by Thomas De Quincey, *New Edinburgh Review* 4 (1823): 273.

15. Geoffrey Harding, *Opiate Addiction, Morality and Medicine: From Moral Illness to Pathological Disease* (New York: St. Martin's, 1988), 53.

16. See de Tott's description of a Turkish opium den (*Memoirs*, 1:160). This Eastern influence also found its way into early British medical writing on addiction, which was based on usage in Asia because it was rare among the English; see, for example, John Jones, *The Mysteries of Opium Reveal'd* (London: R. Smith, 1701), in which he argues that opium gave Turkish men the ability to perform sexually for the harem (p. 23).

17. Thomas Stamford Raffles, *The History of Java*, 2d ed., 2 vols. (London: Murray, 1830). Brian Inglis discusses the unique status of Raffles's moral objection and describes the response to it by the East India Company; see *The Opium War* (London: Hodder, 1976), 58–59.

18. Early nineteenth-century theories of mental structure are dominated by physiological psychology in both England and France. In this theory, all psychological functions are rooted in the material structures of the brain. Phrenology was an important consequence of this approach. See Goldstein, *Console and Classify.*

19. Two important implications of this model reappear in the colonial discourse and the nineteenth-century discourse on addiction. The first is the implication that Asians and/or opium users have surrendered themselves to pure sensual gratification; in this sense, what is being represented is the loss of the capacity for "restraint." Second, and particularly important in the British discourse on public health, is the sense that opium's primary social danger is a loss of the individual's capacity for self-making.

20. The fullest history of the trade and the events leading up to the Opium Wars is Inglis, *Opium Wars.*

21. Algernon S. Thelwall, *The Iniquities of the Opium Trade with China* (London: Allen, 1839), 1.

22. De Quincey, "The Opium and the China Question," *Blackwood's Edinburgh Magazine* 47 (1840): 717–38, 847–53; "War with China, and the Opium Question," *Blackwood's Edinburgh Magazine* 47 (1840): 368–84. The two essays are included in vol. 14 of *Writings*. For a useful discussion of the two essays, see John Barrell, *The Infection of Thomas De Quincey: A Psychopathology of Imperialism* (New Haven: Yale University Press, 1991), 147–56. De Quincey's oldest son died a year later in the same war.

23. De Quincey, "War with China" 369.

24. See Inglis, *Opium War*, 84–89, 126–30.

25. There were, of course, discussions on opium's qualities among the parties immediately concerned in the trade. The silence described here is the absence of any discussion of the trade within Britain itself.

26. See Grevel Lindop, *The Opium-Eater: A Life of Thomas De Quincey* (London: Dent, 1981), 3. De Quincey's full name is Thomas Penson De Quincey.

27. De Quincey describes this episode in the 1856 version of the *Confessions* (*Writings*, 3:312–13). See also Lindop, *Life*, 71–73, and Barrell, *Infection of De Quincey*, 150–51.

28. Lindop, *Life*, 109–10. De Quincey continued to receive this annuity derived from the opium trade for the next thirty-two years, although he was

disappointed in his hopes to inherit the bulk of Penson's estate on his death in 1835; see Lindop, *Life*, 320–21.

29. Quoted from the *Chinese Repository* in Thelwall, *Iniquities*, 22–23. Italics are original.

30. "Opiologia," review of *Confessions of an English Opium-Eater*, by Thomas De Quincey, *Medico-Chirurgical Review* 2 (1822): 887. "Opiologia" is a substantive review of the *Confessions* that directly disputes De Quincey's medical knowledge. See also the review of the *Confessions* in the *Medical Intelligencer* [London] 2 (1821): 613–15, which summarizes De Quincey's narrative as it if were a medical history; as a result, this review is an excellent introduction to the medical frame of reference within which De Quincey operates. De Quincey praises the *Medical Intelligencer* review in his "Letter to the Editor" of the *London Magazine* (*Writings*. 3:465 n. 1). See also the subsequent response to "Opiologia" in *Medical Intelligencer* [London] 3 (1822): 116–18.

31. Review of *Confessions of an English Opium-Eater*, *The Imperial Magazine* 5 (1823): 94.

32. In "Recollections of Charles Lamb," *Writings*, 3:34–92.

33. Ian Jack, "De Quincey Revises His Confessions," *PMLA* 72 (1957): 122.

34. This is an assumption that will be domesticated in public health descriptions of the British working class during the 1860s, mentioned above.

35. *OED*, s.v. "fascinate." These are the primary meanings given by *OED*, which points out that the sense of simple delight in something is a more recent construction. For De Quincey's sense, consider the fascination of the Ancient Mariner over his wedding guests. De Quincey used the term in this same sense in his other writing of the early 1820s. He describes the Roman consul who "*fascinated* the slave, as a rattlesnake does a bird" (*Writings*, 10:56), in his "Letters to a Young Man Whose Education Has Been Neglected," originally published in 1823.

36. As separate paradigms of addiction, these two forms persist throughout the nineteenth century under varying labels. They reappear, for example, in the 1890s as a theoretical distinction between "morphinism," or a simple physical dependency, and the craven enslavement of "morphiomania." See Parssinen, *Secret Passions*, 93–94.

37. *Writings*, 10:57. He contrasted the Romans with the more introspective Greeks in his "Letters to a Young Man." He uses the Roman Consul Marius to illustrate his point.

38. Hayter also recognizes this thematic correlation and shows it at work in "The English Mail Coach" and other essays; see *Opium and Romantic Imagination*, 250–54.

39. Mary Jacobus discusses De Quincey as the daughter and links his *Confessions* to prostitution; see *Romanticism, Writing and Sexual Difference: Essays on* The Prelude (Oxford: Clarendon Press, 1989), 223–30.

40. The importance of this relationship has frequently been overlooked by critics who believe that opium's physiological action enabled De Quincey's writing. Michael G. Cooke, for example, argues that "opium set De Quincey free to talk" ("De Quincey, Coleridge, and the Formal Uses of Intoxication," *Yale French Studies* 50 [1974]: 35).

41. De Quincey attached this story to the *Confessions* in his 1856 revision as the only remaining part of a planned group of dreams and stories meant to complete the work. It bears a formal parallel to the 1822 appendix, which substituted for an unwritten "Third Part" of the *Confessions*, in that both supplements stand for larger proposed but incomplete additions.

42. The phrase is borrowed from Karl Marx's explanation of commodity fetishism in *Capital*.

43. Dropsy is an abnormal saturation of tissues with fluid.

44. This is the only sentence of the conclusion to the *Confessions* that De Quincey deleted in his 1856 revision. Given the introduction of new technical discussions on opium's physical action and advice on how to liberate oneself, it was no longer true, and the humility was out of place.

45. De Quincey first outlined the difference between the literatures of power and knowledge in 1823 in his "Letters to a Young Man Whose Education Has Been Neglected" (*Writings*, 10:46–52). His later discussions are in two essays from 1848, "Oliver Goldsmith" (*Writings*, 4:288–320) and "The Poetry of Pope" (*Writings*, 11:51–95). D. D. Devlin provides an extended discussion of the evolution of De Quincey's thought on the matter in his *De Quincey, Wordsworth and the Art of Prose* (London: MacMillan, 1983), 76–121.

46. I refer to Hayter's popular Penguin edition. Hayter's decision to exclude the Appendix appears to lead to a misstatement in her "Note on the Text" (p. 25). She incorrectly claims to reproduce the periodical text of 1821, when in fact she uses the book text of 1822, as a comparison of her edition with Ian Jack's collation of the two makes apparent. The few differences between 1821 and 1822 are insignificant, as Hayter's own confusion demonstrates. The only textual rationale for claiming to use the periodical text over the slightly corrected book text would be to strengthen a bibliographical justification for treating the Appendix as a superfluity, as Hayter does.

47. The *Confessions* originally appeared in the September and October issues of the *London Magazine* (4 [1821]:293–312, 353–79). The two parts were then reprinted, along with the new Appendix, in book form by the magazine's publishers, Taylor and Hessey, in late 1822.

48. De Quincey's promise is in his "Letter to the Editor," published in the *London Magazine* in December 1821 (*Writings*, 3:464–66).

49. For an example of this complaint about the absence of the autobiographer's self, see Robert L. Platzner's "De Quincey and the Dilemma of Romantic Autobiography," *Dalhousie Review* 61 (1981): 605–17.

50. The quotation refers to his failure to appear with his "Picture of Happiness."

51. Anatomy in England at the time was still used as a postmortem punishment on the bodies of felons; on the social history of anatomy, see Ruth Richardson, *Death, Dissection and the Destitute* (London: Routledge, 1987).

52. De Quincey makes a similar claim in his essay, "Madness," published in the June 1824 *London Magazine*. In it, he contradicts the belief that the brain is the seat of madness (*Writings*, 10:445–47). De Quincey's concept of mechanical sighing was not quite as inventive as it might seem at first glance. The physician Alexander Crichton, writing in 1798, described in

detail how involuntary sighs, moans, and groans are mechanically caused by stomache pains (*Inquiry*, 2: 178–90).

53. Compare this passage to Hélène Cixous's description of hysterical speech: "The great hysterics . . . are decapitated, their tongues are cut off and what talks isn't heard because it's the body that talks, and man doesn't hear the body" ("Castration or Decapitation?" 49).

54. In this, De Quincey is swimming against the historical tide.

55. See Jack's summary of De Quincey's different treatment of the incident ("De Quincey Revises," 127–28).

56. Ibid., 146.

CHAPTER FIVE

1. Edgeworth today has no novels that could be called well known, despite having been the most revered novelist of her day. In an overview of Edgeworth's work in relation to canonicity, Mitzi Myers discusses Edgeworth's continued marginalization in literary studies, including her absence from recent anthologies of early women's writing, and argues persuasively that this reception stems from Edgeworth's lack of self-effacement as a novelist and her insistence on the moral and philosophical significance of her fiction. See Mitzi Myers, "Shot from Canons; or, Maria Edgeworth and the Cultural Production and Consumption of the Late-Eighteenth-Century Woman Writer," in *The Consumption of Culture, 1600–1800: Image, Object, Text,* ed. Ann Bermingham and John Brewer (New York: Routledge, 1995), 193–214. I am grateful to Myers for letting me see a manuscript copy of this article.

2. The writer of the letter, Rachel Mordecai, subsequently held a lifelong correspondence with Edgeworth. Rachel Mordecai to Maria Edgeworth, 7 August 1815, in Edgar E. MacDonald, ed., *The Education of the Heart: The Correspondence of Rachel Mordecai Lazarus and Maria Edgeworth,* (Chapel Hill: University of North Carolina Press, 1977), 3–7.

3. This is Nancy Fowler, the maid's daughter, who looks more like Harrington's childhood maid than the older Fowler herself at this age.

4. In addition to reading widely, Edgeworth was sister-in-law to Thomas Beddoes, one of the leading writers on nervous disorders in the period and a physician trained in the same school as Thomas Trotter. See Butler, *Maria Edgeworth,* 109–11. On Beddoes's career, see Porter, *Doctor of Society.*

5. Maria Edgeworth, *Harrington, a Tale; And Ormond, a Tale,* 3 vols. (London: R. Hunter, 1817), 1:520. I am grateful to the Special Collections at Emory University for permission to work with this volume.

6. For a historical medical explanation of the perceptual mechanism described in this passage, see Crichton, *Inquiry,* 1:254–90 and passim.

7. This evaluative comment on Simon's face is added in the revised edition. In the first edition, Simon's face is a "dark visage," and his voice has a "mysterious tone." Though both of these references remain in the revision, their suggestion of gothic terror is outweighed by the explicit comment on his "good natured countenance." Without that comment, Harrington's fear

seems perfectly justified, and Fowler's narrative becomes almost super-fluous. The problem here is that Edgeworth is repeating, in earnest, an anti-Semitic stereotype by representing Simon as dark and mysteriously threat-ening even as she opens her novelistic attempt to eliminate and expose anti-Semitism. The addition responds to this problem, and it suggests that Edgeworth recognized the implication and made a second attempt to eliminate the vestiges of anti-Semitic representation that continue to litter her tale.

8. A history of narratives in England accusing Jews of murdering Chris-tian children is included in Montagu Frank Modder, *The Jew in the Literature of England to the End of the Nineteenth Century* (1939; New York: Meridian Books, 1960), 1–30. A well-known version is told by the Prioress in Chaucer's *Canterbury Tales.*

9. Michael Ragussis analyzes *Harrington* as an exploration of the social power of representations; see "Writing English Comedy: 'Patronizing Shy-lock,'" chapter 2 in *Figures of Conversion: "The Jewish Question" and English National Identity* (Durham, NC: Duke University Press, 1995), 57–88.

10. Gustave LeBon, *The Crowd* (1879). The most reliable historical ac-count of LeBon is by Robert A. Nye, *The Origins of Crowd Psychology: Gustave LeBon and the Crisis of Mass Democracy in the Third Republic* (London: Sage Publications, 1975). Serge Moscovici, a social psychologist, describes in de-tail the theory of crowd mind and the crowd leader in LeBon's work and re-lates it to the theory of hypnosis; see his *The Age of the Crowd: A Historical Treatise on Mass Psychology,* trans. J. C. Whitehouse (Cambridge: Cambridge University Press, 1985). Susanna Barrows, in *Distorting Mirrors: Visions of the Crowd in Late Nineteenth-Century France* (New Haven: Yale University Press, 1981) offers an important response to scholars who accept LeBon's ideas at face value by researching the nineteenth-century European writers whose theories LeBon appropriated and explaining the cultural function those ideas served. See also Vrettos's discussion of this literature in chapter 3 of *Somatic Fictions.*

11. Emphasis original.

12. The *Oxford English Dictionary* notes that "concert" and "consort" were "confounded . . . down to the Restoration, and often later" (2nd ed., s.v. "concert"). However, given Edgeworth's dual thematic focus on individual and group action in the novel, the use of "concert" is slightly more appro-priate than "consort."

13. Despite the use of quotation marks, the phrase appears to be a para-phrase from memory and not a direct quote. Similar statements appear in *Sylva Sylvarum,* but not in this exact form.

14. *A Late Discourse . . . Touching the Cure of Wounds by the Power of Sym-pathy* (1658); quoted in Hunter and Macalpine, *Three Hundred Years of Psy-chiatry,* 127.

15. Kenelm Digby, *Two Treatises* (Paris, 1644), 335.

16. See Hunter and Macalpine, *Three Hundred Years of Psychiatry,* 124.

17. *The Works of Francis Bacon,* ed. James Spedding, Robert Leslie Ellis, and Douglas Denon Heath (London: Longmans, 1870; Garrett, 1968), 2:660.

18. The explanation of monsters was a problem for the dominant creationist account of origins, which presumed a fixity of all living forms. "Monsters" by definition violated this principle.

19. Catherine Gallagher takes up this issue in "The Changeling's Debt: Maria Edgeworth's Productive Fictions," chapter 2 in *Nobody's Story: The Vanishing Acts of Women Writers in the Marketplace, 1670–1820* (Berkeley: University of California Press, 1994), 257–327. I am grateful to her for her comments on this chapter and for allowing me to see the manuscript of her chapter on Edgeworth.

20. Dora B. Weiner has situated Crichton's ideas in the history of psychiatric concepts and included an exceedingly useful bibliographical essay; "Mind and Body in the Clinic: Philippe Pinel, Alexander Crichton, Dominique Esquirol, and the Birth of Psychiatry," in *The Languages of Psyche: Mind and Body in Enlightenment Thought*, ed. G. S. Rousseau (Berkeley: University of California Press, 1990), 331–402.

21. On the fear of novels in the eighteenth-century, see Taylor, *Early Opposition to the English Novel*, and Altick, *The English Common Reader*. On the dangers of "transport" for the female reader, see Peter de Bolla, "Of the Transport of the Reader: The Reading Subject," chapter 8 in *The Discourse of the Sublime: History, Aesthetics and the Subject* (Oxford: Basil Blackwell, 1989), 230–78. On Maria Edgeworth specifically and her theory of fiction in relation to these fears, see Gallagher, *Nobody's Story*, 273–88.

22. Crichton is unique, at this time, in his sympathy for suicides, and he argued against the punitive treatment of their bodies.

23. Michael Ragussis has a compelling discussion of this issue and Edgeworth's redefinition of "natural" feelings as products of representation; see chapter 2 in *Figures of Conversion*. Catherine Gallagher is more concerned with how Harrington "becomes a creature of representations," as he loses any sense of difference between himself and these descriptions (*Nobody's Story*, 315).

24. See Butler, *Maria Edgeworth*, 197–98.

25. Edgeworth to Mrs. Ruxton, Edinburgh, 30 March 1803, in Mrs. [Frances] Edgeworth, *A Memoir of Maria Edgeworth with a Selection from Her Letters* (London: privately printed, 1867), 1:171–73.

26. For Stewart's theory, see his "Of the Principle or Law of Sympathetic Imitation," part 2, chapter 2 in *Elements of the Philosophy of the Human Mind*, vol. 3 (London: Murray, 1827). All quotations are from *The Works of Dugald Stewart*, 7 vols. (Cambridge, MA: Hilliard, 1829), vol. 3.

27. Jewish Naturalization Act, 26 Geo. 2, c. 26. The act was quickly repealed, in 27 Geo. 2, c. 1.

28. Harrington's relationship with his father is contained in their names. The father is called William Harrington, the son William Harrington Harrington (*TN*, 9:193). The son's name is a double repetition of the name of the father.

29. Edgeworth refers the reader to John Drinkwater's *A History of the Siege of Gibraltar*, from which she borrowed some of her particulars.

Drinkwater's account differs from hers significantly; he blames the "mercenary conduct of the hucksters and liquor-dealers" for raising "a spirit of revenge" among the troops (*A History of the Siege of Gibraltar, 1779–1783*, new ed. [London: John Murray, 1905], 152). This and the later Gordon Riots scene echo the 1798 experience of Richard Lovell Edgeworth, who was nearly lynched in Longford, Ireland, by an anti-Catholic crowd that was convinced he was a French sympathizer; see Butler's account of the incident (*Maria Edgeworth*, 138).

30. A similar example is mentioned by Bacon as an illustration of "the force of the imagination upon other bodies," one form of which is "as if one should imagine such a man to be in the vestments of a Pope, or to have wings" (*Sylva Sylvarum*, 2:653–54).

31. Thomas Holcroft's *A Plain and Succinct Narrative of the Gordon Riots, London, 1780*, ed. Garland Garvey Smith (Atlanta: The Library, Emory University, 1944), 30.

32. The concept of a "crowd mind" is a vexed one. Whether or not such a phenomenon exists, and whether it were individual psychology writ large or something qualitatively different, are fundamental questions defining the disciplinary boundary lines between social psychology and sociology. Historians date the concept itself as a mid- to late-Victorian invention. For a provocative discussion of these issues, see Nye, *Origins of Crowd Psychology*, and Barrows, *Distorting Mirrors*.

33. Catherine Gallagher discusses the significance of filial love in Harrington and relates it to Maria Edgeworth's complex literary relationship with her father; see *Nobody's Story*, 310–11.

34. On the cultural conventions that make up the Man of Feeling, see Todd, *Sensibility*, 88–109.

35. This is the second time that Harrington adopts this position; in the first instance he apologizes for the prejudice in the works of fiction, including Edgeworth's *Moral Tales* (*TN*, 9:13).

36. Crichton viewed arrested attention as significant because it was caused either by an extremely strong external impression, such as a sudden noise, or by a predisposition in the subject to something in the sensations, such as a sympathy or antipathy. In Ormond's case, that prior condition is his sympathy with the character, and in Harrington's case it is his antipathy.

37. For more on this pattern in the tale, see Ragussis's argument that "the Jew as representation, displaces the real Jew," so that Jewish identity exists "only in a performance" (*Figures of Conversion*, 59, 60).

38. Rachel Mordecai called it the one disappointment in the novel (Letter to Maria Edgeworth, 28 October 1817, *Education of the Heart*, 16). Ragussis views it as "a sign of Edgeworth's submission to the ruling ideology" (*Figures of Conversion*, 79); his discussion of it within the context of Jewish conversion figures is sustained and insightful.

39. See Gallagher's discussion, where she notes how Montenero's "obsessive policing of the borderland between realities and representations" ultimately collapses the distinction between them (*Nobody's Story*, 317, 320).

CHAPTER SIX

1. On the fear of novels in the eighteenth century, see Taylor, *Early Opposition to the English Novel*. The different components that produced popular opposition to the novel are discussed in Altick, *The English Common Reader*. See also J.M.S. Tompkins, *The Popular Novel in England: 1770–1800* (London: Constable, 1932; Lincoln: University of Nebraska Press, 1967); Raymond Williams, *The Long Revolution* (New York: Columbia University Press, 1961), 156–72; and Kathleen Tillotson, *Novels of the Eighteen-Forties* (Oxford: Clarendon, 1954).

2. I am grateful to Catherine Gallagher for bringing this to my attention.

3. For the full correspondence, see MacDonald, ed., *Education of the Heart*.

4. Anthony Brundage, *England's "Prussian Minister": Edwin Chadwick and the Politics of Government Growth, 1832–54* (University Park, PA: Pennsylvania State Univ. Press, 1988), 37.

5. Ibid., 77.

6. Edwin Chadwick, *Report on the Sanitary Condition of the Labouring Population of Great Britain*, ed. M. W. Flinn (Edinburgh: Edinburgh University Press, 1965), 423. Subsequent references to this edition are abbreviated *SR*.

7. Brundage discusses Chadwick's bureaucratic career in relation to utilitarianism and discusses how he reconciled his call for state intervention with the laissez faire economics of the utilitarians. On Chadwick's life, see also the two earlier biographies: S. E. Finer, *The Life and Times of Sir Edwin Chadwick* (London: Methuen, 1952); and Richard Albert Lewis, *Edwin Chadwick and the Public Health Movement, 1832–1854* (London: Longmans, 1952). The basic history of the cholera epidemics in early Victorian London is Margaret Pelling's, *Cholera, Fever and English Medicine, 1825–1865* (Oxford: Oxford University Press, 1978); chapter 1 discusses Chadwick's concept of epidemics, and chapter 2 discusses the medical community's response to his *Report*. See also Dorothy Porter's "Enemies of the Race," *Victorian Studies* 34 (1991): 159–78.

8. Charles Kingsley, *Yeast: A Problem* (New York: MacMillian, 1893), 103.

9. Dickens's brother-in-law, Henry Austin, was a friend of Chadwick's and was active in the sanitation movement.

10. Mary Poovey, *Making a Social Body: British Cultural Formation, 1830–1864* (Chicago: University of Chicago Press, 1995), 116. Poovey was the first writer to focus on the *Sanitary Report* as a site for the construction of Victorian domestic ideology, and my own analysis is indebted to her work, first published as "Domesticity and Class Formation: Chadwick's 1842 *Sanitary Report*," in *Subject to History: Ideology, Class, Gender*, ed. David Simpson (Ithaca, NY: Cornell University Press, 1991), 65–83. Anita Levy describes how middle-class intellectuals impose a model of enclosed domestic space on the working class, in her discussion of Peter Gaskell's *Artisans and Machinery* (*Other Women*, 32–35).

11. Robert Brudenell Carter, *On the Pathology and Treatment of Hysteria* (London: J. Churchill, 1853), 152.

12. Mary Poovey uses Kay's *The Moral and Physical Condition of the Work-

ing Classes as a case study to define how this broader group of social reform texts contributed to the formation of national values and the idea of a national identity in the Victorian period; see "Curing the Social Body in 1832: James Phillips Kay and the Irish in Manchester," *Making a Social Body,* 55–72. On the relationship between the Victorian novel and social science discourse generally, see also Anita Levy, *Other Women: The Writing of Class, Race, and Gender, 1832–1898* (Princeton, NJ: Princeton University Press, 1991). On blue books and Victorian novels, see Patrick Brantlinger, "Bluebooks, the Social Organism, and the Victorian Novel," *Criticism* 14 (1972): 328–344; Sheila M. Smith, "Blue Books and Victorian Novelists," *Review of English Studies* 21 n.s. (1970): 23–40. See also Smith's discussion in *The Other Nation: The Poor in English Novels of the 1840s and 1850s* (Oxford: Clarendon Press, 1980). H. J. Dyos tracks the history of the idea of the "slum" in Victorian Britain and defines sanitary literature's centrality to it; see "The Slums of Victorian London," *Victorian Studies* 11 (1967): 5–40

13. On the history of public health, see John V. Pickstone, "Dearth, Dirt and Fever Epidemics: Rewriting the History of British 'Public Health,' 1750–1850," in *Epidemics and Ideas: Essays on the Historical Perception of Pestilence,* ed. Terence Ranger and Paul Slack (Cambridge: Cambridge University Press, 1992), 125–48. See also W. F. Bynum, "Ideology and Health Care in Britain: Chadwick to Beveridge," *History and Philosophy of the Life Sciences* 10, suppl. (1988): 75–87; and Anthony S. Wohl, *Endangered Lives: Public Health in Victorian Britain* (Cambridge, MA: Harvard University Press, 1983), particularly chapters 1–3. For a broad overview of differences between public health in Britain and the United States, see Elizabeth Fee and Dorothy Porter's "Public Health, Preventive Medicine and Professionalization: England and America in the Nineteenth Century," in *Medicine in Society: Historical Essays,* ed. Andrew Wear (Cambridge: Cambridge University Press, 1992), 249–75.

14. On anomic desire and the Victorian construction of the working class, see Christopher Herbert's *Culture and Anomie: Ethnographic Imagination in the Nineteenth Century* (Chicago: University of Chicago Press, 1991). His discussion of Henry Mahew's *London Labour and the London Poor* is particularly relevant to Chadwick, and the difference is instructive. Where Mahew describes a coherent culture among the working class, Chadwick describes a pathology whose primary feature is the resistance to culture.

15. The questionnaires are included as a prefatory appendix to the original *Sanitary Report,* though not included in Flinn's edition. See Chadwick's *Report . . . from the Poor Law Commissioners, on an Inquiry into the Sanitary Condition of the Labouring Population of Great Britain* (London: W. Clowes, 1842), xi–xx. Flinn also omits a lengthy series of interviews with civil engineers and other specialists that Chadwick included as appendices to the 1842 edition, pp. 373–457.

16. Flinn, introduction, *SR,* 48.

17. Joseph W. Childers ("Observation and Representation: Mr. Chadwick Writes the Poor," *Victorian Studies* 37 [1994]: 405–32) similarly notes the way Chadwick "adroitly manipulates" the many voices in his *Report* (p. 416).

18. On the rise of statistics in Britain, see Michael J. Cullen, *The Statistical Movement in Early Victorian Britain: The Foundation of Empirical Social Research* (New York: Barnes and Noble, 1975), and J. M. Eyler, *Victorian Social Medicine: The Ideas and Methods of William Farr* (Baltimore: 1979).

19. Flinn, introduction, *SR*, 54.

20. For a general discussion of the response to sanitary literature, see Nancy Aycock Metz, "Discovering a World of Suffering: Fiction and the Rhetoric of Sanitary Reform—1840–1860," *Nineteenth-Century Contexts* 15 (1991): 65–81.

21. A summation of Chadwick's relationship to the debate over miasmatic contagion and predisposition can be found in Flinn's introduction (*SR*, 62–64). Christopher Hamlin outlines the debate over the nature of disease itself, and his essay is very useful in understanding the models of disease within which Chadwick maneuvers; see "Providence and Putrefaction," *Victorian Studies* 27 (1985): 381–411.

22. See Catherine Gallagher's analysis of Malthus in relation to the Victorian work of Henry Mahew, "The Body Versus the Social Body in the Works of Thomas Malthus and Henry Mayhew," *Representations* 14 (1986): 83–106. My summation of Malthus is based on her work, and her essay was the starting point for my investigation of Chadwick, whose images of the working-class body differ significantly from Mahew's because of the different relationship Chadwick establishes between disease and sexuality.

23. Flinn's introduction provides a useful summary of miasmatic premises, in *SR*, 62–64.

24. As Pickstone notes, this conflation of organic decay with human exhalation is a new approach, articulated by Chadwick's associate Southwood Smith, that becomes central to Chadwick's "reductive, physicalist account of disease" ("Dearth, Dirt and Fever," 147).

25. See Gallagher's analysis of this paradox, in "Body Versus the Social Body."

26. His statistical sources, cited by Flinn, are from Alexander von Humboldt and Francis d'Ivernois.

27. This assumption was a given among Victorian social reformers, as Wohl has pointed out (*Endangered Lives*, 7–9). Dickens for example argues, in 1851, that "Sanitary Reform must precede all other social remedies . . . even Education" (*The Speeches of Charles Dickens*, ed. K. J. Fielding [1960], 129, quoted in Wohl, *Endangered Lives*, 8).

28. That this assumption persists into the twentieth century is certainly apparent within the attitudes literary critics adopt toward Victorian working-class literature. A prominent example is Richard D. Altick, who explains the formal qualities of working-class tastes by claiming as a fact that "their attention spans were short" and that as a result "they needed a running supply of excitements, brief and to the point" (*Victorian People and Ideas: A Companion for the Modern Reader of Victorian Literature* [New York: Norton, 1973], 61). Both of these sentiments could have been taken directly from Chadwick himself. Even Altick's language promotes a physicalist reduction, as when he argues that "the interest of the printed matter which they

actually devoured is sociological, not literary" (*Victorian People*, 62). The language of physical consumption specifically militates against any possible capacity for symbolic forms of comprehension within the working-class reader.

29. Christopher Hamlin, "William Dibdin and the Idea of Biological Sewage Treatment," *Technology and Culture* 29 (1988): 189–218. Hamlin also discusses the conflict between Chadwick's theories in the *Report* and his subsequent problems in actually implementing them, in "Edwin Chadwick and the Engineers, 1842–1854: Systems and Antisystems in the Pipe-and-Brick Sewers War," *Technology and Culture* 33 (1992): 680–709.

30. See Childers's related discussion of the "reified connection between worker and manufacturer" ("Observation and Representation," 419).

31. See chapter 7, "Recognized Principles of Legislation and State of the Existing Law for the Protection of the Public Health," *SR*, 339–410.

32. The centrality of surveillance to Victorian public health is discussed in Nicholas Thomas's "Sanitation and Seeing: The Creation of State Power in Early Colonial Fiji," *Comparative Studies in Science and History* 32 (1990): 149–70.

33. Metz, "Discovering a World of Suffering," 70. Other discussions of the sensationalist qualities of sanitary literature include Dyos, "Slums of Victorian London," and Brantlinger, "Bluebooks."

34. The use of sanitation as a technology of state power has been usefully explored in studies of colonialism. See Nicholas Thomas, "Sanitation and Seeing."

35. This same detail reappears in chapter 6 of Elizabeth Gaskell's *Mary Barton: A Tale of Manchester Life*. In the home of the dying Tom Davenport are seen "three or four little children rolling on the damp, nay wet, brick floor, through which the stagnant, filthy moisture of the street oozed up" (ed. Stephen Gill [New York: Penguin, 1970], 98).

CHAPTER SEVEN

1. This history is summarized from Clarke and Jacyna, *Nineteenth-Century Origins of Neuroscientific Concepts*, 1–58.

2. The division of nerves into those for sensation and those for action was made in the second decade of the century and became widely accepted in Britain as the "Bell-Magendie Law" of 1822.

3. Marshall Hall, *Memoirs of the Nervous System* (London: 1837; Washington, D.C.: University Publications of America, 1978).

4. As I have tried to demonstrate, ideas about neurology intersected with the growing interest in a second level of consciousness that followed Mesmer's experiments and culminated in Freud's theory of the dynamic unconscious. For a comprehensive treatment of this topic, see Ellenberger's "The First Dynamic Psychiatry (1775–1900)," chapter 5 in *The Discovery of the Unconscious*, 110–81.

5. The problem of dissemblance and the related problem of eloquence is discussed in Starr, "'Only a Boy': Notes on Sentimental Novels."

6. George Eliot, *Adam Bede,* ed. Stephen Gill (New York: Penguin, 1980), 199.

7. See Catherine Gallagher, *The Industrial Reformation of English Fiction: Social Discourse and Narrative Form, 1832–1867* (Chicago: University of Chicago Press, 1985), 219–43; and George Levine, *The Realistic Imagination: English Fiction from Frankenstein to Lady Chatterley* (Chicago: University of Chicago Press, 1981), 3–22.

8. On the problem of historical relativism in the philosophy of science, see Jarrett Leplin's introduction to *Scientific Realism* (Berkeley: University of California Press, 1984).

9. George Eliot and Lewes considered themselves husband and wife, though their marriage was never legally recognized.

10. For all subsequent references to this incident, see Gordon S. Haight, ed., *The George Eliot Letters,* 9 vols. (New Haven: Yale University Press, 1954–78), 5:337–38.

11. Sir James Paget (1814–99) was a leading surgeon and had been surgeon-extraordinary to Queen Victoria since 1858; see Gordon S. Haight, *George Eliot: A Biography* (New York: Oxford University Press, 1968), 417.

12. Pierre Victor Renouard, *Histoire de la Medecine,* 2 vols. (Paris, 1846); John Thompson, *An Account of the Life, Lectures, and Writings of William Cullen, MD,* 2 vols. (London, 1832 and 1859); Southwood Smith, *Treatise on Fever* (London, 1830); J. Rutherford Russell, *History and Heroes of the Art of Medicine* (London, 1861). The most extensive guide to her scientific reading in preparation for the novel will be found in the introduction to *George Eliot's Middlemarch Notebooks: A Transcription,* ed. and introduction by John Clark Pratt and Victor A. Neufeldt (Berkeley: University of California Press, 1979). But see also the still useful introduction to *Quarry for Middlemarch,* ed. and introduction by Anna Theresa Kitchel (Berkeley: University of California Press, 1950).

13. Paget met Lewes at Oxford in 1868 and attended his son, Thornton, during the five long months of his fatal illness in 1869 at the Priory, Eliot and Lewes' home. He was undoubtedly familiar, by the time of his remark in 1872, with her extensive knowledge of Victorian science. We know that the two discussed "things medical a propos of *Middlemarch*" as she worked on the novel (Haight, *Biography,* 442).

14. Lewes repeated the claim of Lydgate's fictionality three years later, in 1875 (*Letters,* 6:196). Speculation on historical sources for Lydgate is by no means confined to the science-oriented Paget; because George Eliot frequently used figures drawn from life, *Middlemarch* critics continue to question her claim that there was no original for Lydgate. As examples, see Kitchel, *Quarry,* 2–4; and see Haight, *Biography,* 32–33, 447–48.

15. Recent scholarship on George Eliot and science has located structural relationships between her narrative principles and the concepts of evolution, organicism, pathological anatomy, and physiological psychology. See Beer, *Darwin's Plots;* Simon During, "The Strange Case of Monomania: Patriarchy in Literature, Murder in *Middlemarch,* Drowning in *Daniel Deronda,*" *Representations* 23 (1988): 86–104; George Levine, *Darwin and the*

Novelists: Patterns of Science in Victorian Fiction (Cambridge: Harvard University Press, 1988); Levine, "George Eliot's Hypothesis of Reality," *Nineteenth-Century Fiction* 35 (1980): 1–28; Levine, *The Realistic Imagination*; Lawrence Rothfield, *Vital Signs: Medical Realism in Nineteenth-Century Fiction* (Princeton, NJ: Princeton University Press, 1992), 84–119; and Sally Shuttleworth, "Fairy Tale or Science? Physiological Psychology in *Silas Marner*," in *Languages of Nature: Critical Essays on Science and Literature*, ed. Ludmilla Jordanova (New Brunswick, NJ: Rutgers University Press, 1986), 244–88. Jordanova provides an overview of epistemic shifts in the natural sciences from 1700–1900, with reference to the novel as a genre, in her *Languages of Nature*, 15–47. See also Jordanova's discussion of the language of science in her *Sexual Visions: Images of Gender in Science and Medicine between the Eighteenth and Twentieth Centuries*, Science and Literature (Madison: University of Wisconsin Press, 1989).

16. Her most well-documented collaboration with Lewes is on his *Comte's Philosophy of the Sciences* (1853), which she helped edit and promote; his *Life of Goethe* (1855), where she deserves the full status of co-author; and his *Problems of Life and Mind* (1873–79), which she completed after his death. On Lewes and Eliot's relationship, see Haight's *Biography* and Anna Theresa Kitchel, *George Lewes and George Eliot: A Review of Records* (New York: John Day, 1933). On the aesthetic principles of Lewes's philosophy, see Peter Allen Dale, "George Lewes' Scientific Aesthetic: Restructuring the Ideology of the Symbol," in *One Culture: Essays in Science and Literature*, ed. George Levine (Madison: University of Wisconsin Press, 1987), 92–116.

17. This dichotomy characterized the "Two Cultures Debate" between Thomas Huxley and Matthew Arnold. For a basic critique of this debate, see Levine, *One Culture*, 3–32. On the relationship between literary and scientific discourse in the Victorian period, see Anita Levy, *Other Women*, particularly chapter 1.

18. On the history of pathological anatomy, Lydgate's specialty, and a discussion of its Paris origins and the professional resistance to it in England, see Russell C. Maulitz, *Morbid Appearances: The Anatomy of Pathology in the Early Nineteenth Century* (Cambridge: Cambridge University Press, 1987). See also Rothfield, *Vital Signs*, 84–119.

19. On the structure of the medical profession and the campaign for reform in the first half of the century, see Ivan Waddington, *The Medical Profession in the Industrial Revolution* (Dublin: Gill, 1984). On the medical profession in the later century, see M. Jeanne Peterson, *The Medical Profession in Mid-Victorian London* (Berkeley: University of California Press, 1978).

20. Eliot's notes on the Lancet are reproduced in *Quarry*.

21. All Middlemarch quotations are taken from *Middlemarch: A Study of Provincial Life*, ed. David Carroll (Oxford: Clarendon Press, 1986). Parenthetical references to this edition are abbreviated as *M* and include both chapter and page number for ease of reference.

22. The professionalization of medicine hinged on this fundamental shift of power from client to the physician based on the profession's new claims

to specialized knowledge. On the doctor-client relationship, see Wadding-ton, *Medical Profession*, 9–28; and Dorothy Porter and Roy Porter, *Patient's Progress* (Cambridge: Polity, 1989).

23. On medical "penetration," see Jordanova, *Sexual Visions*, 51–57. See also Michel Foucault's discussion of the epistemic shift in the human sciences from a perception of significance as available on the surface to seeing it as resident within a hidden structure, in *The Order of Things* (New York: Vintage, 1970), 125–65.

24. In this, Lydgate resembles the carpenter Adam Bede, who is first seen repairing the flawed work of his brother Seth, as Elaine Scarry has noted ("Work and the Body in Hardy and Other Nineteenth-Century Novelists," *Representations* 3 [1983]: 121, n. 27). Both men are similarly distinguished as characters by the exceptional quality of their work.

25. On the shifting definition of quackery in relation to orthodoxy, see Roy Porter, *Health for Sale: Quackery in England 1660–1850* (Manchester: Manchester University Press, 1989).

26. See Elaine Scarry's analysis of the manner in which artifacts extend the body's sentient powers and acuity in *The Body in Pain: The Making and Unmaking of the World* (Oxford: Oxford University Press, 1985), 281–85. I am also indebted here to Scarry's concept of "perceptual reach," which she outlines in her discussion of Thomas Hardy and other Victorian novelists, including George Eliot ("Work and the Body," 108–11). Throughout this essay, I rely on the conceptual vocabulary Scarry developed in her own work. On the concept of the boundaries of the human body, see her "Work and the Body" and "Consent and the Body: Injury, Departure, and Desire," *New Literary History* 21 (1990): 867–96. The concepts of sentience and its opposite, perceptual stupidity, are discussed in *The Body in Pain*, 281–96.

27. F. F. Cartwright, *A Social History of Medicine*, Themes in British Social History (London: Longman, 1977), 143.

28. Lydgate and pathological anatomy are considereed in relation to "medical realism" in Lawrence Rothfield's *Vital Signs: Medical Realism in Nineteenth-Century Fiction* (Princeton, NJ: Princeton University Press, 1992), 84–119.

29. Andreas Vesalius (1514–1564), Flemish anatomist regarded as the founder of modern anatomy; Marie Francois Xavier Bichat (1771–1802), French anatomical pathologist and the founder of histology.

30. On the history of anatomy in nineteenth-century Britain, and on the popular association of anatomy with murder following the Burke and Hare trial, see Richardson, *Death, Dissection and the Destitute*.

31. On the importance of this paradox as an historical shift in medicine, see Michel Foucault's discussion of Bichat and anatomy in *The Birth of the Clinic: An Archaeology of Medical Perception*, trans. A. M. Sheridan Smith (New York: Vintage, 1975), 124–46.

32. That Lydgate is indeed studying anatomy in Paris is alluded to several times. "He had known [Pierre] Louis in Paris, and had followed many anatomical demonstrations in order to ascertain the specific differences of

typhus and typhoid" (*M*, 16:161). In her research on historical material for the novel, George Eliot noted that the ability to distinguish between the two types of fever was an achievement of pathological anatomy, Lydgate's specialty (*Quarry*, 29). More generally, the Paris schools were recognized as the place to study anatomy, as bodies were practically unavailable in England but plentiful in Paris, as Eliot also noted (*Quarry*, 24).

33. Simon During regards the enigmatic quality of the act as its central significance; see "The Strange Case of Monomania," 93.

34. In her discussion of "Nature unveiling before science," Jordanova shows how this same paradox functions in Victorian science generally, since the veil both protects and masks (*Sexual Visions*, 87–110).

35. See Levine, *Realistic Imagination*, 252–90; and see Beer, *Darwin's Plots*, 151–52.

36. The Eliot-Lewes library included all of Tyndall's major works, and George Eliot's annotations are found in their copy of Tyndall's "Scientific Limit of the Imagination"; see William Baker, *The George Eliot–George Henry Lewes Library: An Annotated Catalogue of Their Books at Dr. Williams's Library, London* (New York: Garland, 1977), see also Baker's *The Libraries of George Eliot and George Henry Lewes*, English Literary Studies (Victoria, BC: University of Victoria, 1981). Tyndall's relationship to Lewes and George Eliot dates at least back to 1863, when he and Huxley critiqued drafts of Lewes' work on Aristotle (*Letters*, 4:119). In 1874, she calls Tyndall "a favourite of mine. . . . I get on with him delightfully" (*Letters*, 9:183). On Tyndall's life and work, see W. H. Brock, N. D. McMillan, and R. C. Mollan, eds., *John Tyndall: Essays on a Natural Philosopher*, Historical Studies in Irish Science and Technology (Dublin: Royal Dublin Society, 1981).

37. John Tyndall, *Essays on the Use and Limit of the Imagination in Science* (London: Longmans, 1870), 16.

38. Lydgate and the scientific imagination are thoroughly discussed in Levine, *Realistic Imagination*, 252–90, and in Levine's earlier essay, "George Eliot's Hypothesis of Reality." The philosophical debate over the "hypothesizing activity" is discussed in Michael York Mason, "*Middlemarch* and Science: Problems of Life and Mind," *Review of English Studies* 22 (1971): 151–69. See also Beer on the role of imagination in Darwin as well as the scientific imagination in *Middlemarch* (*Darwin's Plots*, 149–80).

39. Beer (*Darwin's Plots*, 152) cites the close parallel of this passage with Thomas Huxley's "The Physical Basis of Life," which originally appeared in *The Fortnightly Review*, ns 5 (February 1869): 132.

40. Wordsworth articulates this belief in his "Preface to Lyrical Ballads" (1802). It is also prevalent in eighteenth- and nineteenth-century medical writing on the social origin of nervous disorders, such as George Cheyne's *English Malady*.

41. One of George Eliot first stories, "The Lifted Veil," describes a protagonist who is cursed by the absence of this perceptual threshold.

42. See Thomas W. Laqueur's discussion of "Humanitarian Narratives," in which he links the function of the realistic novel to the autopsy report, the

clinical report, and the social inquiry. As he points out, each of these narrative forms is a stepchild of the empiricist revolution; "Bodies, Details, and the Humanitarian Narrative," in *The New Cultural History*, ed. Lynn Hunt (Berkeley: University of California Press, 1989), 176–204.

43. "The Natural History of German Life," *Essays of George Eliot*, ed. Thomas Pinney (New York: Columbia University Press, 1963), 270. This essay was originally published in *Westminster Review* 66 (July 1856), 51–79.

44. On positivism, see Leszek Kolakoswki, *Positivist Philosophy from Hume to the Vienna Circle*, trans. Norbert Guterman (Harmondsworth: Penguin, 1972). The influence of Comte on Eliot is much debated. Haight minimalizes it (*Biography*, 301), but T. R. Wright convincingly establishes a far more pervasive influence at work than Haight allows; see Wright's "George Eliot and Positivism," *Modern Language Review* (1981): 257–72.

45. In "The Future of German Philosophy," originally published in *Leader* 6 (July 28, 1855): 723–24.

46. See also her later note, "Historic Imagination," in *Essays*, 446–47.

47. George Levine writes, "The project of the Victorian novel increasingly appeared to me as a cultural twin to the project of Victorian science; even the great aesthetic ideals of fiction writers—truth, detachment, self-abnegation—echoed with the ideals of contemporary science" (*Darwin and the Novelists*, vii).

48. The relationship between George Eliot and Matthew Arnold's writing is discussed in Gallagher, *Industrial Reformation*, 218–52.

49. *Culture and Anarchy*, ed. J. Dover Wilson (Cambridge: Cambridge University Press, 1966).

50. George Eliot discusses *Keepsake* and its genre in "The Natural History of German Life" (*Essays*, 268).

51. On the philosophical structure of naive realism in science, see Levine, *One Culture*, 3–32.

52. On the medical project of professionalization and George Eliot's professional concerns as a female author, see Norman N. Feltes, *Modes of Production of Victorian Novels* (Chicago: University of Chicago Press, 1986), 36–56.

53. The opposite view has dominated *Middlemarch* criticism for years. A prominent example is Gordon Haight's introduction to his edition of *Middlemarch*, in which he compares Rosamond to a siren and claims Lydgate "meant to lash himself to the mast and stop his ears" (*Middlemarch* [Boston: Houghton, 1956], xix). Thus Lydgate, with his scientific view of woman, tries to defend himself from the danger represented by the female. But in fact it is this same scientific view, these same stopped ears, that blinds Lydgate to Vincy's nature, one that other characters in the novel have little difficulty recognizing. Lydgate is represented as the victim of his own illusions about women, which is very different than claiming that he is a victim of the female herself.

54. On Bichat, see Elizabeth Haigh, *Xavier Bichat and the Medical Theory of the Eighteenth Century*, Medical History, Supplement 4 (London: Wellcome Institute, 1984).

55. On the problem of referentiality in science, see the collection of essays in Jarrett Leplin, ed., *Scientific Realism*. I am particularly indebted to two essays: Hilary Putnam, "What is Realism?" (pp. 140–53), and Larry Lauden, "A Confutation of Convergent Realism" (pp. 218–49), which specifically addresses the problem of historical relativism.

56. Ladislaw is describing the futility of Casaubon's project to Dorothea.

57. A similar image appears in the much earlier essay, "The Natural History of German Life," when she discusses the influence of perspective on the observer's interpretation of a group of peasants (*Essays*, 269).

58. Gallagher outlines the centrality of self-referentiality in the later novels of George Eliot, and its connection to the Arnoldian view of culture, much more skillfully than I am able to do here (*Industrial Reformation*, 249–52).

59. In her discussion of Silas Marner, Sally Shuttleworth relates this same sense of magicality to theories of organic social evolution, so that magic represents an earlier stage in social development in George Eliot's novels; see "Fairy Tale or Science?"

60. This circularity is implicit in Arnold's view of culture as an independent sphere representing, ultimately, itself; see Gallagher, *Industrial Reformation*, 236–37.

Bibliography

PRIMARY SOURCES

Arnold, Matthew. *Culture and Anarchy.* Edited by J. Dover Wilson. Cambridge: Cambridge University Press, 1966.

Arnold, Thomas. *Observations on the Nature, Kinds, Causes, and Prevention of Insanity.* 2 vols. 2nd edition. London: Richard Phillips, 1806.

Austen, Jane. *Sense and Sensibility.* Edited by Tony Tanner. New York: Penguin, 1969.

Bacon, Francis. *The Works of Francis Bacon.* Edited by James Spedding, Robert Leslie Ellis, and Douglas Denon Heath. Vol. 2. London: Longmans, 1870; Garrett, 1968.

Beddoes, Thomas. *Hygeia.* 3 vols. Bristol: Mills, 1802–3.

Brown, John. *Elements of Medicine.* Translated by Thomas Beddoes. 2 vols. Portsmouth, NH: 1804.

Burton, Robert. *The Anatomy of Melancholy.* Edited by Holbrook Jackson. 3 vols. London: Everyman's Library, 1968.

Carter, Robert Brudenell. *On the Pathology and Treatment of Hysteria.* London: J. Churchill, 1853.

Chadwick, Edwin. *Report . . . from the Poor Law Commissioners, on an Inquiry into the Sanitary Condition of the Labouring Population of Great Britain.* London: W. Clowes, 1842.

———. *Report on the Sanitary Condition of the Labouring Population of Great Britain.* Edited by M. W. Flinn. Edinburgh: Edinburgh University Press, 1965.

Cheyne, George. *The English Malady.* London, 1733; Delmar, NY: Scholar's Facsimile, 1976.

———. *The Letters of Dr. George Cheyne to Samuel Richardson (1733–1743).* Edited by Charles F. Mullett. Columbia: University of Missouri, 1934.

Review of *Confessions of an English Opium-Eater,* by Thomas De Quincey. *British Critic* ns 18 (1822): 531–34.

Review of *Confessions of an English Opium-Eater,* by Thomas De Quincey. *The Imperial Magazine* 5 (1823): 90–95.

Review of *Confessions of an English Opium-Eater,* by Thomas De Quincey. *Medical Intelligencer* [London] 2 (1821): 613–15.

Review of *Confessions of an English Opium-Eater,* by Thomas De Quincey. *New Edinburgh Review* 4 (1823): 253–74.

Crichton, Alexander. *An Inquiry into the Nature and Origin of Mental Derange-ment*. 2 vols. London: Cadell and Davies, 1798. Reprint, with an introduc-tion by Robert Ellenbogen (2 vols. in 1), New York: AMS Press, 1976.

Cullen, William. *First Lines of the Practice of Physic*. 2 vols. Edinburgh, 1778–84.

De Quincey, Thomas. *The Collected Writings of Thomas De Quincey*. Edited by David Masson. 14 vols. Edinburgh: Adam and Charles Black, 1889–90.

———. *Confessions of an English Opium-Eater*. Edited by Alethea Hayter. New York: Penguin, 1971.

———. "The Opium and the China Question." *Blackwood's Edinburgh Maga-zine* 47 (1840): 717–38, 847–53.

———. "War with China, and the Opium Question." *Blackwood's Edinburgh Magazine* 47 (1840): 368–84.

de Tott, Baron. *Memoirs of the Turks and Tartars*. 1786.

Digby, Kenelm. *Two Treatises*. Paris, 1644.

Drinkwater, John. *A History of the Siege of Gibraltar, 1779–1783*. New edition. London: John Murray, 1905.

Edgeworth, Mrs. [Frances]. *A Memoir of Maria Edgeworth with a Selection from Her Letters*. 2 vols. London: privately printed by Joseph Masters, 1867.

Edgeworth, Maria. *Harrington, a Tale; And Ormond, a Tale*. 3 vols. London: R. Hunter, 1817.

———. *Tales and Novels*. Vol. 9, *Harrington; Thoughts on Bores; and Ormond*. London: Routledge, 1893; Hildesheim, Germany: Georg Olms Verlags-buchhandlund, 1969.

Eliot, George. *Adam Bede*. Edited by Stephen Gill. New York: Penguin, 1980.

———. *Essays of George Eliot*. Edited by Thomas Pinney. New York: Colum-bia University Press, 1963.

———. *The George Eliot Letters*. Edited by Gordon S. Haight. 9 vols. New Haven: Yale University Press, 1954–78.

———. *George Eliot's* Middlemarch *Notebooks: A Transcription*. Edited by John Clark Pratt and Victor A. Neufeldt. Berkeley: University of Califor-nia Press, 1979.

———. *Middlemarch: A Study of Provincial Life*. Edited by David Carroll. Ox-ford: Clarendon Press, 1986.

———. *Quarry for* Middlemarch. Edited by Anna Theresa Kitchel. Berkeley: University of California Press, 1950.

Encyclopaedia Britannica. 10 vols. 2nd edition. Edinburgh: Balfour, 1779.

———. 18 vols. 3rd edition. Edinburgh: Balfour, 1797.

Fenwick, Eliza. *The Fate of the Fenwicks: Letters to Mary Hays (1798–1828)*. Edited by A. F. Wedd. London: Methuen, 1927.

Gaskell, Elizabeth. *Mary Barton: A Tale of Manchester Life*. Edited by Stephen Gill. New York: Penguin, 1970.

Godwin, William. *Caleb Williams or Things as They Are*. Edited by David McCracken. New York: Norton, 1977.

———. *Enquiry Concerning Political Justice: And Its Influence on Modern Morals and Happiness*. New York: Penguin, 1985.

———. *Fleetwood: Or the New Man of Feeling*. Standard Novels, No. 22.

London: Bentley, 1832. Reprint, New York: AMS, 1975.

Hall, Marshall. *Memoirs on the Nervous System.* London, 1837. Reprint, Washington, D.C.: University Publications of America, 1978.

Hays, Mary. *Appeal to the Men of Great Britain in Behalf of Women.* With an introduction by Gina Luria. New York: Garland, 1974.

———. *Letters and Essays, Moral and Miscellaneous.* With an introduction by Gina Luria. New York: Garland, 1974.

———. *The Love-Letters of Mary Hays (1779–1780).* Edited by A. F. Wedd. London: Methuen, 1925.

———. *Memoirs of Emma Courtney.* 2 vols. London, 1796. Reprint, with an introduction by Gina Luria, New York: Garland, 1974.

Hill, John. *Hypochondriasis: A Practical Treatise.* 1766. Reprint, with an introduction by G. S. Rousseau, Los Angeles: William Andrews Clark Memorial Library, 1969.

Hogg, James. *The Private Memoirs and Confessions of a Justified Sinner.* Edited by John Carey. Oxford: Oxford University Press.

Holcroft, Thomas. *Thomas Holcroft's A Plain and Succinct Narrative of the Gordon Riots, London, 1780.* Edited by Garland Garvey Smith. Atlanta: The Library, Emory University, 1944.

Inchbald, Elizabeth. *A Simple Story.* London: Pandora, 1987.

[Jeffrey, Francis.] Review of *Harrington a Tale, and Ormond a Tale: in Three Volumes,* by Maria Edgeworth. *Edinburgh Review* 28 (1817): 390–418.

Jones, John. *The Mysteries of Opium Reveal'd.* London: R. Smith, 1701.

Kingsley, Charles. *Alton Locke: Tailor and Poet.* 2 vols. London: Chapman and Hall, 1850.

———. *Yeast: A Problem.* New York: MacMillian, 1893.

Lewes, G. H. *The Physical Basis of Mind.* London, 1877.

MacDonald, Edgar E., ed. *The Education of the Heart: The Correspondence of Rachel Mordecai Lazarus and Maria Edgeworth.* Chapel Hill: University of North Carolina Press, 1977.

Malthus, Thomas. *An Essay on the Principle of Population.* Edited by Philip Appleman. New York: Norton, 1976.

Mill, John Stuart. *Later Letters of John Stuart Mill.* In *The Collected Works of John Stuart Mill,* Vols. 14–17. Edited by Francis E. Meneka and Dwight N. Lindley. Toronto: Toronto University Press, 1972.

"Opiologia." Review of *Confessions of an English Opium-Eater,* by Thomas De Quincey. *Medico-Chirurgical Review* 2 (1822): 881–901.

Review of "Opiologia." *Medical Intelligencer* [London] 3 (1822): 116–18.

Raffles, Thomas Stamford. *The History of Java.* 2nd edition. 2 vols. London: Murray, 1830.

Review of *Self Control: A Novel* [by Mary Brunton]. *Eclectic Review* 8 (June 1812): 603–20.

Shelley, Mary. *Frankenstein, or The Modern Prometheus.* Edited by Maurice Hindle. New York: Penguin, 1985.

Stewart, Dugald. *Elements of the Philosophy of the Human Mind.* Vol. 3. London: Murray, 1827.

Thelwall, Algernon S. *The Iniquities of the Opium Trade with China*. London: Allen, 1839.

Trotter, Thomas. *An Essay, Medical, Philosophical, and Chemical, on Drunkenness, and its Effects on the Human Body*. 1804. Reprint, with an introduction by Roy Porter, London: Routledge, 1988.

———. *Sea Weeds: Poems, Written on Various Occasions, Chiefly During a Naval Life*. London: Longman; Edinburgh: D. Lizars, 1829.

———. *A View of the Nervous Temperament: Being a Practical Enquiry into the Increasing Prevalence, Prevention, and Treatment of Those Diseases Commonly Called Nervous, Bilious, Stomach and Liver Complaints; Indigestion; Low Spirits; Gout, &c*. London: Longman, 1807. Reprint, New York: Arno, 1976.

Tyndall, John. *Essays on the Use and Limit of the Imagination in Science*. London: Longmans, 1870.

Whytt, Robert. *The Works of Robert Whytt, M.D.* Edinburgh, 1768. Reprint, Classics of Neurology and Neurosurgery Library. Birmingham, AL: Leslie B. Adams, 1984.

Wollstonecraft, Mary. *Mary, A Fiction* and *The Wrongs of Woman*. Oxford: Oxford University Press, 1976.

———. *Vindication of the Rights of Woman*. Edited by Miriam Brody. New York: Penguin, 1985.

SECONDARY SOURCES

Abrams, M. H. *The Milk of Paradise: The Effect of Opium Visions on the Works of De Quincey, Crabbe, Francis Thompson, and Coleridge*. New York: Octagon Books, 1971.

Adams, M. Ray. "Mary Hays, Disciple of William Godwin." *PMLA* 55 (1940): 472–83.

Altick, Richard D. *The English Common Reader: A Social History of the Mass Reading Public 1800–1900*. Chicago: University of Chicago Press, 1957.

———. *Victorian People and Ideas: A Companion for the Modern Reader of Victorian Literature*. New York: Norton, 1973.

———. *Writers, Readers, and Occasions: Selected Essays on Victorian Literature and Life*. Columbus, OH: Ohio State University Press, 1989.

American Psychiatric Association. *Diagnostic and Statistical Manual of Mental Disorders: DSM-III-R*. 3rd edition, revised. Washington, DC: American Psychiatric Association, 1987.

———. *Diagnostic and Statistical Manual of Mental Disorders: DSM-IV*. 4th edition. Washington, DC: American Psychiatric Association, 1994.

Baker, William. *The George Eliot–George Henry Lewes Library: An Annotated Catalogue of Their Books at Dr. Williams's Library, London*. New York: Garland, 1977.

———. *The Libraries of George Eliot and George Henry Lewes*. English Literary Studies. Victoria, BC: University of Victoria, 1981.

Barker-Benfield, F. J. *The Culture of Sensibility: Sex and Society in Eighteenth-Century Britain*. Chicago: University of Chicago Press, 1992.

Barrell, John. *The Infection of Thomas De Quincey: A Psychopathology of Imperialism*. New Haven: Yale University Press, 1991.

Barrows, Susanna. *Distorting Mirrors: Visions of the Crowd in Late Nineteenth-Century France*. New Haven: Yale University Press, 1981.

Beer, Gillian. *Darwin's Plots: Evolutionary Narrative in Darwin, George Eliot and Nineteenth-Century Fiction*. London: Routledge, 1983.

Beizer, Janet. *Ventriloquized Bodies: Narratives of Hysteria in Nineteenth-Century France*. Ithaca, NY: Cornell University Press, 1994.

Bender, John. *Imagining the Penitentiary: Fiction and the Architecture of Mind in Eighteenth-Century England*. Chicago: University of Chicago Press, 1987.

Berridge, Virginia, and Griffith Edwards. *Opium and the People: Opiate Use in Nineteenth-Century England*. New Haven: Yale University Press, 1987.

Brantlinger, Patrick. "Bluebooks, the Social Organism, and the Victorian Novel." *Criticism* 14 (1972): 328–44.

Breuer, Josef, and Sigmund Freud. *Studies on Hysteria*. Translated by James Strachey. New York: Basic Books, 1957.

Brewer, John. *The Sinews of Power: War, Money and the English State, 1688–1783*. London: Unwin Hyman, 1989.

Brock, W. H., N. D. McMillan, and R. C. Mollan, eds. *John Tyndall: Essays on a Natural Philosopher. Historical Studies in Irish Science and Technology*. Dublin: Royal Dublin Society, 1981.

Brundage, Anthony. *England's "Prussian Minister": Edwin Chadwick and the Politics of Government Growth, 1832–54*. University Park, PA: Pennsylvania State University Press, 1988.

Butler, Marilyn. "Godwin, Burke, and *Caleb Williams*." *Essays in Criticism* 32 (1982): 237–57.

———. *Maria Edgeworth: A Literary Biography*. Oxford: Oxford University Press, 1972.

Bynum, W. F. "Ideology and Health Care in Britain: Chadwick to Beveridge." *History and Philosophy of the Life Sciences* 10 (suppl.) (1988): 75–87.

———. "The Nervous Patient in Eighteenth- and Nineteenth-Century Britain: The Psychiatric Origins of British Neurology." In Bynum et al., *The Anatomy of Madness* 1:89–102.

Bynum, W. F., Roy Porter, and Michael Shepherd, eds. *The Anatomy of Madness: Essays in the History of Psychiatry*. 2 vols. London: Tavistock, 1985.

Cartwright, F. F. *A Social History of Medicine. Themes in British Social History*. London: Longman, 1977.

Chartier, Roger. *Cultural History: Between Practices and Representations*. Translated by Lydia G. Cochrane. Ithaca: Cornell University Press, 1988.

Childers, Joseph W. "Observation and Representation: Mr. Chadwick Writes the Poor." *Victorian Studies* 37 (1994): 405–32.

Cixous, Hélène. "Castration or Decapitation?" *Signs* 7 (1981): 36–55.

Clarke, Edwin, and L. S. Jacyna. *Nineteenth-Century Origins of Neuroscientific Concepts*. Berkeley: University of California Press, 1988.

Clej, Alina. *A Geneology of the Modern Self: Thomas De Quincey and the Intoxication of Writing*. Stanford: Stanford University Press, 1995.

Cooke, Michael G. "De Quincey, Coleridge, and the Formal Uses of Intoxication." *Yale French Studies* 50 (1974): 26–40.

Cullen, Michael J. *The Statistical Movement in Early Victorian Britain: The Foundation of Empirical Social Research.* New York: Barnes and Noble, 1975.

Dale, Peter Allen. "George Lewes' Scientific Aesthetic: Restructuring the Ideology of the Symbol." In Levine, ed., *One Culture: Essays in Science and Literature,* 92–116.

de Bolla, Peter. *The Discourse of the Sublime: History, Aesthetics and the Subject.* Oxford: Basil Blackwell, 1989.

Devlin, D. D. *De Quincey, Wordsworth and the Art of Prose.* London: MacMillan, 1983.

Dickson, P.G.M. *The Financial Revolution in England: A Study in the Development of Public Credit, 1668–1756.* New York: St. Martin's, 1967.

Digby, Anne. *Madness, Morality and Medicine: A Study of the York Retreat, 1796–1914.* New York: Cambridge University Press, 1985.

Donnelly, Michael. *Managing the Mind: A Study of Medical Psychology in Early Nineteenth-Century Britain.* London: Tavistock, 1983.

Dumas, D. Gilbert. "Things as They Were: The Original Ending of Caleb Williams. *SEL: Studies in English Literature, 1500–1900* 6 (1966): 575–97.

During, Simon. "The Strange Case of Monomania: Patriarchy in Literature, Murder in Middlemarch, Drowning in *Daniel Deronda.*" *Representations* 23 (1988): 86–104.

Dyos, H. J. "The Slums of Victorian London." *Victorian Studies* 11 (1967): 5–40.

Ellenberger, Henri F. *The Discovery of the Unconscious: The History and Evolution of Dynamic Psychiatry.* New York: Basic Books, 1970.

Evans, Martha Noel. *Fits and Starts: A Genealogy of Hysteria in Modern France.* Ithaca, NY: Cornell University Press, 1991.

Eyler, J. M. *Victorian Social Medicine: The Ideas and Methods of William Farr.* Baltimore: 1979.

Faas, Ekbert. *Retreat into the Mind: Victorian Poetry and the Rise of Psychiatry.* Princeton: Princeton University Press, 1988.

Fee, Elizabeth, and Dorothy Porter. "Public Health, Preventive Medicine and Professionalization: England and America in the Nineteenth Century." In *Medicine in Society: Historical Essays,* edited by Andrew Wear, 249–75. Cambridge: Cambridge University Press, 1992.

Feltes, Norman N. *Modes of Production of Victorian Novels.* Chicago: University of Chicago Press, 1986.

Ferris, Ina. *The Achievement of Literary Authority: Gender, History, and the Waverley Novels.* Ithaca: Cornell University Press, 1991.

Finer, S. E. *The Life and Times of Sir Edwin Chadwick.* London: Methuen, 1952.

Foster, James R. *History of the Pre-Romantic Novel in England.* Monograph Series of the Modern Language Association of America, vol. 12. New York: MLA, 1949.

Foucault, Michel. *The Birth of the Clinic: An Archaeology of Medical Perception.* Translated by A. M. Sheridan Smith. New York: Vintage, 1975.

———. *Discipline and Punish: The Birth of the Prison.* Translated by Alan Sheridan. New York: Vintage, 1979.

————. *The History of Sexuality: Volume I.* Translated by Robert Hurley. New York: Vintage, 1980.

————. *Madness and Civilization: A History of Insanity in the Age of Reason.* Translated by Richard Howard. New York: Vintage, 1965.

————. *The Order of Things.* New York: Vintage, 1970.

Gallagher, Catherine. "The Body Versus the Social Body in the Works of Thomas Malthus and Henry Mayhew." *Representations* 14 (1986): 83–106.

————. *The Industrial Reformation of English Fiction: Social Discourse and Narrative Form, 1832–1867.* Chicago: University of Chicago Press, 1985.

————. *Nobody's Story: The Vanishing Acts of Women Writers in the Marketplace, 1670–1820.* Berkeley: University of California Press, 1994.

Gilman, Sander L., Helen King, Roy Porter, George Rousseau, and Elaine Showalter. *Hysteria Beyond Freud.* Berkeley: University of California Press, 1993.

Goldstein, Jan. *Console and Classify: The French Psychiatric Profession in the Nineteenth Century.* Cambridge: Cambridge University Press, 1987.

————, ed. *Foucault and the Writing of History.* Cambridge, MA: Basil Blackwell, 1994.

Haigh, Elizabeth. *Xavier Bichat and the Medical Theory of the Eighteenth Century.* Medical History, Supplement 4. London: Wellcome Institute, 1984.

Haight, Gordon S. *George Eliot: A Biography.* New York: Oxford University Press, 1968.

————, ed. Introduction to *Middlemarch: A Study of Provincial Life,* by George Eliot. Boston: Houghton, 1956.

Hamlin, Christopher. "Edwin Chadwick and the Engineers, 1842–1854: Systems and Antisystems in the Pipe-and-Brick Sewers War." *Technology and Culture* 33 (1992): 680–709.

————. "Providence and Putrefaction." *Victorian Studies* 27 (1985): 381–411.

————. "William Dibdin and the Idea of Biological Sewage Treatment." *Technology and Culture* 29 (1988): 189–218.

Handwerk, Gary. "Of Caleb's Guilt and Godwin's Truth: Ideology and Ethics in Caleb Williams." *ELH* 60 (1993): 939–60.

Harden, Elizabeth. *Maria Edgeworth.* Twayne's English Authors Series. Boston: Twayne, 1984.

Harding, Geoffrey. *Opiate Addiction, Morality and Medicine: From Moral Illness to Pathological Disease.* New York: St. Martin's, 1988.

Hayden, John O. "De Quincey's *Confessions* and the Reviewers." *Wordsworth Circle* 6 (1975): 273–79.

Hayter, Alethea. *Opium and the Romantic Imagination: Addiction and Creativity in De Quincey, Coleridge, Baudelaire and Others.* Wellingborough, England: Crucible, 1988.

Herbert, Christopher. *Culture and Anomie: Ethnographic Imagination in the Nineteenth Century.* Chicago: University of Chicago Press, 1991.

Hirschman, Albert. *The Passions and the Interests.* Princeton, NJ: Princeton University Press, 1976.

Hobsbawm, E. J. *Industry and Empire.* The Pelican Economic History of Britain, vol. 3. New York: Pelican, 1968.

Hunter, Kathryn Montgomery. *Doctor's Stories: The Narrative Structure of Medical Knowledge.* Princeton, NJ: Princeton University Press, 1991.

Hunter, Richard, and Ida Macalpine. *Three Hundred Years of Psychiatry, 1535–1860: A History Presented in Selected English Texts.* London: Oxford University Press, 1963.

Hyler, Steven E., and Robert L. Spitzer, "Hysteria Split Asunder," *American Journal of Psychiatry* 135, no. 12 (December 1978): 1500–4.

Ignatieff, Michael. *A Just Measure of Pain: The Penitentiary in the Industrial Revolution, 1750–1850.* London: Penguin, 1978.

Inglis, Brian. *The Opium War.* London: Hodder, 1976.

Irigaray, Luce. *Speculum of the Other Woman.* Translated by Gillian C. Gill. Ithaca: Cornell University Press, 1985.

Jack, Ian. "De Quincey Revises His Confessions." *PMLA* 72 (1957): 122–46.

Jacobus, Mary. *Reading Woman: Essays in Feminist Criticism.* New York: Columbia University Press, 1986.

———. *Romanticism, Writing and Sexual Difference: Essays on* The Prelude. Oxford: Clarendon Press, 1989.

Jameson, Fredric. *The Political Unconscious: Narrative as a Socially Symbolic Act.* Ithaca, NY: Cornell University Press, 1981.

Jewson, N. D. "Medical Knowledge and the Patronage System in Eighteenth-Century England." *Sociology* 8 (1974): 369–85.

Jordanova, Ludmilla. *Sexual Visions: Images of Gender in Science and Medicine between the Eighteenth and Twentieth Centuries.* Science and Literature. Madison: University of Wisconsin Press, 1989.

———, ed. *Languages of Nature: Critical Essays on Science and Literature.* New Brunswick, NJ: Rutgers University Press, 1986.

Kahane, Claire. *Passions of the Voice: Hysteria, Narrative, and the Figure of the Speaking Woman, 1850–1915.* Baltimore: Johns Hopkins University Press, 1995.

Kelly, Gary. *The English Jacobin Novel, 1780–1805.* Oxford: Clarendon Press, 1976.

King, Helen. "Once Upon a Text: Hysteria frm Hippocrates." In Gilman et al., *Hysteria beyond Freud,* 3–89.

Kitchel, Anna Theresa. *George Lewes and George Eliot: A Review of Records.* New York: John Day, 1933.

Kolakoswki, Leszek. *Positivist Philosophy from Hume to the Vienna Circle.* Translated by Norbert Guterman. Harmondsworth: Penguin, 1972.

Kristeva, Julia. "Oscillation Between Power and Denial." In *New French Feminisms,* edited by Elaine Marks and Isabelle de Courtivron, 165–7. New York: Schocker, 1981.

Laqueur, Thomas W. "Bodies, Details, and the Humanitarian Narrative." In *The New Cultural History,* edited by Lynn Hunt, 176–204. Berkeley: University of California Press, 1989.

———. *Making Sex: Body and Gender from the Greeks to Freud.* Cambridge, MA: Harvard University Press, 1990.

Lauden, Larry. "A Confutation of Convergent Realism" In Leplin, *Scientific Realism,* 218–49.

Leplin, Jarrett, ed. *Scientific Realism.* Berkeley: University of California Press, 1984.

Levine, George. *Darwin and the Novelists: Patterns of Science in Victorian Fiction.* Cambridge: Harvard University Press, 1988.

———. "George Eliot's Hypothesis of Reality." *Nineteenth-Century Fiction* 35 (1980): 1–28.

———. *The Realistic Imagination: English Fiction from Frankenstein to Lady Chatterley.* Chicago: University of Chicago Press, 1981.

———, ed. *One Culture: Essays in Science and Literature.* Madison: University of Wisconsin Press, 1987.

Levy, Anita. *Other Women: The Writing of Class, Race, and Gender, 1832–1898.* Princeton, NJ: Princeton University Press, 1991.

Lewis, Richard Albert. *Edwin Chadwick and the Public Health Movement, 1832–1854.* London: Longmans, 1952.

Lindop, Grevel. *The Opium-Eater: A Life of Thomas De Quincey.* London: Dent, 1981.

Lloyd, Christopher, ed. *The Health of Seamen: Selections from the Works of Dr. James Lind, Sir Gilbert Blane and Dr. Thomas Trotter.* London: Navy Records Society, 1965.

Luria, Gina. "Mary Hays's Letters and Manuscripts." *Signs* 3 (1977): 524–30.

Lutz, Tom. *American Nervousness, 1903: An Anecdotal History.* Ithaca: Cornell University Press, 1991.

MacDonald, Michael. *Mystical Bedlam: Madness, Anxiety and Healing in Seventeenth-Century England.* Cambridge: Cambridge University Press, 1981.

Marshall, Peter H. *William Godwin.* New Haven: Yale University Press, 1984.

Martin, Philip W. *Mad Women in Romantic Writing.* New York: St. Martin's, 1987.

Mason, Michael York. "Middlemarch and Science: Problems of Life and Mind." *Review of English Studies* 22 (1971): 151–69.

Maulitz, Russell C. *Morbid Appearances: The Anatomy of Pathology in the Early Nineteenth Century.* Cambridge: Cambridge University Press, 1987.

Metz, Nancy Aycock. "Discovering a World of Suffering: Fiction and the Rhetoric of Sanitary Reform—1840–1860." *Nineteenth-Century Contexts* 15 (1991): 65–81.

Micale, Mark S. *Approaching Hysteria: Disease and Its Interpretations.* Princeton, NJ: Princeton University Press, 1995.

Miller, D. A. "*Cage aux folles:* Sensation and Gender in Wilkie Collins's *The Woman in White.*" In *The Novel and the Police.* Berkeley: University of California Press, 1988.

Modder, Montagu Frank. *The Jew in the Literature of England to the End of the Nineteenth Century.* 1939; New York: Meridian, 1960.

Moscovici, Serge. *The Age of the Crowd: A Historical Treatise on Mass Psychology.* Translated by J. C. Whitehouse. Cambridge: Cambridge University Press, 1985.

Mullan, John. *Sentiment and Sociability: The Language of Feeling in the Eighteenth Century.* Oxford: Oxford University Press, 1988.

Murray, Patrick. *Maria Edgeworth: A Study of the Novelist*. Cork: Mercier, 1971.

Myers, Mitzi. "Godwin's Changing Conception of Caleb Williams." *SEL: Studies in English Literature, 1500–1900* 12 (1972): 591–628.

———. "Shot from Canons; or, Maria Edgeworth and the Cultural Production and Consumption of the Late-Eighteenth-Century Woman Writer." In *The Consumption of Culture, 1600–1800: Image, Object, Text*, edited by Ann Bermingham and John Brewer, 193–214. New York: Routledge, 1995.

Newcomer, James. *Maria Edgeworth the Novelist: 1767–1849, A Bicentennial Study*. Forth Worth: Texas Christian University Press, 1967.

Nye, Robert A. *The Origins of Crowd Psychology: Gustave LeBon and the Crisis of Mass Democracy in the Third Republic*. London: Sage Publications, 1975.

Oppenheim, Janet. *"Shattered Nerves": Doctors, Patients and Depression in Victorian England*. New York: Oxford University Press, 1991.

Papay, Twila Yates. "A Near-Miss on the Psychological Novel: Maria Edgeworth's Harrington." In *Fetter'd or Free: British Women Novelists, 1670–1815*, edited by Mary Anne Schofield and Cecilia Macheski, 359–69. Athens, OH: Ohio University Press, 1986.

Parssinen, Terry M. *Secret Passions, Secret Remedies: Narcotic Drugs in British Society, 1820–1930*. Philadelphia: ISHI, 1983.

Pelling, Margaret. *Cholera, Fever and English Medicine, 1825–1865*. Oxford: Oxford University Press, 1978.

Peterson, M. Jeanne. *The Medical Profession in Mid-Victorian London*. Berkeley: University of California Press, 1978.

Pickstone, John V. "Dearth, Dirt and Fever Epidemics: Rewriting the History of British 'Public Health,' 1750–1850." In *Epidemics and Ideas: Essays on the Historical Perception of Pestilence*, edited by Terence Ranger and Paul Slack, 125–48. Cambridge: Cambridge University Press, 1992.

Platzner, Robert L. "De Quincey and the Dilemma of Romantic Autobiography." *Dalhousie Review* 61 (1981): 605–17.

Pocock, J.G.A. *The Machiavellian Moment: Florentine Political Thought and the Atlantic Republican Tradition*. Princeton, NJ: Princeton University Press, 1975.

———. *Virtue, Commerce, and History: Essays on Political Thought and History, Chiefly in the Eighteenth Century*. Cambridge: Cambridge University Press, 1985.

Pollin, B. K. "Mary Hays on Woman's Rights in the *Monthly Magazine*." *Etudes Anglaises* 24 (1971): 271–82.

Poovey, Mary. "Domesticity and Class Formation: Chadwick's 1842 Sanitary Report." In *Subject to History: Ideology, Class, Gender*, edited by David Simpson, 65–83. Ithaca, NY: Cornell University Press, 1991.

———. *Making a Social Body: British Cultural Formation, 1830–1864*. Chicago: University of Chicago Press, 1995.

———. *The Proper Lady and the Woman Writer: Ideology as Style in the Works of Mary Wollstonecraft, Mary Shelley and Jane Austen*. Chicago: University of Chicago Press, 1984.

———. *Uneven Developments: The Ideological Work of Gender in Mid-Victorian England.* Chicago: University of Chicago Press, 1988.

Porter, Dorothy. "Enemies of the Race." *Victorian Studies* 34 (1991): 159–78.

Porter, Dorothy, and Roy Porter. *Patient's Progress: Doctors and Doctoring in Eighteenth-Century England.* Stanford: Stanford University Press, 1989.

Porter, Ian Alexander. "Thomas Trotter, M.D., Naval Physician." *Medical History* 7 (1963): 155–64.

Porter, Roy. "Addicted to Modernity: Nervousness in the Early Consumer Society." In *Culture in History: Production, Consumption and Values in Historical Perspective,* edited by Joseph Melling and Jonathan Barry, 180–94. Exeter: Exeter University Press, 1992.

———. *Doctor of Society: Thomas Beddoes and the Sick Trade in Late-Enlightenment England.* London: Routledge, 1992.

———. *Health for Sale: Quackery in England 1660–1850.* Manchester: Manchester University Press, 1989.

———. *Mind-Forg'd Manacles: A History of Madness in England from the Restoration to the Regency.* Cambridge, MA: Harvard University Press, 1987.

Putnam, Hilary. "What Is Realism?" In Leplin, *Scientific Realism,* 140–53.

Ragussis, Michael. *Figures of Conversion: "The Jewish Question" and English National Identity.* Durham, NC: Duke University Press, 1995.

Rajan, Tilottama. "Autonarration and Genotext in Mary Hays's *Memoirs of Emma Courtney.*" *Studies in Romanticism* 32 (1993): 149–76.

———. *The Supplement of Reading: Figures of Understanding in Romantic Theory and Practice.* Ithaca: Cornell University Press, 1990.

———. "Wollstonecraft and Godwin: Reading the Secrets of the Political Novel," *Studies in Romanticism* 27 (1988): 221–51.

Richardson, Ruth. *Death, Dissection and the Destitute.* London: Routledge, 1987.

Risse, Guenter B. "Brunonian Therapeutics: New Wine in Old Bottles?" *Medical History,* Supplement 8 (1988): 46–62.

———. "Hysteria at the Edinburgh Infirmary: The Construction and Treatment of a Disease, 1770–1800." *Medical History* 32 (1988): 1–22.

Rogers, Katharine M. "The Contribution of Mary Hays." *Prose Studies* 10 (1987): 131–42.

Rolleston, Humphry. "Thomas Trotter, M.D." In *Contributions to Medical and Biological Research Dedicated to Sir William Osler in Honour of His Seventieth Birthday, July 12, 1919, by His Pupils and Co-Workers,* 1:153–65. New York: Hoeber, 1919.

Rosenberg, Charles E. and Janet Golden, eds. *Framing Disease: Studies in Cultural History.* New Brunswick, NJ: Rutgers University Press, 1992.

Rosenberg, Edgar. *From Shylock to Svengali: Jewish Stereotypes in English Fiction.* Stanford: Stanford University Press, 1960.

Rothfield, Lawrence. *Vital Signs: Medical Realism in Nineteenth-Century Fiction.* Princeton, NJ: Princeton University Press, 1992.

Rothman, David J. *The Discovery of the Asylum: Social Order and Disorder in the New Republic.* Boston: Little, Brown, 1971.

Rousseau, G. S. "Nerves, Spirits, and Fibres: Towards Defining the Origins of Sensibility." In *Studies in the Eighteenth Century III*, edited by R. F. Brissenden and J. C. Eade, 137–57. Canberra: Australian National University Press, 1976.

Scarry, Elaine. *The Body in Pain: The Making and Unmaking of the World*. Oxford: Oxford University Press, 1985.

———. "Consent and the Body: Injury, Departure, and Desire." *New Literary History* 21 (1990): 867–96.

———. "Work and the Body in Hardy and Other Nineteenth-Century Novelists." *Representations* 3 (1983): 90–123.

———, ed. *Literature and the Body: Essays on Populations and Persons*. Baltimore: Johns Hopkins University Press, 1988.

Schneider, Elisabeth. *Coleridge, Opium and "Kubla Khan."* Chicago: University of Chicago Press, 1953.

Scull, Andrew, ed. *Madhouses, Mad-Doctors and Madmen: The Social History of Psychiatry in the Victorian Era*. London: Athlone, 1981.

Showalter, Elaine. "On Hysterical Narrative." *Narrative* 1 (1993): 24–35.

Shuttleworth, Sally. "Fairy Tale or Science? Physiological Psychology in *Silas Marner*." In Jordonova, *Languages of Nature*, 244–88.

———. *George Eliot and Nineteenth-Century Science: The Make-Believe of a Beginning*. Cambridge: Cambridge University Press, 1984.

———. "'Preaching to the Nerves': Psychological Disorder in Sensation Fiction." In *A Question of Identity: Women, Science, and Literature*, edited by Marina Benjamin, 192–222. New Brunswick, NJ: Rutgers University Press, 1993.

———. "'The Surveillance of a Sleepless Eye': The Constitution of Neurosis in *Villette*." In Levine, *One Culture*, 313–35.

Simms, Karl N. "'Caleb Williams' Godwin: Things as They Are Written." *Studies in Romanticism* 26 (1987): 343–63.

Slavney, Phillip R. *Perspectives on "Hysteria."* Baltimore: Johns Hopkins University Press, 1990.

Smith, Sheila M. "Blue Books and Victorian Novelists." *Review of English Studies* 21 n.s. (1970): 23–40.

———. *The Other Nation: The Poor in English Novels of the 1840s and 1850s*. Oxford: Clarendon Press, 1980.

Smith-Rosenberg, Carroll. "The Hysterical Woman: Sex Roles and Role Conflict in Nineteenth-Century America." *Social Research* 39 (1972): 652–78.

Sontag, Susan. *Illness as Metaphor*. New York: Vintage, 1977.

Starr, G. A. "'Only a Boy': Notes on Sentimental Novels." *Genre* 10 (1977): 501–27.

Stephanson, Raymond. "Richardson's 'Nerves': The Physiology of Sensibility in *Clarissa*." *Journal of the History of Ideas* 44 (1988): 267–86.

Taylor, John Tinnon. *Early Opposition to the English Novel: The Popular Reaction from 1760 to 1830*. New York: King's Crown Press, 1943.

Thomas, Nicholas. "Sanitation and Seeing: The Creation of State Power in Early Colonial Fiji." *Comparative Studies in Science and History* 32 (1990): 149–70.

Tillotson, Kathleen. *Novels of the 1840s*. Oxford: Clarendon, 1954.
Todd, Janet. *Sensibility: An Introduction*. London: Methuen, 1986.
———. *The Sign of Angellica: Women, Writing and Fiction, 1660–1800*. New York: Columbia University Press, 1989.
Toews, John. "Foucault and the Freudian Subject: Archaeology, Genealogy, and the Historicization of Psychoanalysis." In Goldstein, *Foucault and the Writing of History*, 116–34.
Tompkins, J.M.S. "Mary Hays, Philosophess." In *The Polite Marriage*, 150–90. Cambridge: Cambridge University Press, 1938.
———. *The Popular Novel in England: 1770–1800*. London: Constable, 1932.
Ty, Eleanor. *Unsex'd Revolutionaries: Five Women Novelists of the 1790s*. Toronto: University of Toronto Press, 1993.
Veith, Ilza. *Hysteria: The History of a Disease*. Chicago: University of Chicago Press, 1965.
Vrettos, Athena. *Somatic Fictions: Imagining Illness in Victorian Culture*. Stanford: Stanford University Press, 1995.
Waddington, Ivan. *The Medical Profession in the Industrial Revolution*. Dublin: Gill, 1984.
Watson, Nicola J. *Revolution and the Form of the British Novel, 1790–1825: Intercepted Letters, Interrupted Seductions*. Oxford: Clarendon Press, 1994.
Watt, Ian. *The Rise of the Novel: Studies in Defoe, Richardson and Fielding*. London: Chatto, 1957.
Weiner, Dora B. "Mind and Body in the Clinic: Philippe Pinel, Alexander Crichton, Dominique Esquirol, and the Birth of Psychiatry." In *The Languages of Psyche: Mind and Body in Enlightenment Thought*, edited by G. S. Rousseau, 331–402. Berkeley: University of California Press, 1990.
Williams, Raymond. *The Long Revolution*. New York: Columbia University Press, 1961.
Wohl, Anthony. *Endangered Lives: Public Health in Victorian Britain*. Cambridge, MA: Harvard University Press, 1983.
Wright, T. R. "George Eliot and Positivism." *Modern Language Review* (1981): 257–72.
Zimmern, Helen. *Maria Edgeworth*. London, W. H. Allen, 1883.

Index

Abrams, M. H., 74
Adam Bede (Eliot), 169, 170
Adams, M. Ray, 207–8n. 5
addiction, 78–93, 96–103, 105–8
Addison, Joseph, 35
aestheticism: class specificity of, 27, 158;
  and science, 98, 107, 173, 186, 190–94;
  and truth, 130–32, 137–38
agency: and addiction, 88–92, 96–97,
  102, 105–7; and narration, 68–69; and
  party spirit, 122–23
alcoholism, 15, 202n. 20
Altick, Richard D., 210n. 13, 220–21n. 28
Alton Locke, Tailor and Poet (Kingsley),
  145
American Notes (Dickens), 146
anatomy, science of, 180, 192
anesthesia, 178
anti-Catholicism, 125–26
anti-Semitism, 109–10, 112–14, 122–30,
  132–36
aphasia, 9, 17
*Appeal to the Men of Great Britain in Behalf
  of Women* (Hays), 60
aristocracy, 1, 18, 21–22, 31, 78
Arnold, Matthew, 184–86, 223n. 17,
  227n. 60
Arnold, Thomas, 1, 197n. 1
art. *See* aestheticism
Artisans and Machinery (Gaskell), 147
Asian opium-eater, images of, 80, 89
audience, 128–30, 137–38, 192.
  See also readers
autobiography, 75

Bacon, Francis, 12, 115, 125; *Sylva Syl-
  varum; or, A Natural History*, 115, 116
Baker-Benfield, F. J., xiii
Barrows, Susanna, 215n. 10
Beddoes, Thomas, xii, 1, 210n. 8, 214n. 4
behaviors: of groups, 114–15, 121–22,
  127–28; as products of environment,
  48
"Bell-Magendie Law" (1822), 221n. 2
Bender, John, 205n. 3

Bentham, Jeremy, 145
Bibliothéque Universelle, 152, 153
Bichat, Marie Francois Xavier, 179,
  188–90, 193, 194
birth rates, 150
Blackwood's Edinburgh Magazine, 15, 83
bodies: concepts of, xi, 1–12, 143–44,
  166–70; in De Quincey, 73–75, 92–97,
  99, 100–101, 103–4, 107, 108; in Edgeworth, 113–14, 116–18, 121, 131, 134–
  37, 143–44; in Eliot, 177–81, 188–90;
  in Godwin, 48, 50–53; in Hays, 59, 68,
  71; in Trotter, 22–31, 34
Boswell, James, 201n. 16
Breuer, Joseph, 8, 9
Brown, John, 77
Brundage, Anthony, 218n. 7
Burton, John, 146
Burton, Robert, 20
business. *See* commerce
Butler, Marilyn, 205n. 9

Caleb Williams (Godwin), 3–4, 45–58;
  and *Confessions of an English Opium
  Eater*, 74, 102; and *Harrington*, 110;
  and *Memoirs of Emma Courtney*, 60, 62,
  65–66, 68–69
capitalism, and nervous disorders,
  31–36
Carbery, Susan, 85
Carter, Robert Brudenell, 146–47
Cassandra (Nightingale), 67
cautionary tales, 65, 87, 193
Chadwick, Edwin, 144; *Report on the
  Sanitary Condition of the Labouring
  Population of Great Britain*, 145–64
Channel Fleet (British), 36
Charcot, Jean Martin, 41
Cheyne, George, xi, 34, 40, 146; *The
  English Malady*, 1, 18–19, 166
Childers, Joseph W., 219n. 17, 221n. 30
children, 117–18, 159–60
chloroform, recreational usage of, 79
city, and nervous disorders, 34
Cixous, Hélèn, 213–14n. 53

243

class. *See* social class
coal mines, 203n. 36
Coleridge, Samuel Taylor, 83, 103
colonialism, and opium, 80–84, 89–90
commerce, 31–37, 39, 82–84
Comte, Auguste, 226n. 44
Confessions of an English Opium-Eater (De Quincey), 4, 46, 71, 73–108, 206n. 20
Cooke, Michael G., 212n. 40
credit society, critique of, 31–33
Crichton, Alexander, 208n. 13, 213n. 52, 216n. 22, 217n. 36; *An Inquiry into the Nature and Origin of Mental Derangement*, 118–19
crime, 155
crowd psychology, 114–15, 121, 127–28, 138. *See also* party spirit
Cullen, William, 17–18, 197n. 1
The Culture of Sensibility (Barker-Benfield), xiii

De Quincey, Thomas: *Confessions of an English Opium-Eater*, 4, 46, 71, 73–108, 206n. 20; "Recollections of Charles Lamb," 103
de Tott, Baron, 80
Defoe, Daniel, 35
deformity, physical, 117–18, 152–53
Diagnostic and Statistical Manual of Mental Disorders: DSM-III-R (American Psychiatric Association), 8
Diagnostic and Statistical Manual of Mental Disorders: DSM-IV (American Psychiatric Association), 8
Dickens, Charles, 146, 220n. 27; *American Notes*, 146
didacticism, and realism, 170
Digby, Kenelm, 115–17; *Two Treatises*, 116
disease, 47–48, 150–51, 153, 159, 161. *See also* nervous disorders
doctors: fictional representations of, 171–72, 175–76, 195; and nervous disorders, 30, 41; Trotter on, 37–38, 39–40
drains, as public intervention, 161
dreams, opium, 90, 96–97, 108
Drinkwater, John, 216–17n. 29
Dumas, D. Gilbert, 206n. 17
During, Simon, 225n. 33

Earl of Mar life insurance trial, 78
East India Company, 82, 83
echopraxia, 116
economy. *See* social conditions
Edgeworth, Maria, 143–44; *Forester*, 120; *Harrington*, 4, 45, 109–39, 144; *Moral*

Tales, 120; *Ormond*, 131
Edgeworth, Richard Lovell, 109, 216–17n. 29
education, 70, 156–58, 173
effeminization: medicalization of, 24–26, 40, 41; of narratives, 53, 56, 94, 95; of narrators, 50, 55, 91, 104, 108; of national character, 32, 33, 154
Eliot, George, 170–73; *Adam Bede*, 169, 170; *Middlemarch*, 5, 171–83, 185–96
Encyclopaedia Britannica, 115–16, 117–18
The English Malady (Cheyne), 1, 18–19, 166
Enquiry Concerning Political Justice (Godwin), 47, 60
environmental conditions. *See* social conditions
Esquirol, Jean-Étienne-Dominique, 41
An Essay on Drunkenness (Trotter), 15
Essay on the Principle of Population (Malthus), 149–50
ether, recreational usage of, 79
exercise, 24, 30–31, 135

Factory Inspector's Report, 147
Falret, Jean Pierre, 201n. 7
fashion, and party spirit, 128
feelings. *See* sensibility
Female Biography (Hays), 60
female bodies, 23–26, 29, 50, 53. *See also* women
feminization. *See* effeminization
Fenwick, Eliza, 60
fiction, attitudes toward, 143. *See also* realism
Fielding, Henry, 179
Fleetwood (Godwin), 45
folk medicine, 77
Forester (Edgeworth), 120
Foster, James R., 207n. 5
Foucault, Michel, 11, 27, 201–2n. 17, 202n. 22, 224n. 23
framing devices: in De Quincey, 94, 102; in Eliot, 179; in Godwin, 56; in Hays, 65, 70
Frankenstein (Shelley), xii, 45, 57
Freud, Sigmund, 8, 10, 204n. 42

Gallagher, Catherine, 216n. 23, 217nn. 33, 39, 220n. 22, 226n. 48, 227nn. 58, 60.
Gaskell, Elizabeth, 145, 221n. 35
Gaskell, Peter, 144; *Artisans and Machinery*, 147
gender. *See* effeminization; female bodies; male bodies; masculinity; men; women

Gibbon, Edward, 25
Godwin, William, xii, 64, 143, 202–3n.
 28; *Caleb Williams*, 3–4, 45–58, 60, 62,
 65–66, 68–69, 74, 102, 110; *Enquiry
 Concerning Political Justice*, 47, 60;
 Fleetwood, 45; *Political Justice*, 61
Gordon riots, 125–26, 144

Haight, Gordon, 226n. 53
Hall, Marshall, 167–68
Hamlin, Christopher, 220n. 21
Handwerk, Gary, 206–7n. 23
Harrington (Edgeworth), 4, 45, 109–39,
 144
Hayden, John O., 78
Hays, Mary, 91, 93–94; *Appeal to the Men
 of Great Britain in Behalf of Women*, 60;
 Female Biography, 60; *Letters and Essays,
 Moral and Miscellaneous*, 60; *Memoirs of
 Emma Courtney*, 3–4, 45, 57, 59–72, 74,
 102, 110; *Memoirs of Queens Illustrious
 and Celebrated*, 60; *The Victim of Preju-
 dice*, 60
Hayter, Althea, 74, 212n. 38, 213n. 46
Herbert, Christopher, 219n. 14
heredity, 21, 24–25, 48, 89
Histoire de la Medecine (Renouard), 172
History and Heroes of the Art of Medicine
 (Russell), 172
History of Java (Raffles), 81
Hobsbawm, E. J., 204n. 39
Hogg, James, 46
Holcroft, Thomas, 126
home, and disease, 159, 161–63
Howard, John, 46
Howe, Adm. Richard, 15, 36
Huxley, Thomas, 223n. 17, 225n. 39
hypochondria, xii, 17, 19, 32, 93, 94.
 See also nervous disorders
hypodermic syringe, 79
hysteria: cures for, 34, 135; description
 of, xii, 8–10, 16–17, 23, 94, 113, 114;
 susceptibility to, 1, 146–47. *See also*
 nervous disorders
Hysteria: The History of a Disease (Veith),
 10

ideas, impressions from, 119
imagination, and science, 173, 181–82,
 186, 190–91
imitation, 115–21
Imperial Magazine, 86
impressions, 28–29, 53, 95–96, 112,
 118–19
Inchbald, Elizabeth, 2, 168
independence: in De Quincey, 89,

95, 105; in Edgeworth, 133; in Eliot,
 185–86; in Hays, 63–64, 69; in Trotter,
 32–33, 38–39
Inglis, Brian, 82, 83
*The Iniquities of the Opium Trade with
 China* (Thelwall), 83
insane asylums, 46, 77
intellect, 95, 105

Jack, Ian, 87, 107
Jacobus, Mary, 9, 212n. 39
Jewish Naturalization Act (1753), 122
Johnson, Samuel, 201n. 16
Jones, John, 85, 210–11n. 16; *The Myster-
 ies of Opium Reveal'd*, 85
Jordanova, Ludmilla, 225n. 34

Kahane, Claire, 199n. 14
Kay, James Phillips, 147
Keepsake, 186
King, Helen, 198n. 9
Kingsley, Charles, 145–46

Lamb, Charles, 104
Lamb, Mary, 104
Laqueur, Thomas W., 6, 225–26n. 42
laudanum, 76, 77
LeBon, Gustave, 115
*Letters and Essays, Moral and Miscella-
 neous* (Hays), 60
Levant Company, 76
Levine, George, 226n. 47
Levy, Anita, 218n. 10
Lewes, George Henry, 171, 173, 181,
 222nn. 13, 14
Life of William Cullen (Thompson), 172
Lindop, Grevel, 84
Lister, Joseph, 178
London Magazine, 99
lower classes. *See* working class

male bodies, 25–26, 29, 53. *See also* men
Malebranche, Nicolas de, 117
Malthus, Thomas, 149, 151–52, 156;
 Essay on the Principle of Population,
 149–50
Manchester Grammar School, 84, 90,
 106–7
Martineau, Harriet, 146
Mary: A Fiction (Wollstonecraft), 2
Mary Barton: A Tale of Manchester Life
 (Gaskell), 145, 221n. 35
masculinity, 26, 50, 56, 75, 95
mass psychology. *See* crowd psychology
maternity, 70–71. *See also* mothers
McCracken, David, 205n. 12

medical profession: authority of, 41;
fictional representations of, 174–75,
192–93; and opium, 77, 79; and patronage, 36–39, 187
medical science: discourse of, xi, 4, 5, 98,
100, 107, 170–71; in Eliot, 173–81, 185;
texts of, 11, 15–16, 166
medicine. *See* medical science
Memoirs of Emma Courtney (Hays), 3–4,
59–72; compared with *Caleb Williams*,
45, 57; compared with *Confessions of an
Opium Eater*, 74, 102; compared with
Harrington, 110
*Memoirs of Queens Illustrious and Cele-
brated* (Hays), 60
Memoirs of the Nervous System (Hall),
167–68
Memoirs of the Turks and Tartars (de Tott):
80
men, nervous disorders among, 25, 117
Merchant of Venice (Shakespeare), 128,
129
mercury, and nervous temperament, 37
Micale, Mark S., 8–9, 12, 198nn. 11, 12,
201n. 10
middle class: morphine usage among,
79; and nervous disorders, 1, 4, 5, 19,
21–22, 66, 144, 165; values of, 30–31,
35, 36, 89, 90–91; and working class,
11, 163–64
Middlemarch (Eliot), 5, 171–83, 185–96
Mill, J. S., 146, 148
Milton, John, 186
*The Moral and Physical Condition of the
Working Classes* (Kay), 147
Moral Tales (Edgeworth), 120
morality, 81–82, 83, 150–51, 155–56
Mordecai, Rachel, 144, 214n. 2, 217n. 38
morphine, 79
Moscovici, Serge, 215n. 10
mothers, 24, 117–18. *See also* maternity
Myers, Mitzi, 206n. 17, 214n. 1
The Mysteries of Opium Reveal'd (Jones),
85

narration: and the body, 71, 95, 101; as
symptom of nervous disorder, 29, 38,
45, 68–69
narrative authority: in De Quincey, 73,
74–75, 93, 96, 99–100, 101–2, 105, 107;
in Edgeworth, 110, 138; in Godwin,
47, 54–55; in Hays, 68, 71; and the
nervous body, 2–3, 29–30
nervous bodies. *See* bodies
nervous disorders: causes of, 7–8, 15,
21–25, 28, 66; class-specificity of, 1, 4,
5, 18–23, 48, 66, 144, 146–47, 165; di-

agnosis of, xii, 16, 20, 22–23, 40; and
doctors, 37, 38; and narrative, 29, 38,
45, 68–69; as tool of social criticism,
2, 135–36
nervous narratives: and De Quincey,
73, 92–93, 101–2, 105; description of,
2–3, 29, 45–46, 75; and Edgeworth,
109, 110; and Godwin, 46, 54–56; and
Hays, 68–70
nervous system: conceptions of, 4–5,
6–8, 17–19, 20, 27, 166–68, 171; and
gender, 23–24
neuroses, 18. *See also* nervous disorders
New Edinburgh Review, 80
New Poor Law (1834), 145
Nightingale, Florence, 67
nitrous oxide, recreational usage of, 79
novels, attitudes toward, 143
Nye, Robert A., 215n. 10

*Observations on the Nature and Origins
of Mental Derangement* (Crichton),
118–19
Observations on the Scurvy (Trotter), 15
Observations (Whytt), 23
opium, 4, 37, 74, 76–92, 96–107
Opium War, 82–83
Ormond (Edgeworth), 131
Other, staging of, 128–29, 136
outward-directed activity, 68, 70, 135

Paget, Sir James, 171, 196
Paradise Lost (Milton), 186
Parssinen, Terry M., 78
party spirit, 114–15, 122–28, 132–34,
139. *See also* crowd psychology
patent medicines, 79
patronage system, 36–37, 187
Penson, Thomas, 84, 85
philosophers, 74, 95
Pickstone, John V., 220n. 24
Pocock, J. G. A., xiii, 32–33
Poisons and Pharmacy Act (1868), 79
Police Report, 145
Political Justice (Godwin), 61
Poor Law Commission, 145, 147
Poovey, Mary, 146, 218n. 12
Pope, Alexander, 202n. 24
population growth, 149–54
Porter, Roy, 197n. 2
predisposition, for nervous disorders,
21–24
*The Private Memoirs and Confessions of
a Justified Sinner* (Hogg), 46
production, among working class,
153–54, 160
psychoanalytic theory, 9–10, 17

psychology, of crowds, 114–15, 121, 127–28, 138. *See also* party spirit
public credit, critique of, 31–33
public health movement, 78–79, 145–64

Raffles, Thomas Stamford, 84, 85, 88, 89; *History of Java*, 81
Ragussis, Michael, 215n. 9, 216n. 23, 217nn. 37, 38
Rajan, Tilottama, 209n. 15
readers: and Chadwick, 163–65; and De Quincey, 91, 97–98, 104–5; and Edgeworth, 131–34, 137–38; effect of fiction on, 118–19, 143–44; and Godwin, 49–50, 57
realism, 165, 172–73, 183–84, 186, 191–96
reason: and the body, 114, 116, 120, 129; narrative of, 51–54, 56–57; and party spirit, 122–24; and self-delusion, 62, 64–65, 71
"Recollections of Charles Lamb" (De Quincey), 103
referentiality. *See* signifier / signified
reflex system, 167–68
Renouard, Pierre Victor, 172
Report on Handloom Weavers, 147
Report on the Employment of Children in Factories, 147, 159
Report on the Sanitary Condition of the Labouring Population of Great Britain (Chadwick), 145–64
reproduction, 70, 153, 160. *See also* population growth
Ricardo, David, 94
Richardson, Samuel, xi, 1
Risse, Guenter, 202n. 19
Rogers, Katharine M., 60, 202n. 24
Rothman, David J., 205n. 3
Royal College of Physicians, 36
Royal College of Surgeons, 100
Rural Constabulary Act, 145
Russell, J. Rutherford, 172

sanitation reform, 78–79, 145–64
savage, as contrast to urban body, 25–27, 34–35
Scarry, Elaine, 224n. 26
Schneider, Elizabeth, 74
science: and aesthetics, 98, 107, 173, 186, 190–94; and realism, 184. *See also* medical science
self-control, 111, 120, 135–36
self-delusion, 62, 64–65, 71, 101–2
self-violence, 59–72
sensibility: and commerce, 35–36, 39–40; and nervous disorders, 63, 65–66, 70, 112–13, 165; paradox of, 26–28, 47,

50–51, 95–96, 132; among working class, 147, 158–59, 163
sentimental ideology, 60
sexuality: among women, 66–67, 69–70, 71; among working class, 151–54, 156, 164
Shakespeare, William, 128, 129
Shelley, Mary, xii, 45, 57
Showalter, Elaine, 198n. 14
Shuttleworth, Sally, 227n. 59
sighs, as bodily speech, 103–4
signifier / signified, 114, 123–27, 169–70, 187–92, 194
silence, 83–84, 104
Simms, Karl N., 207n. 24
A Simple Story (Inchbald), 2, 168
Smith, Southwood, 144, 220n. 24; *Treatise on Fever*, 172
Smollius, G., 200n. 6
social class, 2, 129, 185. *See also* aristocracy; middle class; working class
social conditions: for medical profession, 192–93; and nervous disorders, 1–2, 18–19, 21, 29, 31, 46, 47–48, 50; for women, 62, 64, 65–67; for working class, 145–65
social critique: in Edgeworth, 114; in Godwin, 46–47, 49, 55; nervous narratives as, 2
Society of Apothecaries, 76, 79
speech: of the body, 101–2, 103–4; and nervous disorders, 2, 9, 16–17, 56–57, 59, 92–93; suppression of, 52, 53–54, 72
Stewart, Dugald, 120–22
Stewart, Mrs. Dugald, 120
Studies in Hysteria (Breuer and Freud), 9
surveillance, 161–64
Sydenham, Thomas, 77, 200–201n. 6, 201n. 14, 202n. 18
Sylva Sylvarum; or, A Natural History (Bacon), 115, 116
symbolic order, 9, 157
sympathetic imitation, 115–21
sympathy, 115–16, 183–85

Taylor, John Tinnon, 210n. 13
tea trade, with China, 82
Ten Hours Bill, 159
Thelwall, Rev. Algernon, 83
Thompson, John, 172
Todd, Janet, 64, 209n. 15
Treatise on Fever (Smith), 172
Trotter, Thomas, xii, 1, 47–48, 73, 111, 197n. 5; *An Essay on Drunkenness*, 15; *Observations on the Scurvy*, 15; *A View of the Nervous Temperament*, 15–42, 146

truth, and representation, 52–53,
  130–32, 137–38, 169
Tuke, William, 46
Two Treatises (Digby), 116
Ty, Eleanor, 209n. 15
Tyndall, John, 181–82, 190, 191, 194

urban bodies, 23, 26, 34. See also bodies
utopia, 50, 52, 53, 124, 134

Veith, Ilza, 10
Vesalius, Andreas, 179
The Victim of Prejudice (Hays), 60
A View of the Nervous Temperament
  (Trotter), 15–42, 146
Vindication of the Rights of Woman
  (Wollstonecraft), 66–67, 69–70
Virtue, Commerce and History (Pocock),
  xiii

Wakley, Thomas, 173
Watson, Col. Henry, 84
Watson, Nicola J., 209n. 15
wealth, and nervous disorders, 1–2
Weiner, Dora B., 216n. 20
wet nurses, 20

Whytt, Robert, 18, 20, 23; Observations, 23
Wohl, Anthony, 220n. 27
Wollstonecraft, Mary, 60, 91, 93–94,
  205n. 11, 208n. 9; Mary: A Fiction, 2;
  Vindication of the Rights of Woman,
  66–67, 69–70; The Wrongs of Woman,
  2, 45, 74
women: in Chadwick, 162–63; in De
  Quincey, 94; in Eliot, 187–88; in Godwin, 50; in Hays, 59–64, 65–67, 70, 72;
  and nervous disorders, 9, 79, 117–18;
  in Trotter, 19, 23–24, 26, 34. See also
  female bodies
Wordsworth, William, 91, 225n. 40
working class: middle-class conceptions
  of, 4, 5, 11; nervous disorders among,
  1–2, 18–19, 48, 144; opium usage
  among, 77, 78–80; social conditions
  for, 145–65
work-place, and disease, 159, 160, 161
Wright, T. R., 226n. 44
The Wrongs of Woman (Wollstonecraft), 2,
  45

Yeast (Kingsley), 145–46
York Retreat, 46, 77

Compositor:	G&S Typesetters, Inc.
Text:	10/13 Palatino
Display:	Palatino
Printer:	Maple-Vail Book Manufacturing Group
Binder:	Maple-Vail Book Manufacturing Group